Six Days and a Day

The Creator's Blueprint to Make Us Like Jesus

Marvin Byers

Treasure House

An Imprint of
Destiny Image® Publishers, Inc.
P.O. Box 310
Shippensburg, PA 17257-0310

"For where your treasure is
there will your heart be also." Matthew 6:21

ISBN 1-56043-263-2

For Worldwide Distribution
Printed in the U.S.A.

1-800-LAST DAY
(1-800-527-8329)

Treasure House books are available through these fine distributors outside the United States:

Christian Growth, Inc.
Jalan Kilang-Timor, Singapore 0315

Rhema Ministries Trading
Randburg, South Africa

Salvation Book Centre
Petaling, Jaya, Malaysia

Successful Christian Living
Capetown, Rep. of South Africa

Vine Christian Centre
Mid Glamorgan, Wales, United Kingdom

Vision Resources
Ponsonby, Auckland, New Zealand

WA Buchanan Company
Geebung, Queensland, Australia

Word Alive
Niverville, Manitoba, Canada

Inside the U.S., call toll free to order:
1-800-722-6774
Or reach us on the Internet: **http://www.reapernet.com**

Acknowledgments

I recognize that we have nothing of spiritual value that has not been given to us by a gracious God. I thank God for opening my blind eyes to see the truth that leads me to love Him more and to know Him in a deeper way.

I am eternally indebted to my loving wife, Barbara. She has faithfully walked with me these many years, although many times it would have been easier for her not to do so. She has often carried a greater burden than I have, and she surely deserves a greater reward.

I would also like to express my deep appreciation for the outstanding editing work that was done by Tom and Holly Erickson. Out of their hearts of love for me and for God's Word, they worked many long, hard hours to help make this book what it is.

Contents

Introduction

For most of us, recalling our personal history is like looking back over the horizon of time and picking out certain outstanding experiences that rise from our past like mighty mountains. Those landmark experiences are the first things that come to mind whenever we begin to tell others about our lives. As Christians, those experiences often become part of our personal testimony of God's goodness, mercy, and truth. Even Christ's earthly life was marked by a number of such experiences that come to mind immediately when we recount the story of His life. For example, although few Christians would immediately remember what Jesus taught His disciples at Caesarea Philippi, most can remember the accounts of His baptism in the Jordan, His transfiguration, the Last Supper, His crucifixion, and His resurrection.

Without a doubt, one of the landmark experiences in my own life was the gracious and sovereign way in which the Lord opened my understanding to the account of the seven days of Creation in Genesis. I am living proof that the Lord Jesus Christ still opens the eyes of the blind and the ears of the deaf. Today, almost 30 years after the Scriptures came alive to me in this area of truth that I now share in *Six Days and a Day*, I still marvel at God's ability to speak to someone so spiritually deaf as myself, or give spiritual sight to one so blind!

After reading this book, many serious students of God's written Word will discover that the seven-step process of bringing us from spiritual infancy to spiritual maturity is repeated in numerous other parts of the Bible that are not included in this study. Some will observe that many, if not most, of the books of the Bible can be outlined in accordance with these seven steps. Over and over, God's message to us is that He not only wants to save us from hell, but He also wants to save us from ourselves—from what we are—so that we can be filled with what He is. He will accomplish that purpose as what we are decreases and what He is increases within us through these seven steps. My prayer is that God will meet with you in a new way as you open your heart to His plan for every new creation in Christ Jesus.

Chapter 1

Something Out of Nothing

It was a beautiful day on the island of Palawan in the Philippines, but I could not see the cloudless sky above me because clouds of despair filled my heart. I had just finished teaching my final class of the day in the Palawan Bible Training Center, where I lived with my wife and our four small children. Palawan is the most primitive of the five major islands in the Philippines, and we were living in one of its most isolated areas. In front of our house was the South China Sea, and to the rear was dense jungle. Many of the natives living in that jungle wore only loincloths, and these often looked so old one had to assume they had been inherited from a previous generation. Many times our only meat was wild pig that the natives hunted and sold to us. Poisonous snakes were commonplace. In fact, on two different occasions cobras invited themselves into our house. The only welcome they received was administered through the end of a broom handle. With four small children present, there was no time for careful consideration of other means to deal with them!

The Bible school was so secluded that the nearest dirt road was 50 miles away. Those 50 miles could be crossed only by boat on what was frequently a very treacherous sea. The outcome of the journey was not always certain due to the stormy seas, the dark nights, and the crude navigational methods available to steer us safely through the rock-filled waters. Even getting on and off the Bible school's ten-ton cargo boat was a risky proposition if the waves were big—especially at night with four small children. Since we did not even have a dock, we anchored 50 yards offshore and used a small dugout canoe to shuttle people and cargo between boat and shore.

One particularly dark night when the waves were crashing onto the beach, my wife and I, with our four small children, were being shuttled from the boat to the shore in the dugout. Suddenly, just before we reached the shore, we were capsized by a large wave that plunged us all into the water. Our children were not wearing flotation gear, even though the younger three were unable to swim. During our three years in the Philippines, I never saw one life jacket; I suppose no one there had ever heard of them. We could not see our children anywhere. The darkness was so thick we couldn't even *guess* where they had fallen into the sea. With all four children in the sea, my wife and I began to grab for them frantically in the blackness of the night, reaching into the churning waters that were even darker than the night itself. By the time we had rescued three of the children, I still had no idea where our three-year-old daughter was, because I hadn't caught even one glimpse of her since the boat had capsized. Just as she was being rapidly swept out to sea, under three feet of water, I just "happened" to thrust my arm down in the right place at the right time. God surely intervened in saving the lives of our children that night!

Traveling was generally a trial, but staying at the Bible school for long periods of time also had its disadvantages because there was no mail, no telephone, no newspapers, and no electricity apart from what we produced ourselves with small generators. My wife could never go to the mall because there was no mall to go to. In fact, not a single store of any kind existed in the area. Anything we wanted or needed had to be grown by us or brought in from the outside every three or four months.

Although we faced many difficulties in the natural realm, my despair did not result from our trying and often dangerous living conditions. Instead, the cloud upon my heart as I finished teaching my course that afternoon was the result of the spiritual condition and great need in my own life. I knew that I had failed to give my students an impartation from the Lord. The class had been dry and filled with information *about* the Lord, rather than a revelation *of* the Lord. I had filled their *heads* with facts and doctrines, but their *hearts* had remained untouched and unchanged. For some reason, I knew that I had not become a channel for the living word that morning—the word that causes our hearts to burn and our lives to be changed. The hungry heart longs to hear what *He* is speaking; it has very little interest in hearing what *we* desire to speak, even if it is the deepest doctrinal discourse ever heard (and my students definitely were not getting anything close to that either).

I did not *always* leave my classes in despair. Many times the Spirit of the Lord would be present in a very wonderful way to impart life to all of us. Although my students did not know it, God had placed me in those classes to teach me as much or more than He was teaching them. I felt despair only when the Lord's apparent blessing did not come during the class. At times it seemed like the Lord left me to my own devices to remind me gently of what I could accomplish without Him—nothing! He was also showing me that the blessing comes from Him, and not from my abilities or thorough preparation. One of the most humbling things about teaching God's Word is that we are never sure whether His presence will come. Furthermore, all the fasting, prayer, study, and earnestness in the world will never guarantee success! Although we should continue doing these spiritual exercises, we must not put our confidence in them. God's mercy alone decides when and where He will visit and to what extent. This truth He also taught me in those dry, difficult classes; and continues to do so to this day.

Yes, I left class that day in despair because once again He had left me to myself and my own "extensive" notes. As I walked along the path leading to our house, I said to Him, "Lord, You certainly don't have much to work with in me." He responded instantly in a way that left me no doubt about who was speaking. It could not have been clearer if He had spoken audibly. He said, "I don't have *anything* to work with in you, and the sooner you learn that I am the Creator who makes something out of nothing, the sooner I will be able to make something beautiful with your life." As only His word can do, this truth broke my heart with a spirit of repentance. It revealed to me how self-confident I was, and to what extent I still trusted in the flesh. Yet, at the same time, it filled my heart with joy and expectancy, knowing that a better day was coming—a day in which He alone would be my confidence, and He alone would be seen and heard through my life and ministry.

This gentle rebuke from the Lord also amplified and confirmed a truth that He had previously opened to me from Genesis 1. At that moment, I understood in a new way the importance of Genesis 1:1 and saw in it the Bible's most important revelation. Why is this simple declaration, "In the beginning God created the heavens and the earth," of vital importance? It is most important because it is the first thing God says to mankind in the Scriptures. A study of the teaching methods of *the* teacher, the Lord Jesus Christ, reveals that He always goes straight to the point and states the most important thing first. He then develops the truth and ends by repeating the key thought. We will see in a moment that by starting the written Word with Genesis 1:1, God went straight to the point.

When Nicodemus came to Jesus, his long greeting was typical of man's tendency to use polite conversation. He began, "Rabbi, we know you are a teacher who has come from God. For no one could perform the miraculous signs you are doing if God were not with him" (Jn. 3:2 NIV). Significantly, Jesus did not answer by saying, "Thank you, Nicodemus. That is very kind of you. Please, won't you come in? It is a pleasure to get to know you. Would you like something to drink? It's a beautiful night to-night, isn't it?" No, the first thing Jesus said to Nicodemus was, "I tell you the *truth*, no one can see the kingdom of God unless he is born again" (Jn. 3:3 NIV). He started with the *truth*. Not only was it truth but it was also the most important truth Nicodemus needed to hear at that moment.

Going straight to the point is not something the Lord did only with Nicodemus. Rather, this reflects God's nature as seen in His dealings with mankind since the beginning. In Genesis 1:1, the very first verse of Scripture, God speaks to man the message man needs to hear most. This truth is so deep that we need to resort to the very best Old Testament commentary available. I call it "God's Divine Commentary on the Old Testament." Another name for this divine commentary is "The New Testament." Besides giving a revelation of one *main* message—the new covenant the Lord made by shedding His blood on the cross—the New Testament Scriptures serve several other purposes. One of those purposes is to give God's divine commentary on the Old Testament.

God's commentary on Genesis 1:1, as found in John 1:1,3, explains it this way: "In the beginning was the Word, and the Word was with God, and the Word was God...All things were made by him." Since "the Word" is Christ, and He made all things, then according to the Apostle John, Genesis 1:1 is a revelation of Christ, the most important person in the Bible.[1] Another divine commentary on this verse is given in Hebrews 11:3. We are told, "By faith we understand that the worlds were framed by the word of God, so that the things which are seen were not made of things which are visible" (NKJV). In simple English, this means that **God made something out of nothing**. This is a revelation of His glory as the Creator. Mankind can *make* things. We do this by working with raw materials and changing them into the finished product. Only God can *create* things. Without the use of raw materials, He can create things that never existed before. He is a God that makes something out of nothing!

This is the message I received from the Lord that day He spoke to me in the Philippines. He does not need our help, our natural abilities, nor our

---

1.   God the Father is a person also, and He is greater than Christ (Jn. 14:28; 1 Cor. 15:27-28). However, He is not the central figure of the Bible. In fact, whereas Christ is revealed continually throughout the Scriptures, there are very few clear revelations of the Father. Obviously, father Abraham is one of the few clear revelations of the Father and His nature. For example, the offering of Isaac by father Abraham is a glorious revelation of the Father.

flesh. He can make something out of nothing. The only thing He asks from us is total surrender to His will. What is His will? His will for us is the same as it was for our example, the Lord Jesus Christ. That "will" is revealed in Hebrews 10:5-10. There we are told that Jesus came into the world to offer His body as a sacrifice on the cross. Can His will for us, His Body, be anything different? He is asking us to take up our cross daily and follow in His footsteps. The cross is defined by the Lord Himself to be a denial of our self-life (Mt. 16:24). It is simply the process of becoming nothing so He can fill our temples with *His* glory. As John the Baptist declares, "He must increase, but I must decrease" (Jn. 3:30).

Does He want just a little of what *we* are to decrease so just a little of what *He* is may be formed in us? Or, is He looking for total commitment and the crucifixion of what we are so that we might be "filled with all the fullness of God"—the goal that Ephesians 3:19 (NKJV) sets before us? The answer is self-evident. Those who are willing to be reduced to nothing in their own eyes, seeing that they can accomplish nothing and are worth nothing outside of Christ, will soon come to know the Creator who makes something beautiful out of nothing.

I have often heard people declare, "The Lord and I make a good team." This concept is not new. This was Peter's idea of how things worked. He just had a hard time convincing the Lord how valuable he really was. The truth is, the Lord makes an even *better* "team" without us! In other words, without our carnal ideas and input, the Lord can do much, much, more in and through us. Only when we have become so reduced that we continually see our weakness and His strength, our smallness and His greatness, can He flow through us freely. Then and *only* then, will we be able to declare with Paul, "When I am weak, then am I strong" (2 Cor. 12:10).

God's ability to make something out of nothing in us is a revelation of His grace. Grace can be defined as divine ability or enabling flowing in and through mankind.[2] There are at least two simple reasons why this message of grace—God making something out of nothing—is the most important truth in the Bible. First, we desperately *need* what He is because what we are isn't the answer for anyone or anything in this world. Second, God's grace works in us to replace what we are with what He is so that

---

2. Although grace can also be defined as unmerited favor, many Scriptures reveal it as the power of God that comes to us from the Spirit of grace (Heb. 10:29). It is this power that enables us to obey, and actually makes us what we are in God. Paul said, "But by the grace of God I am what I am" (1 Cor. 15:10a). Ezekiel 36:26-27 reveals what the Lord does for us in the age of grace. He gives us the Spirit of grace that enables us to obey the Lord. See also Romans 1:5; 12:6; Zechariah 4:6-7; Acts 4:33; 20:32, etc.

God alone gets all the glory. His reason for making something out of nothing is clearly explained in First Corinthians 1:26-29. We are told that God chooses that which is nothing to bring to nothing that which is, *so that no flesh will glory in His presence.*

Are we willing to be reduced to nothing? To zero? Or do we still believe that we have something of real value to offer Him, or others, outside of Christ? **If there is any part of our lives and abilities that we still consider to be worthwhile, we will one day seek to share His glory for what we have helped Him accomplish.** We must allow all that we are to die, both the positive and negative aspects, so that He alone might live within us.

At the end of life's journey, if we continue to believe that "the Lord and I make a good team"—that is, if we continue to believe that we can somehow add something to what He already is within us, we will be greatly embarrassed when we enter Heaven. Imagine what this type of declaration will sound like in the presence of the saints and the angels. Imagine how we will feel when we see His greatness and our smallness, and when we fully understand that we, like Peter, never added anything to God's purposes, but many times actually detracted from them. May God help us to humble our hearts before Him now so that He can reach *His* goal in our lives. He wants to become the fullness and strength of every area of our lives—to be our "all in all"! (Eph. 1:23)

There is a very wonderful positive side to all this: Regardless of what failures we have been, regardless of what our weaknesses may be, regardless of how long we have failed to measure up or have gone around the same mountain, and regardless of how long we have warred against the same enemies in our lives, His grace can make something out of nothing in all of us! He can exalt our valleys, or weak areas, and bring down all the mountains that stand in our way. He can make something beautiful with our lives if we are willing to stop hoping in our own strength to change what we are and start hoping in His mercy. He actually *delights* in those who hope in His mercy (Ps. 147:11). Therefore, regardless of what we are, we can delight His heart if we start hoping in the power of the Creator to make *something out of nothing* in us and stop trusting in our own determination to change ourselves. God revealed to Moses a simple yet profound truth: "So then it is not of him that willeth, nor of him that runneth, but of God that sheweth mercy" (Rom. 9:16).[3]

---

3.   There is an intimate link between mercy and grace, although they are not precisely the same. As Hebrews 4:16 reveals, if we obtain mercy, then we find grace. Divine grace is inherent in divine mercy.

Maybe we have believed that the difference between where we are today and where the Lord wants us to be is just a little gap. Maybe we have even thought that if we could just polish up a few more rough spots in our character we could close that gap. The truth is, an enormous gulf lies between us and the place the Lord has ordained for us. Only a sovereign act of God's mercy can take us across that chasm. If we can only accept our own nothingness and fix our hope in His tender mercy, He will delight in carrying us across—in His arms! The Lord doesn't just want us to see what *we* are. Primarily, He wants us to see what *He* is—the mighty God of Creation!

Our end does not depend on what we are able to accomplish in our lives, but rather on what the Creator is able to do with us if we recognize our great "nothingness." Many have received wonderful promises from God concerning what He wants to do in and through them. They have received high callings in the Spirit. This is usually followed by doubts and fears that those things can never take place in a life that is so frail and so far from being like the Lord. The truth is, the Creator can make us to be *anything* that He wants us to be. He doesn't need to use good raw material, or even *any* raw material, to make us into a new creation in Christ Jesus. The Lord recognized that there was nothing good in us from the day He called us, yet He called us and promised to bring the power of the Creator to bear on our nothingness. The question is whether or not we believe *all* His Word, including Romans 7:18, which says that there is **no** good thing in our natural man. The testimony that will delight all Heaven will be the testimony that reveals this simple truth: "The Lord maketh poor, and maketh rich: he bringeth low, and lifteth up. He raiseth up the poor out of the dust, and lifteth up the beggar from the dunghill, to set them among princes, and to make them inherit the throne of glory" (1 Sam. 2:7-8a). The attitude of all who enter Heaven will be, "I made it to Heaven because of His kindness toward a beggar." Imagine the mercy of our God that places beggars on the throne! He has chosen to do this because He wants us to be eternal testimonies of His infinite mercy, not testimonies of our own merits and worth (Eph. 1:5-6).

So then, the first verse of the Bible reveals the most important person in the Bible, the Lord Jesus Christ. It also reveals the most important truth, the grace of God that makes something out of nothing.[4] This message is

---

4. The message of God's grace can be summed up in one word—the cross. We will see this in later Chapters. The cross is the only source of God's grace—His divine enabling or power. Paul declares that the cross *is* the power of God (1 Cor. 1:17-18). No wonder the age of grace actually began at the cross of Christ! Nor is it any wonder that Paul's preaching continually centered in Christ and the cross (1 Cor. 2:1-2).

repeated over and over throughout the Scriptures in many different ways because He desires to amplify and clarify His truth. He has revealed His gentleness and kindness by doing everything possible to help us grasp the truth. The message of the grace of our Lord Jesus Christ is so important that the Apostle Paul *begins and ends* almost every one of his 13 Epistles with these two central issues (the most important person and the most important truth).[5] Furthermore, the revelation with which the Lord began the Bible is the revelation with which He also ends it in Revelation 22:21: "The grace of our Lord Jesus Christ be with you all. Amen." Here, too, God points to the most important person and the most important truth.

---

5. In 26 beginnings and endings to 13 different Epistles there are only three exceptions to this pattern, and even in those three Paul ends with the words, "Grace be with you," but without referring to Jesus Christ. See Colossians 4:18; First Timothy 6:21; and Titus 3:15 for the exceptions.

Chapter 2

Day One—Salvation Light
Dispels the Darkness of Our Earth

"Dr. Carver, would you please tell us how you managed to discover over 200 different uses for the peanut?" This question was once asked George Washington Carver, the black scientist who actually discovered over 200 uses for the peanut and, thereby, saved the southern United States from financial disaster in the nineteenth century. His answer revealed not only Carver's humility but also the wisdom of God—wisdom that is often overlooked by the Church and the world alike. He said, "I once asked the Lord, 'God, why did You make the universe?' The Lord responded, 'That's too big a question for you to ask, little man. Ask something simpler.' I then asked Him, 'Lord, why did You make me?' Again the Lord responded, 'That's still too big a question for you to ask, little man. Ask something simpler.' So then I asked Him, 'Lord, why did You make the peanut?' That answer He was willing to give me."[1]

Discovering God's purpose for making the peanut ultimately became the way Dr. Carver discovered God's purpose for making him. He lived to help others, and one of the many ways God fulfilled that purpose in his life was to show him the purpose for the lowly peanut. Have you ever asked God why He made something? Is it possible that we, like Dr. Carver, will never really understand the purpose of God for our own lives unless we receive some measure of understanding of His purpose for the things around us that are part of His creation? Does this sound preposterous? The Apostle Paul didn't seem to think so.

---

1. This story was condensed and paraphrased from David R. Collins, *George Washington Carver* (Milford, MI: Mott Media, 1981), pp. 105-106.

Consider what Paul tells us: "The wrath of God is being revealed from heaven against all the godlessness and wickedness of men who suppress the truth by their wickedness, since what may be known about God is plain to them, because God has made it plain to them. For *since the creation of the world* God's invisible qualities—*his eternal power and divine nature— have been clearly seen, being understood from what has been made*, so that men are without excuse" (Rom. 1:18-20 NIV). Paul is declaring that men actually suppress the truth, and that knowledge about God is evident to all, having been made plain by the Lord Himself through the things He has created. Paul goes on to say that even God's "invisible qualities" are "clearly seen" and understood by means of the things God has created. Therefore, we can understand both the greatness of God (His "eternal power") and what He is like (His "divine nature") by considering the creation. One of the many aspects of the divine nature that we can understand through the creation is truth, because He *is* truth (Jn. 14:6).

King Solomon, known for his great wisdom, must have asked the Lord often, "Lord, why did You make this particular thing? Lord, what revelation of divine wisdom and truth do You have for us in this part of Your creation?" Scripture shows us that much of Solomon's wisdom came as he considered the things that were made by God—things both great and small. "And he spake of trees, from the cedar tree that is in Lebanon even unto the hyssop that springeth out of the wall: he spake also of beasts, and of fowl, and of creeping things, and of fishes. And there came of all people to hear the wisdom of Solomon, from all kings of the earth, which had heard of his wisdom" (1 Kings 4:33-34).

Is it any wonder, then, that the greater Son of David, the Lord Jesus Christ, taught us by continually using the creation around us as an object lesson? In fact, He *never* taught the multitudes anything without doing so through a parable (Mt. 13:34-35; Mk. 4:33-34). He spoke of trees, beasts, fowl, creeping things, fishes, sand, fire, rocks, the wind, the waves, sowing, reaping, fishing, baking bread, farming, buying and selling land, shepherding, and much more.

Natural man needs object lessons. In fact, any preacher who does not use examples from real life is a preacher whose sermons are dead, and who is often hard to understand! Are you hungry enough for the truth that you meditate on the creation around you and its object lessons, as the psalmist often did? (Ps. 143:5; 8:3) Do you allow the Holy Spirit and the Scriptures to teach you the object lessons found in creation? The Scriptures are so full of truths that are based on the things God created that it is difficult to find even one thing in the creation that is not mentioned in the Bible. Of course, the Bible must also be accepted as the only source of interpretation. However, almost without exception, the Bible explains what those things represent in the spiritual realm. For example, water speaks of the Word (Eph. 5:26), fire speaks of the Spirit (Mt. 3:11), the rock speaks of Christ (1 Cor. 10:4), sand speaks of a multitude of men (Gen. 22:17), trees speak of men (Is. 61:3; Song 2:3; Mk. 8:24), and grass also speaks of men (Ps. 90:5-6), etc.

We will probably never need to understand the peanut as Dr. Carver did. Nevertheless, if we do not receive the wisdom and understanding the Lord desires to show us through His creation, we may very well lack the wisdom we need to fulfill God's purposes for our lives. If we never understand why He created the things around us, what chance is there that we will have a clear understanding of why He created us, mankind?

We saw one example of the importance of understanding the creation: In the previous Chapter, we saw how the New Testament writers unveil the tremendous revelation of truth that is found in the simple declaration, "God created the heavens and the earth" (Gen. 1:1 NKJV). This very first verse in the Bible is exploding with truth that can change our lives. Therefore, it would be appropriate to inquire whether the entire divine account of the Creation story in Genesis 1 may also have many precious gems of truth for those hungry enough to search for them. Romans 1:18-20 and many other New Testament Scriptures show us that there are countless gems of truth in Genesis 1 and the Creation story. How could it be otherwise? As Believers, we often take the miracles and parables of Jesus and dissect them, considering the spiritual message of each little detail. This is good and proper because He is the living Word and every jot and tittle of the Word is significant (Mt. 5:18). Therefore, everything He does, and how He does it, is very important and reveals truth. Surely, then, one of His greatest works of all time, the Creation, must also be exploding with truth!

If the details of the Creation reveal truths, then all those truths must also be clearly explained in the New Testament just as Genesis 1:1 is explained. No valid interpretation of an Old or New Testament Scripture can be arbitrary or founded on personal revelation; it must be firmly based on other Scriptures that clearly state what we are saying. If we are willing to limit ourselves to this standard, we will avoid most of the strange and spurious doctrines that are taught today.

Many years ago the Lord gave me a wonderful experience. Through it He enabled me to comprehend the simple yet profoundly important fact that the Creation story in Genesis 1 is more than merely a revelation of how God created the earth. It is also a revelation of the very nature of God—His ways, ideas, methods, etc. My understanding of His purposes, and of the message of the Scriptures, was forever changed. I trust that the same awakening will occur in your heart as you read this testimony and the rest of the book.

One day when I was mowing the lawn of the church where my wife and I were pastoring, I suddenly heard a little voice say to me, "Go inside and read Genesis 1, and everywhere it says 'earth,' put in its place 'the spirit of man.' " I thought to myself, "Now *that* is a crazy thought!" and I continued to mow the grass. A few minutes later, I again heard a little voice saying, "Go inside and read Genesis 1, and everywhere it says 'earth' put in its place 'the spirit of man.' " Again I considered the thought to be ridiculous and continued to mow.

Like Balaam, we are sometimes too busy going our own way to recognize the voice of the Lord when it comes to us. Balaam was so determined to go his own way that he instinctively began to argue with the donkey, instead of recognizing the miracle—that his donkey was actually talking! (Num. 22:28-30) I was too busy mowing the grass to stop and obey, but when that little voice came to me again for the third time, I said to myself, "Well, I suppose I can't lose too much if I do it. I guess I'll just go inside and see what happens." I soon discovered that the little voice had come from the Lord. (I often marvel at the Lord's ability to speak to someone as deaf as I am, and at the mercy He shows to open our blinded eyes even when we are so proud that we think we can already see plainly.)

Is it biblically sound to compare the natural earth the Lord created with man's spiritual life? Could it be that the way God created the natural earth is a revelation of how He makes us into "a new creation" in Christ Jesus? (2 Cor. 5:17 NIV) Hebrews compares us with the "earth which drinketh in the rain that cometh oft upon it…" (Heb. 6:7). Likewise, Moses speaks to the earth, saying, "…hear, O earth, the words of my mouth. My doctrine shall drop as the rain, my speech shall distil as the dew, as the small rain upon the tender herb, and as the showers upon the grass" (Deut. 32:1-2). Obviously, the natural earth does not have ears and cannot hear, but *this* "earth" in Deuteronomy 32 can. Surely *we* are that earth, and upon our earth falls the rain of God's doctrine and speech, or the living Word. Many times, when the Scriptures speak about the "earth," they are not only referring to the ball of clay we call the natural earth, but also to another ball of clay—man.[2] Adam, who was actually taken from the earth, was literally a piece of earth into which divine life entered.

---

2.   The "earth" of the Bible not only can hear, but also can see (Ps. 97:4) and sing (Ps. 96:1); have emotions such as fear (Ps. 76:8) and joy (Ps. 97:1); be satisfied (Ps. 104:13) and melt at the sound of God's voice (Ps. 46:6).

Thus, as I began to read Genesis 1, replacing "the earth" with "the spirit of man," the message became clear. I realized for the first time that God's Creation of the natural earth reveals how God deals with man to make him a new creation in Christ Jesus. In the first verse we are told, "In the beginning God created the heavens and the earth." Then, in verse 2, we are immediately shown the spiritual condition of mankind before the Creator's power is directed toward us to transform us into a new creation: "And the earth was without form, and void; and **darkness was upon the face of the deep.**"

The Light of the Gospel Comes to Our Earth

As I continued reading the next verse—"And God said, Let there be light: and there was light"—immediately I was reminded how the Apostle Paul applies this event in the Creation to our salvation experience, where the light of the gospel enters our spiritual being. This is the new birth, which is the first step toward becoming a new creation in Christ Jesus. Paul certainly sees the first Day of Creation as a symbol of the new-birth experience when he says, "The god of this age has blinded the minds of unbelievers, so that they cannot see the light of the gospel of the glory of Christ, who is the image of God...For God, who said, 'Let light shine out of darkness,' made his light shine in our hearts to give us the light of the knowledge of the glory of God in the face of Christ" (2 Cor. 4:4,6 NIV). Therefore, we have indisputable New Testament evidence that the Spirit of God, through Paul, compares the work of the first Day of Creation with man's salvation experience and the entrance of the gospel. This begins our spiritual walk with God.

Day One Begins Our Spiritual Journey Toward Day Seven

At this point in my reading of Genesis 1, I also recalled that the seventh and last Day in the Creation account, called the "Day of Rest," is shown to be the spiritual **goal** of the Christian life in a well-known passage from the Book of Hebrews (Heb. 3:7–4:11). This New Testament divine commentary on Israel's journey from Egypt to Canaan is principally concerned with the importance of entering "God's rest." In fact, "rest" is mentioned in this short passage 11 times. In the most unmistakable terms, it is directly linked to the rest of Day Seven in the Creation account, "For He has spoken in a certain place of the seventh day in this way: 'And God rested on the seventh day from all His works' " (Heb. 4:4 NKJV). Instead of referring to the goal of Israel's wilderness journey as "Canaan," the writer of

Hebrews calls it "God's rest." He first does this in Hebrews 3:9-11 when he refers to the oath God made in Numbers 14:21-24 against rebellious Israel. He is actually quoting from Psalm 95:8-11, which refers to the same oath. In Numbers, God swore that, because Israel had tempted or tested Him in the wilderness, they would not enter into the "**land**" (Canaan) He had promised to their fathers. In Hebrews and Psalm 95, this divine oath seems to be changed slightly. In both places, God's oath declared that Israel would not enter into God's "**rest**" because they had tempted God in the wilderness. Neither the psalmist nor the writer of Hebrews were being presumptuous when they interchanged the concept of inheriting Canaan with the concept of entering God's rest. God Himself, through Moses, had shown Israel that these two concepts were really one and the same. (See Deuteronomy 3:20 and 12:9-10.) From the beginning of their walk, God was leading Israel toward His rest, or Canaan, the promised land. Are you headed that direction in your own spiritual journey?

In First Corinthians 10:1-11, Paul gives a summary of Israel's journey from Egypt to Canaan, and then declares that their journey is an example for all Believers. He writes, "Now all these things happened to them as examples, and they were written for our admonition, upon whom the ends of the ages have come" (1 Cor. 10:11 NKJV). This key verse, which demonstrates that the history of Israel is a pattern for the Church, shows us that we, too, must leave Egypt—the world—and journey toward the promised land of God's rest. Therefore, we are made to understand that just as Israel's goal was represented by the rest of the seventh Day, so is ours. We begin our spiritual journey on Day One with the new birth. We then move toward God's rest on the seventh Day as we yield our lives to the process of God's dealings in our wilderness journey.

Regarding the goal of entering rest, Hebrews gives us an awesome warning. Israel failed to reach this goal because of unbelief (Heb. 3:17-19), and we are warned not to repeat their mistake (Heb. 4:1-2). This stern warning was spoken to Believers and *not* to the world. This makes it clear that it is possible for us to fail to reach God's rest, the very goal that God has established for our Christian life! Even so, Hebrews encourages us by declaring that at least some Believers will ultimately enter that rest (Heb. 4:6), as also happened with God's people under Joshua.

Could it be that many do not finish their spiritual journey and enter God's rest simply because they do not know that spiritual rest exists or that it is the primary goal in life? Or, maybe you know that God has a place of rest for you, but you aren't sure of the steps to enter that rest. We can only "enter into His rest" through faith (Heb. 4:1-2). Many Christians today do not realize that they are on a spiritual journey that is symbolized by Israel's natural journey; nor do they understand the steps or the goal of that journey. How sad! What is the probability that we will have the faith to reach a goal in life we do not even know exists? And if we do not know that rest exists, what is the probability that we will heed the exhortation found in Hebrews to "make every effort to enter that rest"? (Heb. 4:11 NIV)

Many Scriptures show that God's rest is actually the primary goal of our spiritual lives. Could it be for this precise reason the Lord began His Word with Genesis 1 and 2, revealing that rest and the steps to enter it? It seems likely. After giving that initial revelation, God repeated it and amplified it time and again throughout the Bible. Wouldn't it be tragic if, in spite of all His efforts to help us, we would remain blind to what it all means? Have you considered what His rest really means and how you plan to enter it?

Some Christians have concluded that God's rest refers to Heaven, the eventual home of His people. Of course, this doctrine does not fit at all with Israel's journey and the example they left us. Canaan could not represent Heaven, because their greatest battles began once they got to Canaan! Hebrews 4:3-4 shows what God's rest really was from the beginning—a time when He ceased from all His works on the seventh Day. Hebrews 4:10 then applies that same concept of rest to us, saying that those who have entered into *God's* rest have done the same thing—they have ceased from *their* own works. Paul tells us what our own works are; they are the works of the flesh (Gal. 5:19). Of course, for those who long to have the character and life of Christ manifested in and through their lives, any and every work of the flesh brings inner conflict, turmoil, and sorrow. Clearly these things are anything but rest. Therefore, as long as we continue to do the works of the flesh, there can be no lasting rest in our spirits.

There is only one way for us to enter that true spiritual rest: The works of the flesh must be conquered in us. This begins to happen in our "earth" as God's light dispels the darkness of our ways on Day One of His creative work in us. As we allow Him to continue His work in us, the cross will reduce us to nothing so that Christ's life may increase in us and fill our temple with His glory. We considered this process in Chapter 1, but it is not enough to tell someone, "Brother, just embrace the cross; then you will decrease, and He will increase." We need to know, in practical terms, the necessary steps for this to become reality in us. These steps are revealed to us in the six Days of Creation that lead us to the seventh Day—the "Day of Rest." Each Day will bring us a fresh revelation of the cross of Christ. For this reason we need a clear understanding of what each of those spiritual works of God represents in our lives. Throughout these Chapters we will often refer to the seven Days of God's creative work in our spiritual lives as the "**redemptive week**." The seven Days of this "redemptive week" reveal how God works in six creative steps or "Days" to bring our spiritual lives or "earth" into His rest on the seventh Day. This redemptive process transforms a sinful, fallen man into a mature Believer. When His work is finished in our earth, we will know by experience His complete redemption in every area of our lives.

Once I had clearly seen the above truths, I continued to read Genesis 1 with a new understanding and a new assurance. I was confident that the steps God took in the Creation of the natural earth indeed revealed the steps He must take in making us a new creation in Christ. I felt certain that the other five Days of Creation also have a message to give us. If this is true, we must allow the Scriptures to interpret each of the Days for us.

We will see that the interpretation of the spiritual significance of each Day is firmly based on the Scriptures from Genesis to Revelation. If we long for the Lord to finish His creative work in our spiritual lives, then we need to understand His ways and yield to those ways with all our hearts.

King Solomon said, "It is the glory of God to conceal a thing: but the honour of kings is to search out a matter" (Prov. 25:2). God conceals things so that only those who are truly hungry will search for and discover the gems of truth hidden in His Word. The wisest man in the Old Testament told us that wisdom will reveal its secrets to us if we love it enough to discover its gems (Prov. 8:17). Do you love the truth? Do you love it enough to spend quality time in the intimacy of His presence where understanding is birthed as you search out His hidden secrets?

Genesis 1 is an extremely profound chapter that desperately needs to be searched out. The amazing quantity of spiritual information that is hidden there is very much like the storehouse of natural information found in a seed. But the same God who speaks light into our darkness on Day One, wants the brightness of His light to increase within us. For those who love the truth, His light will shine ever brighter to reveal the things He has hidden in dark places. The Lord promises, "And I will give thee the treasures of darkness, and hidden riches of secret places" (Is. 45:3a). His Word also promises, "But the **path of the just** is like the shining sun, that **shines ever brighter** unto the perfect day" (Prov. 4:18 NKJV).

Has the spiritual darkness of your earth been dispelled by the entrance of the light of His gospel on Day One? If so, then His plan is to accomplish further creative works within your earth until you experience the glory of His light on the "perfect day." However, if your heart is still living in spiritual darkness, why not ask the Creator to speak light into your "earth" today as you repent of your ways, asking Him to forgive your sins and take full control of your life and your future?

Chapter 3

The Miracle of a Seed

Jesus tells us that the Word of God is like a seed (Lk. 8:11). Every time a farmer plants seed in his field, he is involved in a miracle that is one of the greatest confirmations of God's existence that there is. When God created the first seed, it was a tremendous divine miracle. That miracle is no less a miracle today than it was when He first performed it. It continues to give testimony to His greatness. Since we have planted seed for so many generations without considering what is involved, many would laugh at the idea that the seed we plant is truly a miracle.

This type of spiritual blindness surely pervaded the Israelites in their wilderness journey regarding the miracle of manna. It was an amazing miracle from anyone's perspective when they awoke one morning to find bread from heaven spread all over the ground. For the new generation that was born and raised in the wilderness, manna was simply a natural, daily occurrence. For them, the *real* miracle occurred the day they crossed the Jordan into Canaan and never again found manna on the ground! As so often happens in "modern times" when God manifests His power in the earth, the miracle of manna was soon relegated to "an act of Mother Nature," instead of being appreciated as the provision of a gracious God! Manna had become simply a fact of life.

Ponder the miracle of a seed for just a few moments. It is more than sufficient proof that an awesome and wonderful God created this world. Consider, for example, a tiny apple seed. Within that little seed is stored an incredible wealth of information. When planted in damp, dark, warm soil, the little seed has within it all the necessary information to split its hull open, shoot its roots downward, and push a stalk upward. Imagine what would happen if the seed shot roots upward and a stalk downward! In addition, the seed contains all the specific information needed to cause the cells of its stalk to continue to multiply in just the right way so that it develops two or more small leaves. It also has the information necessary to begin the process of photosynthesis when it reaches the light so that the leaves are green. Next, for no apparent reason, the new plant begins to sprout branches on all sides with new leaves on those branches, each one similar yet unique.

As the little tree continues to grow, the original trunk and the new branches are provided with the information needed to protect themselves by forming bark. The wisdom that was resident in that little seed also instructs the new tree that it is still too young to bear fruit, so it spends several years simply growing and getting stronger. (It is too bad that the trees the Lord plants, as mentioned in Isaiah 61:3, sometimes try to bypass this wise choice.) Then, one spring morning, after a number of years that is predetermined by the information in the seed, new growths suddenly begin to appear along the sides of all the branches. This is old, yet new, because although those branches were always sprouting this way, continually forming more new branches, this is different! These are not new branches; they are buds that turn into flowers after a certain number of days! How could that seed have had enough information to wait for so many years and then form beautiful, delicate flowers? Then, miracle of miracles, a tiny green apple forms under each flower within a few days. Imagine how much stored information the seed needed to change a flower into an apple! The miracle does not stop there. The new apple is provided with all the information necessary to grow to a specific size and shape, depending on the species of apple seed that was planted. After a certain number of months, it has all the information it needs to mature and turn red (or maybe yellow). Finally, the farmer comes along and picks the apple, eats the fruit, and finds tiny new seeds inside. Stored within those new little seeds is every detail of the information that had been stored in the original seed the farmer planted, even though that seed had broken apart and ceased to exist years before!

Imagine the many different types of cells that were formed throughout this process: cells for the stalk, leaves, bark, buds; cells for each of the many parts of the flowers and the apples. Man does not have, nor will he ever have, enough information or wisdom available to him to create even *one* single living cell—even though a little seed is capable of forming a multitude of cells of countless varieties, each with a specific purpose. In spite of this, many men continue to ignore the miracle of the seed and deny the existence of God. It is no wonder the psalmist tells us, "The fool has said in his heart, 'There is no God'…" (Ps. 14:1 NKJV). Therefore, if we say that there is no miracle-working God behind the seed, we must confess that the insignificant little apple seed is much wiser than we are, since we are not wise enough to make even one cell. Then where does that leave us? As very ignorant fools! We aren't talking here about having a "pea brain," as the saying goes, but rather of having a brain much smaller than a tiny apple seed!

What does all this have to do with the Word of God, and why does Jesus compare the Word to a seed? Because, like a seed, His Word is exceedingly full of vital information. Genesis 1, the first Word that God revealed to man, is an example. It is like a seed from which all the rest of the Book of Genesis springs, and then, the rest of the Bible. In fact, every major doctrine of the Scriptures can be found in seed form in Genesis 1. How can so much information be stored in such a small place? That is the miracle of a seed! It is no wonder that Jesus, speaking of the Old Testament Scriptures, said that every jot and tittle would be fulfilled. In the Creation account of Genesis 1, each word of each verse, as well as the order of events, must be carefully considered.

Is it possible that first Genesis, then the entire Bible, spring from the Creation account like a tree from a seed? To catch at least a small glimpse of this wonderful truth before reading on, consider this: After the Lord reveals to us the truth of the *seven Days* of Creation and the story of Adam, He dedicates the rest of the Book of Genesis to the lives of the *seven men* of faith listed in Hebrews 11. Who are they and what do they tell us?

The Seven Men of Faith in Genesis

There are only seven men of faith about whom Genesis gives us details, all of whom are listed in Hebrews 11. They are as follows: 1) Abel, 2) Enoch, 3) Noah, 4) Abraham, 5) Isaac, 6) Jacob, and 7) Joseph. Some may ask why Adam is not included in this list. The first reason is that Adam is an integral part of what we have called "the seed," or the Creation account. Like a tree springs from a seed, the seven men of faith literally sprang from Adam, the father of all humanity. The second reason Adam is not found in our list is that he is not found in the Holy Spirit's list either. He is not included among the men of faith listed in Hebrews 11.

Why are there seven men of faith after the seven Days of Creation? These men emerge next because their lives give us a deeper understanding of the message of the seven Days of Creation, by revealing how that message can be experienced in our lives in a practical way. For example, on the

third Day we are told, "And God said, Let the waters under the heaven be gathered together un... one place, and let the dry land appear: and it was so" (Gen. 1:9). Precisely the same event is repeated in the life of Noah, the **third man** of faith. We will examine these types of comparisons throughout the book.

The Seven Feasts of the Lord

Not only does the entire Book of Genesis, including the seven men of faith, spring from the seven Days of Creation, but the rest of the Bible also springs from the Creation account. The Book of Exodus, which follows immediately after Genesis, along with Numbers and Deuteronomy, gives the account of Israel's journey from Egypt to Canaan. Are seven steps also revealed in this part of the Bible? God Himself divided Israel's journey into seven principal events or steps, which He commanded Israel to remember forever and commemorate each year through the celebration of the seven feasts of the Lord (Lev. 23). These feasts were and still are Israel's national holidays. Like most national holidays, Israel's holidays celebrate important events in the history of their nation.

The first feast is Passover, which commemorates the Israelites' deliverance from death and slavery in Egypt. Their journey began at the first Passover. The complete list of the seven feasts is as follows: 1) Passover, 2) Unleavened Bread, 3) Firstfruits, 4) Pentecost, 5) Trumpets, 6) Day of Atonement, and 7) Tabernacles.

We will discover that the same seven spiritual steps are revealed in both the seven Days of Creation and the seven feasts. No wonder, then, that Hebrews 3–4 refers to the "rest" of the seventh day as the goal of Israel's journey, instead of calling it "Canaan." Clearly, the seven steps in the journey and the seven Days of Creation both bring us to the same place in God! Thus Exodus, the second book of the Bible, (dealing with Israel's journey), is governed by the information from the original "seed" found in Genesis 1–2. One brief example of this amazing truth is that God created the first fruits on the **third Day** of Creation (Gen. 1:11), and the **third feast** is the "Feast of Firstfruits!" Coincidence? We will see.

Seven Steps in the Tabernacle of Moses

The pattern of seven steps in our walk toward spiritual maturity continued to be the "seed" from which the Scriptures grew long after Israel's seven-step journey to Canaan ended. Those seven steps were also revealed in the Tabernacle of Moses, which was at the heart of Jewish life and Scriptures for the rest of Old Testament history.[1] God gave Israel the Law and the Tabernacle as described in the last part of Exodus and most of Leviticus. The central issue in the observance of that Law revolved around the Tabernacle and the priests who ministered there. It is no surprise that there are seven principal steps or truths revealed in the Tabernacle. They include the door of the Tabernacle and the six furnishings found inside. The seven steps of the Tabernacle are the following: 1) the door, 2) the laver, 3) the brazen altar, 4) the candlestick, 5) the table of showbread, 6) the altar of incense, and 7) the ark of the covenant (found in the Holy of Holies). This is the order of the steps that the priests followed in their daily ministry, except they were not permitted to enter the Holy of Holies on a daily basis. All those who desire to draw near to God must begin at the door, which is symbolic of man's salvation experience. (John 10:9 shows us that Christ is the door.) Without this absolutely essential first step, no one will ever experience the glory that the six furnishings of the Tabernacle symbolize. God's goal for us is that we move from the door to the ark of the covenant in the Holy of Holies. This is the place where God's glory dwells—the place of true spiritual rest.

Throughout the rest of this book, we will compare the seven Days of Creation with the seven men of faith in Genesis, the seven feasts, and the seven steps in the Tabernacle of Moses. We will note that each of these groups of seven reveal precisely the same progression in our spiritual walk. (Refer to the chart at the end of the book for a complete summary.) Throughout the Bible, the Lord gives us the same message over and over by using different methods. There are at least two reasons for this: First, He does so to **emphasize** the truth; second, He does so to **amplify** and **clarify** the truth. His truth, like a beautiful diamond, has many facets or faces. It is impossible to take in its full beauty by concentrating our attention on only one facet. As we do with a diamond, we must look at the truth from many different angles. We will see that there are so many amazing parallels between the various lists of seven steps that we can be sure each speaks of the same spiritual process. Interestingly, each list also contributes details that are not found in the other lists. This permits us to view the major stages in our spiritual walk from slightly different perspectives to deepen our understanding of each one.

---

1. From the outside, the Tabernacle of Moses appeared to be nothing more than a common tent. However, God chose to dwell in that tent and fill it with His glory. After almost 500 years of use, the Tabernacle was replaced by the Temple. However, the Temple contained the same furniture and the same basic layout as the Tabernacle. They both reveal the same principal truths. The major difference was that the Tabernacle was moveable and the Temple was not.

Chapter 4

The Message of Genesis and Evolution

Did you know that hydrogen gas, given enough time, turns into human beings? Does that sound preposterous? I have "scientific proof" that this is what really happened! You see, in college I majored in science; my "scientific proof" is that my science professors and many of my science textbooks unabashedly declared this to be so. Of course, *their* only "scientific proof" for teaching me this ludicrous idea was that *their* science teachers and textbooks taught *them* the same thing. We were all assured that those people were respected scientists and that the textbooks were all based on scientific facts. Therefore, we knew we could depend on that information as being trustworthy and believable.

Many teachers of evolution are simply parroting what they have been taught, without ever questioning its logic. Therefore, they are not guilty of deceiving their students *on purpose*, but they *are* guilty of deceiving their students—unwittingly. Furthermore, if we make an honest attempt to reduce the theory of evolution down to its most basic premise, we can see that it is actually telling the world that hydrogen gas, all by itself, has turned into human beings!

Let's reduce this so-called "scientific theory" down to two of its principal declarations (without getting bogged down in the details). First, the most popular "scientific" explanation for the origin of the universe is known as "the big bang theory." Among other things, this theory states that in the beginning the only thing that existed was the most basic of all earth's elements—hydrogen gas—which emerged from a huge explosion. Supposedly, through nuclear reactions, the other elements were gradually formed from the original hydrogen. Then, in the process of time, with the formation of planets and other heavenly bodies, our earth emerged out of this chaos. The second basic premise of the theory of evolution is that the earth gradually cooled down until a hot thin soup existed upon its surface. Allegedly, it was out of this soup that the most basic forms of life emerged. Then we are told that over a period of time these life forms evolved into human beings. If we put these two basic concepts together, the obvious conclusion is that hydrogen gas turned into human beings.

This theory of the origin of life is taught in most western nations of the world today, all in the name of science, and with no shame or hesitation whatsoever. In fact, many of the "authorities" that teach these things even laugh at Christians who believe that God created us. Their scoffing proves that they honestly believe that hydrogen gas could have turned into people on its own—something that they say our God couldn't possibly have done!

In every age of known history, including our so-called "modern" day, members of the authoritative scientific community of the world have been guilty of believing one or more preposterous theories. In the days of Columbus, most believed that the earth was flat. Later on, it was taught in respectable universities that certain materials on earth were capable of burning due to the fact that they contained a substance known as "phlogiston," which actually produced the flames. No one had ever seen this substance, but the "authorities" assured their students that it existed. Why else would things burst into flames? It was not until the discovery of oxygen that the shame of these "authorities" and their ignorance was exposed. Then, a mere 130 years ago, the scientific world laughed Louis Pasteur to scorn when he declared his new concept that *only life can beget life*. He proved that germs exist in everyday life; they do not just suddenly materialize. The great men of the day didn't even flinch when they confidently taught that life was the result of "spontaneous generation." In other words, they believed that a pile of garbage, when left alone for a time, was capable of producing mice! In their eyes, they had scientific proof. All the proof they needed was to observe a pile of garbage for a few days, and sure enough, mice would be found there! After all, personal observation is admissible scientific proof of a theory, isn't it?

Today, the "modern" scientific world has, in some ways, simply regressed 130 years to the days of Pasteur. Evolution is nothing more than a greatly-refined version of the theory of spontaneous generation—the same thing the scientific world foolishly believed 130 years ago! Today we know that a pile of garbage cannot produce mice, but we are absolutely sure that hydrogen gas, given enough time, can produce human beings. It's all a matter of time; hydrogen gas simply needs more time to produce life than the pile of garbage had available to it. In other words, to the "great scientific minds" of our day, the world-renowned experts of Pasteur's day made one vital mistake; they were under the erroneous impression that garbage could produce life very quickly, when in fact it takes about five billion years for that to happen. Oh, how blind and foolish humanity is when we choose to ignore the Creator—the One who is truth and light!

Unfortunately, some Christians try to reconcile the Creation account of Genesis 1 with the "false science" of evolution.[1] **But the two concepts cannot be reconciled.** Some would have us believe that a "Day" in Genesis 1 refers to a very long period of time, maybe thousands or millions of years. However, it is important to note that the Hebrew term used here refers specifically to a 24-hour period of time.[2] Consider just a few irreconcilable differences between what God says and man's ideas. First, evolution claims that the earth had sunlight before plants evolved, but Genesis 1 says that plants were created on the third Day and the light of the sun was given on the fourth Day. That plants existed for thousands or millions of years without the light of the sun is an impossibility in nature! On the fourth Day, fish and birds were created at the same time, *not* millions of years apart as evolutionists would tell us. On the sixth Day, the "creeping things" were made *after* the birds of the fourth Day—not before (as evolutionists assert).

Maybe we have never considered just how serious the debate over the Creation account of Genesis 1 really is. In the first place, Genesis 1 reveals the greatness and glory of the Creator. If we do not accept the Word of God in Genesis 1 at face value, we will be plagued continually with the spirit of unbelief as we read the rest of God's Word and seek to experience it. Either Genesis 1 is trustworthy, or it is not. If it is not, then neither is the rest of God's written Word. Although our *mouths* may declare that we believe what God says, if we do not believe the *first* thing He tells us in His Word, how can we say that we believe the rest? Our spiritual man will have difficulty believing what He says to us later if we doubt what He told us in the beginning. The Bible emphasizes that we must *confess with our mouths;*

---

1. The existence of dinosaurs in the past is part of the reason this is done. However, it would be extremely faulty reasoning to attempt to prove the validity of evolution by pointing to the fact that entire classes of animals existed in the past that no longer exist today. The subject of where the dinosaurs came from and what happened to them is outside the scope of this book. However, I do believe that there is a very logical explanation for them without resorting to evolution—without trying to explain the unknown by means of the absurd!

2. "Evening and morning" here actually mean "the night and the day," and refer to the shining of the sun (*Strong's Hebrew Dictionary* #6153 and #1242). Therefore, this expression refers to one cycle of nighttime and daylight to form a day of 24 hours.

but that is not enough because we must also *believe in our hearts* (Rom. 10:9). If we do not believe Genesis 1, we do not really believe.

Can we see the subtlety of Satan in seeking to plant doubts in our hearts about the very first chapter of God's written Word? If he can destroy our faith there, he has succeeded in destroying our faith in the rest of the Bible. It is little wonder that many Christians never really grow and prosper in their spiritual lives; they have been filled with unbelief. They have allowed the enemy to plant doubts in their spirits about the very first thing God revealed to mankind—where man came from! How, then, can they believe God when He tells them where man is headed—God's goal for his life—and the only way to get there?

There is another vital issue involved here in the enemy's tactics. As a science major myself, I have observed that **true science** always ends up confirming what the Bible says. Nevertheless, because of the false "scientific noise" Satan has made about the origin of man, many of us, when reading Genesis 1, give more thought to refuting evolution, or to comparing evolution with the Creation, than to the real importance of this chapter. Satan desperately wants to muddy the waters concerning the true importance of Genesis 1—and all the rest of Genesis for that matter. If he succeeds in focusing our minds on other things as we read about the Creation, then maybe we will never see the gems of truth that are found there nor the primary message of Genesis that springs from this "seed." We need not continue being blinded by his smoke screen!

The Message of Genesis

So, what is the message of Genesis? Obviously, Genesis reveals where we came from. It also shows us where we are going and how we must get there. It gives us *a vision of God's goal for us—to enter the **inheritance** He offers us*. In the Bible, our inheritance is often referred to as "Canaan" and also as the "rest" of the seventh Day. We may then ask, "What exactly is our spiritual inheritance?" Genesis gives us the answer.

There are two basic sections in Genesis. The first part deals with man's ancient history from the Creation up through Noah and his descendants (chapters 1–10). The second part deals with Abraham and his descendants. In the first ten chapters, the "**rest**" of God is a recurring theme. In Genesis 11–50, the recurring theme is "**Canaan.**" In this second part, the men of faith were promised Canaan as an everlasting inheritance; finally, after entering Canaan, they were filled with the desire to remain in Canaan forever.

The Bible explains how "rest" and "Canaan" are related. As I already mentioned, the concepts of "rest" and "Canaan" are intimately linked by Hebrews 3 and 4, where "rest" is actually used to refer to "Canaan," the goal of Israel's journey and the promised inheritance. We understand, then, that both these terms are used to refer to the inheritance God promises His people. Consider what the real crux of that inheritance is. In Numbers 18:20, the Lord tells the priests that *He* is their inheritance; then He repeats this thought for *all* members of the New Testament priesthood in Romans 8:17, where we are told that we are "heirs of God." In other words, we inherit God Himself!

The concept of man inheriting God is awesome, but the concept of God inheriting man is shocking. He is not only *our* inheritance, but we are *His* inheritance! (Ex. 34:9) The psalmist must have been overwhelmed as he meditated on that blessing. He declared, "Blessed is the nation whose God is the Lord; and the people whom he hath chosen for his own inheritance" (Ps. 33:12). It is understandable that man would want to inherit God, but why would God ever want to inherit us? The only answer is infinite love and kindness. He has chosen us as His eternal bride. In our marriage with the Lord, as in any earthly marriage, the husband belongs to the wife, and the wife belongs to the husband, as they become one flesh (1 Cor. 7:4). It is no wonder, then, that the biblical terms used for our inheritance ("rest" and "Canaan") are also both directly linked to the thought of "marriage" in the Scriptures. In the mind of a Hebrew person, "rest" and "marriage" are synonymous terms, as seen in Ruth 1:9, where Naomi says to Ruth and Orpah, "The Lord grant you that ye may find rest, each of you in the house of her husband...." Furthermore, the promised land, Canaan, is also linked with marriage in Isaiah 62:4, where the Lord promises His people, "...neither shall thy land [Canaan] any more be termed Desolate: but thou shalt be called Hephzibah, and thy land Beulah: for the Lord delighteth in thee, and *thy land shall be married*." The word *Beulah* actually means "married," so that the land of Canaan shall be called "married." Once we have truly caught a glimpse of Him and experienced the glory of His presence, we will long to inherit Him and all that He is by being united with Him in marriage. Therefore, the thought of God's rest—or Canaan— being our inheritance carries with it the thought of the life of Christ becoming our eternal spiritual inheritance, as we become joined to Him in a husband-wife relationship.

Paul prays in Ephesians 1:18 that we would know "...*the riches of the glory of his inheritance in the saints.*" Remember that the inheritance is two-way: God inherits us and we inherit God. Later, in Ephesians 3:3-6, Paul goes on to speak of a wonderful divine "mystery"—that the "inheritance" will be received by the Gentiles as well as the Jews. In Colossians 1:27, Paul tells us that God desires to "...make known what is the *riches of the glory of this mystery* among the Gentiles; *which is Christ in you*, the hope of glory." So if Canaan and rest are our inheritance, and "Christ in us" is our inheritance, then we know that Genesis, when it refers to inheriting the land of Canaan or entering rest, is revealing the fullness of the life of Christ being formed in us.

The goal or inheritance that Genesis sets before us is to grow up into the maturity and character of Christ—to be transformed into His likeness. Only when we are like Him can we experience true spiritual rest. The world urgently needs to see the beauty of Jesus in and through the Church. Manifestations of our flesh and our own sinful ways can only bring death to others. Consequently, unless we understand how to reach the place where we are "filled with all the fullness of God" (Eph. 3:19 NKJV), His purposes in us will be frustrated. The Lord warns us, "My people are destroyed for lack of knowledge" (Hos. 4:6a). How many Christians have the necessary knowledge to progress from being a spiritual baby to a mature, spiritual father?

In the Church today, there seems to be much talk about winning the world, but very little is shared on the kind of Christian life that will succeed in doing so. We want to *preach* the gospel without *living* the gospel. We want to be involved in delivering others when we don't really have liberty ourselves (2 Pet. 2:19; Jn. 8:34). We want to give birth to many spiritual children, but we don't have time to enter the chambers of the King and participate in an intimate love relationship with Him. Only that relationship can cause children to be conceived and birthed in the spiritual life, just as happens in the natural life.

In short, we want to *be* someone without *becoming* someone in Him. We want to be someone in *man's* eyes without becoming someone in *His* eyes—without being like Christ. We want spiritual success without paying the price it requires, and without choosing the way that leads us there. We are so busy building the Kingdom that we don't have the time to read the blueprints that show us how to build it *His* way. Of course, the enemy doesn't mind if we busy ourselves for the rest of our lives building a 100-story spiritual skyscraper for the Lord. As long as it does not have the right foundation, he knows that it will ultimately come crashing down, as so many works and their respective ministries have done over the past few years. Jesus tells us that only a house built on the right foundation, the Rock, will last. Woe to any spiritual house that has been built on the sand of man's opinions and ways (Lk. 6:46-49). Sand is often likened to man, as in Genesis 22:17. Jesus explains that a house built on the Rock is built by the man who comes to Him, hears how He wants the house to be built, and then follows His instructions. Therefore, a house on the sand is built some other way. *Any* other way is man's way—a way that will never prosper in the end. We are sometimes so busy working *for* the Lord that we fail to spend time *with* the Lord to receive His instructions.

Moses spent 80 days on the mountain with the Lord before he even began to build God's house, the Tabernacle of Moses. The Lord solemnly warned him to build it precisely in accordance with the pattern and vision he had received in the presence of the Lord (Heb. 8:5). God did not say that He would smash the whole work if Moses did not build it according to the divine blueprint. That is not what was in God's heart. Rather, He was telling Moses to build the house God's way, or it would not have a foundation that could endure the flood the enemy, and time itself, would bring against it.

So many well-known ministries have crashed recently! Would they not have continued to prosper without eternal loss if the leaders had just laid the foundation and built the house according to direct guidance from the Lord? These ministries did not end as they did because God forsook them or failed them, or because He is a hard God who gets angry and smashes everything that is not built His way. To the contrary, God's heart is one of compassion, mercy, and love. He wants *all* our works to endure and receive an eternal reward. Nevertheless, He has established the laws of the Kingdom just as He established the laws of nature. Regardless of how sincere little three-year-old Johnny is when he leaps from the second floor window with a sheet tied to his back, convinced that he can fly, he is going to have a hard landing! God did not fail him. Rather, he tried to break one of God's laws of nature, and that law broke him. If we build according to our way and not His, God will not judge us in anger, but instead, He will mercifully let us go from failure to failure until we discover why we need to repent of our ways. As any true father would do, He will also weep for us in our times of distress.

The Lord *pleads* with us to come to Him and get the understanding of His laws and ways that we desperately need to mature. If, in our rush to have spiritual or ministerial success, or because of our love for the world, we ignore His invitation, then His law will eventually break us. Genesis 1 is a very good place to begin our search for His ways. It gives us a revelation of each essential step in the work of God to fully form Christ's life in us as Ephesians 3:19 promises the Believer. The succeeding chapters of Genesis further develop this revelation by giving us examples of seven men who learned by experience the lessons revealed in Genesis 1.

Let's briefly summarize the two main sections of Genesis—Genesis 1–10 and Genesis 11–50. They deal with two biblical concepts: "rest" and "Canaan," respectively. If we analyze the first section, we see that in Genesis 1–2 the six Days of Creation show the way into the seventh Day, His rest. In Genesis 3–5 we see how man lost his rest (and still loses it today) when he was removed from the Garden of Eden and God's presence. In Genesis 6–10 we read about Noah and his descendants. The word "Noah" in Hebrew actually means "rest." It signified that he would lead the world into rest, a rest from the sin and violence that filled the earth (Gen. 5:29). How desperately we need our heavenly Noah, Christ, to do the same for us in these last days! Thankfully, Jesus assures us that the events of Noah's day will be repeated in the last days (Mt. 24:37-44). At that time, this earth will experience rest from its spiritual convulsions and the violence that fills it.

In the second section of Genesis (chapters 11–50), the central issue is the inheritance of Canaan promised to Abraham and his descendants. God promised Canaan to Abraham, and the Book of Genesis ends with both Jacob and Joseph insisting that their bodies be returned to Canaan and be buried there after their deaths. Let's return now to the six Days of Creation, which illustrate the path God uses to bring us into rest or Canaan. This rest is our spiritual and eternal inheritance—Christ's life formed in us.

Chapter 5

God Alone Can Grant the Light of Life

"When my Christian friends go their own way, God always disciplines them and deals with them, but when I go my own way, God never does anything to stop me. What do you think is wrong?" asked a concerned young woman. We know that God loves His children so much that He faithfully disciplines everyone He receives; only illegitimate children receive no discipline (Heb. 12:6-8). Therefore, I asked this young woman how she had been born again. She explained that she had attended a Christian concert ten years before, where someone told those present to come up to the front if they wanted to be saved and go to Heaven. She responded—because like most people, she really did want to go to Heaven, especially if it was that easy. She said that she felt nothing while she was up front. From that day on she regularly attended a church, yet she noticed a vast difference between her life and that of other Believers. I was very hesitant to tell her that maybe she had never really been born again, even though that was what I felt. However, when she said, "Recently a leader told me that I need to be sure I have been born again," I immediately confirmed that counsel to her. We then prayed together that the Lord would meet with her in a very real way to give her a genuine new-birth experience. She eventually met the Lord, and her life was never the same.

The light of life must enter our earth on Day One of God's "redemptive week" in His way. It will never come to us if we seek to receive it in *our* way. Proverbs 14:12 tells us that there is a way that *seems* right to us, but the end of that way leads to death. We need to examine the foundation of our spiritual lives to be sure it has been laid according to God's Word, and not according to man's words or ideas. We have already discovered that Paul applies God's creative miracle of this first Day of Creation to the light of the gospel entering our lives (2 Cor. 4:6). Since His life is light (Jn. 1:4), the entrance of His light into our earth simply means that His divine life enters our hearts. This is our salvation experience or the new birth.

In the Church-world today, there are many doctrinal positions concerning when and how the creative miracle of the new birth takes place in the life of a Believer. Some claim that it happens when a newborn baby is baptized by the sprinkling of water. Others tell us that this life is given to all who are old enough to know right and wrong if they are willing to repeat the sinner's prayer. Still others declare that only those who belong to their particular organization can be saved. However, there is only one way to get to Heaven, and thankfully that way does not depend on man's opinions or ideas. That way has been offered to all who are willing to search for it, and it depends on only one truth—His. Are we concerned enough about our own eternal destiny, and that of others, that we are willing to search the Scriptures with an open heart and align our way with the Lord's way?

Remember, sincerity is not enough. Many Christians fall into the trap of believing that our great sincerity will somehow cause everything to work out just fine. I do not know of a single Christian who would assure a Hindu that he will somehow be saved from hell because of his deep sincerity. Rather, with great conviction we would tell the Hindu person, "There is no other name under Heaven given among men by which we must be saved but the name of Christ. Your great sincerity will never save you from infinite destruction and loss." Yet, we sometimes pacify our consciences by believing something for our own lives that we would never believe to be true for the Hindu man—believing that our own sincerity is all that really matters! Do not be deceived. Just as the Hindu's sincerity cannot save him from an eternity in hell, our mistaken sincerity cannot save us from the great spiritual loss of failing to experience the fullness of the Lord's life in His way. Otherwise, God would not be a just judge. If the Hindu is wrong, he loses his life forever; and if I, a true Christian, am wrong in some areas, I will lose forever at least some of the blessings God has prepared for those who love Him. This is a terrifying thought if you are *really* hungry for God and all that He desires to give you!

If we have truly seen the beauty of the Creator, and His grace that can make something out of nothing in us (Gen. 1:1), then a cry has been birthed in our hearts to become partakers of that grace and to be changed. Then, as we see what He is, we also see what we are, and we are made aware of the great gulf that separates a holy God from a sinful soul. Fortunately, the Lord, in His infinite kindness, immediately reveals in Genesis 1:2-3 how our earth can come into His light and life through a genuine salvation experience. This can happen only in accordance with the pattern He reveals in these verses.

Day One and the First Feast

The way into a genuine new birth is also the first revelation God gives us in the seven feasts of the Lord. The first feast is Passover. During this feast a lamb was slain, and its blood was placed on the door posts and lintels of the houses of all true Israelites. Most Christians know that the Passover is symbolic of the Lamb of Calvary, through whose shed blood our sins are forgiven and our lives are redeemed from death. Paul explains this by saying, "For indeed, Christ, our Passover, was sacrificed for us" (1 Cor. 5:7b NKJV). Therefore, the act of slaying a lamb and applying its blood to their houses was symbolic of Christ's life being poured out for us and His blood being applied to our lives to save us. Therefore, the first feast, clearly represents our salvation experience, the same message found in the first Day of Creation.

Day One and the Tabernacle of Moses

Entering through the door is the first step of the seven steps that are revealed in the Tabernacle of Moses. Jesus said, "I am the door: by me if any man enter in, he shall be *saved*, and shall go in and out, and find pasture" (Jn. 10:9). Once again, we see that our first step is the experience of salvation.

Day One and the First Man of Faith

The first of the seven men of faith in Genesis is Abel. Abel offered a lamb upon the altar. This act is associated with our salvation through the Lamb of Calvary. Even more important, Abel's blood was shed by wicked Cain, just as Christ's blood was shed by the wicked. In the Book of Hebrews, Christ's death and Abel's death are compared. We are told that we have come "to Jesus the mediator of a new covenant, and to the sprinkled blood that speaks a better word than the blood of Abel" (Heb. 12:24 NIV). Abel's blood spoke a word to God from the ground and called for vengeance toward his murderer (Gen. 4:10), but Christ's shed blood speaks a word to the Father from the ground calling for forgiveness toward His murderers. Oh, what grace He brought to sinful man!

The Condition of Fallen Man Is Revealed

Before the Lord begins His creative work in us, we are "without form" (Gen. 1:2). Actually, this Hebrew word is most often translated as "vain" or "vanity" in the authorized version, as in Isaiah 40:17: "All nations before him are as *nothing*; and they *are counted to him less than nothing, and vanity.*" The human being without Christ is "less than nothing" and completely vain. He may reach the pinnacle of success in man's eyes, but if he loses his own soul, what has he accomplished? He may receive an Oscar award in this life, but will he be applauded in hell? Most people who sell their souls are willing to do so for a much more vain reason than the bowl of porridge for which Esau sold his! Your life will have eternal purpose if you give it to Christ.

The earth without Christ is also said to be "void" (Gen. 1:2). This word simply means "empty." This was the deep emotion I felt as a young man when I finally achieved one of my first big goals in life—to buy a very powerful motorcycle. I will never forget the empty feeling I had after parking it in my driveway for the first time. I had expected the motorcycle to fill me with real joy, but I felt nothing but emptiness. Emotionally, it was as though someone had let the air out of a huge, over-inflated balloon. Many people react to this void by simply spending the rest of their lives pursuing one goal after another in search of lasting joy. They conclude that maybe a motorcycle isn't the answer. What they really need is a new car, next a boat, later a house, and then maybe a bigger car. On and on they go. What they *really* need is a meeting with the Lord where they discover that only the Creator, not the creation, can satisfy them. Only He can fill that void!

God's Answer: His Way Into the New Birth

The condition of man's spiritual life revealed here seems to be hopeless. This situation requires a mighty miracle from Heaven, and that is precisely what began to take place as "the Spirit of God moved upon the face of the waters!" (Gen. 1:2b) It is extremely important that we understand this first step toward becoming a new creation in Christ. It all begins with a work of the Holy Spirit. The New Testament confirms this truth in many places (Jn. 3:5-8; Gal. 4:29; Rom. 8:9). Here is the one ingredient that was missing in the life of the young woman who didn't understand why God never disciplined her. This ingredient has been ignored and left out of the salvation equation in the lives of many who call themselves Christians. The result is that many in the Church are **convinced but not converted**. What does all this mean for us, in practical terms?

The Spirit moves on the *waters*. Water is used to represent the Word of God. We saw in Deuteronomy 32:1-2 that God's doctrine and speech fall on our earth as rain. In Ephesians 5:26 we are told that the Lord is sanctifying and cleansing the Church "with the washing of water by the word." Therefore, in Genesis 1:2, the picture we are given is that of an earth on which the water of God's word has fallen. The waters of His word are covering the earth. Many have taught that all we have to do is believe the written Word and we are born again, but *"water" is not enough*! If the Spirit of God does not move on those waters, we will never be brought into the light of the next verse. Jesus declared this to Nicodemus, saying, "Except a man be *born of water **and** of the Spirit*, he cannot enter into the kingdom of God" (Jn. 3:5b). Both these agents must be involved in the new birth! In First Peter 1:23, we are told that we must be born by the incorruptible seed of the *word of God* (water), but Jesus says that we must be born by the *Spirit* also.

At this point, you might say that the Spirit and the Word are the same thing. When *Christ* speaks, this is true (Jn. 6:63). Even Satan can quote the Scriptures; but when he does, they do not carry the life-giving anointing of the Holy Spirit. When I quote Scripture without the anointing and presence of the Spirit, I am quoting the dead letter that brings death rather than life. Paul makes this clear in Second Corinthians 3:6 (NKJV) when he says that the Lord has "made us sufficient as ministers of the new covenant, not of the letter but of the Spirit; for the letter kills, but the Spirit gives life." The Greek word translated here as "letter" is the same Greek word translated as "Scriptures" in Second Timothy 3:15, where Paul tells Timothy, "…from a child thou hast known the holy scriptures." No wonder Paul said that he didn't preach the gospel only with words, but in the power and demonstration of the Spirit (1 Cor. 2:1-6). As we share the gospel with others, are we ministering only the Scriptures (waters), or is the Spirit involved, moving upon the waters and causing them to be life to the hearers?

Inoculated Against the Gospel

Unfortunately, many sincere Christians do not understand these things, and they have unintentionally "inoculated" a great number of people against the gospel. Some do not understand that having the water of the Word present in our spiritual earth is not enough; the water may be present long before the Spirit decides to move on it, as He did in Genesis 1:2. There *must* be a moving of the Holy Spirit in our lives to bring conviction for sin and a genuine spirit of repentance. True conviction and repentance are both gifts that come through the ministry of the Holy Spirit (Jn. 16:8; Acts 5:31). Since most people would like to go to Heaven, they are generally quite willing to repeat a simple sinner's prayer if that is the passport needed to get there, as they are sometimes told by well-meaning Believers. However, unless the Spirit is present to grant them the miracle of the new birth, they remain untouched and consequently unchanged.

Consider what often happens to these people if they find themselves in a meeting where the Spirit of God is, in fact, "moving on the waters." The

Spirit is bringing life to the preaching of the Word. The living Word is being heard and not only the dead letter. The preacher may invite the unsaved to come to the front and be born again by water and the Spirit. The person, who was previously instructed that simply repeating the sinner's prayer is enough to be born again, does not respond. He thinks, "I already tried this once and it didn't work." We cannot expect unbelievers to be theologians. They do not understand Genesis 1:2-3, but *we* should! They do not realize that on this second occasion they are being invited to come to the feet of Christ by the call of the Spirit. They have been inoculated against God's call by a zealous Christian who did not understand His ways.

This is one reason why the Church today has so many members within it who are convinced but not converted. If we truly have been born again ourselves, it is not difficult to recognize those who have had a genuine meeting with the Lord Jesus Christ. It soon becomes apparent whether they have mere religion or marvelous reality. One can easily detect if they are speaking from the depths of a transformed heart or are simply mouthing theological words. Unfortunately, there are many who can only do the latter because they have been misinformed and simply do not understand that they need to ask God to meet them in a very real way.

Am I saying that we should not witness to others? Not at all. Rather, I am saying that we must learn to be led by the Holy Spirit instead of being moved simply by the need around us. We should learn to lead people through the sinner's prayer only when the Holy Spirit is "moving on the waters" of the Word that we are sharing with them. When we are conscious of His presence flowing upon what we are sharing, then we can be sure that He is present to grant the miracle of the new birth in our listeners. Often, when the Spirit is present, we will not even need to lead them in prayer, because they will be crying out to God themselves for His forgiveness and salvation.

Several years ago, another pilot and I were asked to fly some businessmen to a meeting in another city. While our passengers were in their meeting, we waited for them in the lobby of the hotel where the meeting was held. My pilot friend was not a Believer, but while we waited, the subject of the gospel came up. Suddenly, the Spirit began to "move upon the waters." I knew that the presence of the Lord was falling upon what I was sharing with him, and that he could also feel the Lord's presence. After a few moments, when God's presence was almost palpable, I said to him, "At this moment you are feeling something in your heart that you have never felt before. It is the Spirit of God inviting you to surrender your life to Him." The pilot responded, "Yes, you are right. I have never felt what I am feeling right now. Could we pray?" Right there in the hotel lobby, a pilot who had previously manifested only pride and self-assurance began to pray and ask the Lord to forgive him and to come into his heart! *This* is the work of the Spirit, not of man. *This* I could never have accomplished myself, even if I had quoted to him every Scripture in the Bible; and I didn't even have to talk him into repeating the sinner's prayer!

In Acts, Peter did not have to convince the multitude to accept the Lord—the Spirit did that. When they heard the anointed message of Peter, their hearts were convicted of sin and they cried out, "Men and brethren, what shall we do?" (Acts 2:37b) If the Lord's presence does not fall on what we are sharing with someone, then maybe we are only called to plant the seed in his heart. Very likely it is not the right time to lead him in the sinner's prayer. We need not be discouraged. The harvest always requires several stages, some of which we may not be personally involved in. Paul said, "I have planted, Apollos watered; but God gave the increase" (1 Cor. 3:6).

We must not live and move among men simply looking for one more person who will permit us to lead them in the sinner's prayer. May God open our eyes to see people as eternal souls destined to eternal damnation unless they enter the Kingdom through a genuine new-birth experience. May God purify our hearts so that our motives are right in His sight. Listening to some Christians talk about their exploits in soul-winning, I have often wondered if at least part of their goal in witnessing is the honor that comes from telling about how many "decisions for Christ" were reached through their ministry. Sometimes it sounds like the goal is simply to add another notch to the handle of their spiritual six-shooters after winning another duel! Our goal must be to exalt the Lordship of Christ over the earth as we save another soul from eternal suffering. Oh, that we may do so with a heart that is broken with the burden of what it means to die without Christ and without hope—destined to hell.

Only the Living Word Brings Life

One of the reasons so many people are inoculated against the gospel is that Christians have learned to preach the gospel without the help of the Holy Spirit. After all, anyone can quote Scripture texts. Why do we need His help for that? Even worse, we have learned to live the Christian life without a daily, personal relationship with Christ. One of the rebukes of Christ toward the Church—not the world—is, "...thou hast a name that thou livest, and art dead" (Rev. 3:1). Could it be that we carry the name of Christ and Christian but are spiritually dead? Paul warns against "having a form of godliness, but denying the power thereof" (2 Tim. 3:5a). Has our spiritual life become a Christian front that has the form or appearance of godliness without the power of Christ's life flowing in us? In the same context, Paul goes on to explain that the root of this problem is *"ever learning*, and never able to come to the *knowledge of the truth"* (2 Tim. 3:7). Truth is a person, the Lord Jesus Christ. It doesn't matter how much we *learn*. If we do not know Him personally, we have no life in us. You may have had a relationship with Him yesterday, but do you have one today? Is the life of the Vine flowing in you *today*?

We have learned so many Scripture verses and so many religious clichés that we can communicate to people's intellect a gospel message that resides only in our heads. Sometimes we can even convince them. The true gospel must reside in our *hearts*; it can only be communicated from heart to heart as the power of the Spirit flows. When that happens people are converted. The psalmist understood this well. He declared, "Deep calleth unto deep at the **noise** of thy waterspouts" (Ps. 42:7a). Water only makes noise when it is moving, and the moving force on God's "waters" is always the Holy Spirit. The depths of one *heart* speak to the depths of another *heart* when there is a moving of the Spirit on His Word. Without the Spirit, our communication remains strictly on an intellectual level. Oh, Spirit of God, come and move on Your Word and on us today!

If we desire life in the Spirit, we must not only read and know the Scriptures but we must also hear the living Word. When the living Word descended on Mount Sinai and spoke directly to Israel, their reaction to that living Word was tragic! Basically they told Him to go back to Heaven and never speak to them again (Deut. 18:16). They wanted Moses to give them the rules, so he wrote them all down for the people. From that day forward, one of the favorite declarations of the children of Israel was, "It is written." About 1,500 years later, the Pharisees condemned the living Word to death, and to their way of thinking, they did everything in strict obedience to what had been written by Moses!

In the wilderness, Israel attempted to feed their spiritual lives with the Scriptures alone, *void of a personal relationship with the Savior*. This is what the Pharisees were still doing when the living Word visited Israel again. Are we doing that today? This will bring death at *any* stage of our walk from Day One through Day Seven. This does not mean that the Scriptures are unimportant. We must read them daily if we hope to be a king (Deut. 17:15,18-19). Rather, I am seeking to emphasize the importance of relationship. Jesus told the Pharisees, "You diligently study the Scriptures because you think that by them you possess eternal life. These are the Scriptures that testify about me, yet you refuse to come to me to have life" (Jn. 5:39-40 NIV). They were ever learning (the Scriptures), but they never came to the knowledge of the truth! They never experienced His life. May we not make the same mistake. May the **written Word** continually bring us closer to the **living Word** throughout the seven Days of the "redemptive week."

In the Body of Christ this life-and-death issue is sometimes overlooked. The hymn writer, Mary A. Lathbury, must have had a deep understanding of this truth. She so beautifully expressed it in the hymn "Break Thou the Bread of Life." The first verse prays:

> Break Thou the bread of life,
> Dear Lord, to me,
> As Thou didst break the loaves beside the sea;
> *Beyond the sacred page,*
> I seek Thee, Lord,
> My spirit pants for Thee,
> *O living Word.*

Chapter 6

Can We Go On to Day Two Now?

Now that we are born again by the water of the Word and the power of the Spirit, are we ready to go on to the redemptive work of God revealed in the second Day of Creation? The answer is no. Sometimes God does give us a little foretaste of the glorious experiences that await us on future Days giving us an incentive to press on. However, these seven Days of Creation reveal a **progressive work**, so it is impossible to continue on to Day Two until all God's purposes for Day One have been fulfilled. If we examine Genesis 1:4, there is something further that must be accomplished in our lives on Day One. God must divide the light from the darkness.

It is important to understand that we must *permit* God to accomplish each work in our lives. Not only must the Spirit come to offer us the new-birth experience but the Spirit of grace must also come to bring us the grace of God for every future redemptive work the Lord wants to accomplish in us. With each successive and deeper visitation of the Spirit, as He comes and touches our lives to give us greater grace, we have the option of accepting or rejecting His grace at that moment. He never forces Himself or His will on anyone. That would neither express nor produce true love. On the other hand, if we do not permit Him to have His way, then He will not permit us to continue on to deeper things in Him. He will not permit us to proceed to the blessings of the other Days in His redemptive work. Recall Hebrews 6:1,3, which says, "…let us go on unto perfection… and this will we do, if *God permit*." May God continually help us to make a total surrender of our will to His will. May we always be quick to say yes to the dealings of the Spirit in our hearts so that our "earth" will one day be "filled with all the fullness" of His life and glory (Eph. 3:19 NKJV).

Many Christians get stuck in the division of light from darkness on Day One and never grow any further in God. Some will simply not permit God to have His way on this issue so that Day One can be finished in their lives. If they caught a glimpse of the glory that awaits them on Days Two through Seven, they would be more likely to surrender their wills to God. Let's consider what else we must *permit* the Lord to accomplish on this first Day so that we are *permitted* to continue on to the second Day.

The Light Must Be Divided From the Darkness

"And God saw the light, that it was good: and *God divided the light from the darkness*" (Gen. 1:4). The New Testament also picks up this aspect of truth found in the "redemptive week" and gives us **three areas in which we must allow God to make a division** between the light and darkness in our lives.

1. Our Friends Bring Either Light or Darkness

"Be ye not unequally yoked together with unbelievers: for what fellowship hath righteousness with unrighteousness? and *what communion hath light with darkness?* And what concord hath Christ with Belial? or what part hath he that believeth with an infidel?" (2 Cor. 6:14-15—"unbelievers" and "infidels" are from the same Greek word). Very often this Scripture is applied to the unequal yoke of marriage between a Christian and non-Christian. Although this exhortation can certainly be *applied* to marriage, the issue is far deeper. Paul is speaking about *fellowship* and *communion*. We must allow God to be Lord over this area of our lives.

"Know ye not that the friendship of the world is enmity with God? whosoever therefore will be a friend of the world is the enemy of God" (Jas. 4:4b). This is a very solemn warning. Far from being permitted to grow in their relationship and communion with the Lord, those who choose friendship with the world are considered enemies of the Lord. Abraham was not the only "friend of God" who was required to leave his family, his friends, and his country to walk with God. This is a basic requirement for all God's friends and all Abraham's children. Some Christians have chosen to delay this decision until they are a little further down the Christian pathway. As in the life of Abraham, this is a choice that must be made at the beginning of our walk with God, on the first Day of the "redemptive week," not at the end, upon reaching maturity. We must make this decision: Who is more appealing to us—our old friends or the God of Heaven?

Do you desire to be special in the eyes of the Lord—someone whose spiritual beauty is irresistible to the Lord? You *can* be that way from the very beginning of your walk with God if you will follow the counsel of Psalm 45:10-11: "Hearken, O daughter, and consider, and incline thine ear; *forget also thine own people*, and thy father's house; so shall the king greatly desire thy beauty: for he is thy Lord; and worship thou him." If you will simply follow the example of Abraham and leave your family and friends, the Lord will greatly desire your spiritual beauty. Isn't it a tragedy that many Christians never go beyond the blessing of the new birth and the first Day of the new creation in Christ only because their unbelieving friends are more attractive to them than the King of glory?

We are not talking about cutting off all contact with unbelievers, because then we would be unable to reach them for Christ. The concept here is clearly *fellowship*. I believe that the line of demarcation between spending time with an unbeliever[1] to win him for Christ and being with him for fellowship is quite easy to discern. As long as an unbeliever wants to spend time with me because he has at least some interest in what I have to offer him spiritually, then I should be willing to be with him. I have crossed the line when either of two things happen: 1) He is no longer interested in being with me because of who I am and what I have in the Lord; or 2) I am now interested in being with him because of who he is and what he has in the world. In other words, I enjoy being with that person because we have common interests such as sports, hobbies, cars, business, school, family, etc. When that happens, my spiritual life stagnates, and I will soon be considered an enemy of God instead of His intimate friend.

Unacceptable fellowship is frequently a problem with boyfriend-girlfriend relationships. Many young Christian girls say, "I believe that my friendship with him is God's will because I believe God wants to use me to win him to Christ." What they do not understand is that *they* are the ones who need to be won to Christ because they have already fallen from grace by disobeying the Lord and have become an enemy of God. We can never rescue another person who has fallen into a pit by jumping into the pit with him; this is precisely what a Christian girl does with an unbelieving boyfriend.

2. Our Works Bring Either Light or Darkness

A missionary friend of mine was rebuking a local pastor because the pastor had told him a lie. He said, "Brother, you are a pastor, and you lied to me! Don't you know that lying displeases the Lord?" The pastor

---

1. Biblically speaking, an "unbeliever" is anyone who has not been genuinely born again (2 Cor. 6:14-15).

responded, "Yes, but all the pastors in our country tell lies." My friend responded, "If that is so, then all the pastors in this country will spend eternity in hell because the Bible says that all liars will have their part in the lake of fire" (Rev. 21:8).

In Ephesians 5:3-11 the Apostle Paul gives a list of works that are unacceptable to the Lord. He also exhorts us, "For ye were sometimes *darkness*, but now are ye *light* in the Lord: *walk as children of light*" (Eph. 5:8). He goes on to say, "And have no fellowship with the unfruitful *works of darkness*, but rather reprove them" (Eph. 5:11). Paul is speaking here of a separation between light and darkness in the context of our works. After God speaks light into our hearts, we are called "children of light." To wear this title, we are then required to separate the darkness of our past works from the light of our new life in Him.

We know that the creative work of the Lord in our personal lives on the first Day does not bring us into perfection. Clearly, the separation between light and darkness is not complete on the first Day because we see that God further separates light and darkness on the fourth Day (Gen. 1:18). However; if we want to progress beyond Day One, there are certain things in our lives that the Lord will insist on dealing with first. The idols in each individual life are different, and He will deal with each person in a different way. The separation between light and darkness that He requires in our individual lives in order to continue on to the second Day does not have to meet anyone else's approval; only the Lord knows the heart of each one of us.

We are not talking here about legalism. There is a tendency in some churches to think that a true Christian has to line up with the laws men have laid down. If a new Christian does not line up with the local standards, he is considered to be unspiritual or even unsaved. Acts 15:28-29 gives us a short list of four requirements for a new Christian. Many Christians in the early Church were imposing all sorts of rules and regulations on new Gentile Believers. Therefore, the principal leaders of the Church met, prayed about this matter, and concluded that the only necessary rules were these four things. If we add even one rule to this list for a new Christian, we have placed ourselves in the camp of legalistic Christians, according to the Bible, and we are an enemy of the cross of Christ.

Not only are we enemies of the cross but also enemies of the souls of men. How can that be? I have often heard unsaved people say, "Well, I could never be a Christian because I drink, smoke, go to movies, and dance." Who ever laid *those* laws on them? Certainly not the Holy Spirit or the apostles. The *apostles* said that there are only four laws, and not one of these things is included in their list! Sadly, these laws have been set by legalistic Christians. Indeed, many churches have a list of don'ts much longer than the Holy Spirit gave, and it is nailed to their front doors, so to speak, so that everyone will know what their "standards" are. The result is that souls are kept out of the Kingdom because they see only the many laws they do not feel capable of keeping. How sad that they never meet the One who died for them. They would soon find out that He changes our desires and gives us the grace to surrender to Him things that we thought we could never stop doing. This is the result of love instead of law.

We know that the law kills us (Rom. 7:9-10). Unfortunately, some Christians, like the Apostle Paul before he had a real meeting with the Lord, walk around murdering others spiritually, all in the name of holiness and the law of God. Such people have not yet learned one of the principal lessons God wants us to receive from the life of Paul, a man who kept the law to the letter. He was as righteous as a person could be under that law (Phil. 3:6). Paul, the best disciple the law ever produced, manifests to us the end result of that way—he dedicated his time to murdering Christians. The more legalistic we are, the more people we murder! How does this happen in our churches today?

John Doe and Sister Most Holy

John Doe comes into our church off the street and is touched by the Lord. As he begins his new life in Christ, he is filled with unspeakable joy. Then the Lord pulls out a divine list of the works of darkness that are in John and begins to clean up John's life as He deals with one thing after another. Thus John discovers that grace *and* truth come through Jesus Christ, and not just the law that brings sorrow and death (Jn. 1:17). In other words, when the Lord says to him, "John, I would like to deal with your tongue and give you victory over gossiping," John responds, "Lord, I have never liked the way I gossip, but I haven't been able to control my tongue. I would be so thankful if you would change me in this area." The Lord then says to him, "Don't worry, John. You and I are going to work together on this weakness, and I am going to give you the grace you need to win the battle. Just trust and obey Me" (remember, "grace" is divine ability or enabling). John is delighted and walks in even greater joy as he sees the Lord's mercy and kindness changing his life. Later, the Lord says, "Today, John, we are going to work on your gluttony. I'm going to give you the grace to conquer that area in your life." Once again, John responds with joy to this new challenge, believing that the Lord will give him victory over this part of his life that has caused him trouble for years. So it goes with John in his new Christian life as he proceeds from victory to victory over his enemies. In spite of the Lord dealing with one thing after another, John continues to know deep joy and a growing love for the Lord.

Suddenly, things begin to go terribly wrong for John because one of the members of the church, Sister Most Holy, pulls out *her* list of priorities regarding the works of darkness that she just *knows* John needs to change—for his own good, of course. We have all met a Brother or Sister Most Holy. They are the ones who always have a word of counsel for everyone, whether it is wanted or not. John's new-found "friend," Sister Most Holy, has a problem. She is well-known both in the church and out of the church for having the longest and most dangerous tongue in the city. She has been a Christian for 40 years, even though she lost the joy of the Lord about 39 years ago. She has been a continual "help" to the pastor and an unmovable "bulwark" in the church.

John comes to church one fine morning filled with his usual joy in the Lord, and suddenly, Sister Most Holy buttonholes him and says, "John, don't you know that a Christian isn't allowed to smoke?" Yes, John is still smoking, but he had not even considered smoking to be a problem. Some may think that it is impossible to be a Christian and not know that smoking is wrong. To those who condemn smokers, I would recommend a study of the life of Charles Spurgeon, often called "the prince of preachers." He won multitudes of souls to Christ through his powerful ministry that spanned many years. I have never heard of anyone that doubted he was a true Christian, even though he smoked up to the last day of his life and never considered it to be wrong.

I was once pastored by a wonderful man of God who had come from a well-to-do family and had not been exposed to Christians as he grew up. (Unfortunately, this can be a real advantage.) He was gloriously born again, and was seeking God with all his heart. He had been fasting and praying for some time, asking God to grant him a specific spiritual blessing. One day as he earnestly prayed, and smoked, God spoke to him almost audibly and said, "If you will stop smoking I will give you the desire of your heart." Without thinking twice, he threw away his cigarettes and said yes to the Lord, knowing in his heart that he would never return to smoking. God responded to his obedience by fulfilling the longing of his heart that very same day. Isn't this a much better way for a new Christian to be cleansed from the past, than to have someone lay the law on him?

If John would have known as much theology as Sister Most Holy, he could have looked her straight in the eye and said, "Jesus said that it is not what goes into a man that defiles him, but rather what comes out. Which do you think does more harm: The smoke I take in, or the gossip, backbiting, and sowing of discord among the brethren that comes out of your heart?" Even if John had been a theologian, the meekness of the Lord that emanated from him would not have allowed him to treat her the way she treated others. Instead, John said nothing and went home with a heavy heart.

For the first time since he had become a Christian, John lost his joy. He had not considered the issue of smoking before. He knew that Sister Most Holy was right, of course. If only he had thought of it before! He should have known! He would have to stop smoking immediately! And so the struggle began. Day after day John's attention is glued to his battle with smoking. He just doesn't seem to have the strength to conquer this weakness. He lives under continual condemnation as he throws away one pack of cigarettes, only to soon buy another pack. Meanwhile, he cannot understand what is happening to him. He thought that he loved the Lord with all his heart, and that he would do *anything* for the Lord, but he can't even give up smoking! (I know many Christians who are in this kind of battle with some law that another Christian has placed on them.) Why has John lost the joy of the Lord? Why can't he conquer this habit?

First, John is simply experiencing the reality of the Apostle John's declaration, "The law was given by Moses, but grace and truth came by Jesus Christ" (Jn. 1:17). When *Christ* speaks to John to stop doing something, that expression of truth comes with the necessary grace (divine enabling) to conquer the enemy. John joyfully responds to His living Word and is also thankful to be freed from another enemy. Law comes through man. When *man* opens John's eyes to see a failure or weakness in his life, instead of receiving grace to conquer it, he comes under the condemnation of the law. The law can only condemn us; it *cannot* change us. Grace will *only* come when the Lord speaks to us. The law has killed John and robbed him of his joy in the Lord. For all of us, the question becomes, "Do I want to be a lawgiver or a channel for the life of Christ, who is the source of grace and truth?"

The second consequence of being given the law is probably even more tragic for John. Do you remember the *Lord's* list of priorities to cleanse and sanctify John's life—to separate light from darkness? Well, John isn't working on that list any longer. He is totally consumed with Sister Most Holy's list. He is following *her* priorities and *her* program to conquer the enemies in his life. In addition to smoking, she has given him several other things he needs to stop doing.

The Lord *rarely* asks us to fight against two enemies at once. He knows the risk of defeat when our strength and attention are divided between two fronts. David discovered two great secrets to success in war. First, he only fought the enemies *God* told him to fight. Second, he obtained the victory over his enemies by fighting them one at a time. On one occasion, he fought on two fronts at once and risked losing his kingdom (2 Sam. 10:6-12).

John is also at risk, with battles raging on several fronts. He isn't winning his battles any longer, nor is he growing spiritually. He isn't winning battles because he isn't receiving God's grace to be changed. To the contrary, He is now fighting enemies that God has not directed him to fight, and he is actually losing the battles. In fact, his attention and strength have become divided between several "problems" in his life.

What will happen to John? Because the joy of the Lord is our strength, he no longer has any strength in his spiritual walk. He has lost his joy. Also, since he is now under continual condemnation, he lacks the warm feeling he used to enjoy in the Lord's presence. Indeed, he doesn't feel comfortable drawing near to the Lord anymore. He avoids praying and reading the Bible because these things actually make him feel more guilty. Like many Christians who have been murdered spiritually by legalism, John will probably end up either falling away from the Lord, or else he will stay in the church and *pretend* to have a living, loving relationship with the Lord. He will no longer enjoy being a Christian, but none of his fellow Believers will notice because they, too, lost their joy through legalistic demands. John will continue to say the right things, but in his heart he will now feel so empty. If John isn't careful, he could actually turn into a Brother Most Holy! What would be worse—to fall back into sin and openly recognize that we are a sinner in need of God's mercy, or to continue *acting* like a good Christian? If we do the latter, we will end up being the only one who is deceived. How sad!

Naturally speaking, what sane parent would walk into the room of a newborn baby and pull out a list of ten requirements the baby must keep? Sadly, this is precisely what many spiritual newborns face in our churches. Maybe you are a Christian who has faced the onslaughts of a Brother or Sister Most Holy, and you have come under a spirit of condemnation. What should you do? First, recognize that the Lord wants you to know the joy of His intimate love in spite of what you are or are not. Remember: If our good works cannot bring us into His presence, then our failures certainly cannot keep us out. We can enter only by grace, through the shed blood, and that blood can cover *all* our sins (Heb. 10:19). Second, ask God what is the *one* enemy *He* wants you to war against at this time. The next time someone confronts you with your failure to pass spiritual lesson "333," it will be all right to let them know that, presently, you are working real hard on lesson "33"!

I would like to share one final word of advice on this matter. We *all* have what the psalmist calls "secret sins" that are clearly seen only in the light of the Lord's countenance (Ps. 90:8). Not only can the Lord see them, but our family and friends can usually see a good number of them also. Fortunately for us, the Lord does not open our eyes to show us all the ugliness of our flesh at one time! If He did, we might throw in the towel, spiritually speaking, and give up all hope of ever pleasing Him. I am sure that none of us want this to happen. Therefore, if we do not want the Lord to show all our weaknesses at once, we should be careful not to do this to others—especially to the Lord's newborns. It is easy for an older Christian to see things in the life of a newborn that need to be changed. The Holy Spirit is capable of doing that in His own time. If the newborn is sincere, then the Lord will cleanse him according to His own divine list of priorities. However, if that newborn is *not* sincere, then neither our help nor the Lord's will do him any good. Either way, we should leave the separation of light and darkness to the Holy Spirit. It is a very personal and very wonderful time, if the Lord is the One who does the work!

3. Our Attitude Toward Brethren Brings Either Light or Darkness

"I am the pastor of this work. God called *me* to this place, and I am the one who founded this work. I invited you to come along with me; now you are trying to take over. Who do you think you are? You are treading on very dangerous ground to rise up against the person God has called to accomplish His purposes in this place. When you came here with me, you were broke; now, because you have shared in the blessing God has poured on me, you are very well off. How can you have the nerve to turn around and use those riches to throw your weight around? You haven't even been called by God to be here, yet you are demanding your rights and trying to take over the work!"

Probably some of these thoughts passed through the mind of Abraham when his nephew Lot rose up against him. (See Genesis 13.) Though these things were true, Abraham committed his cause to the Lord, and said, "Lot, you choose." Imagine; the one called to inherit the whole land of Canaan is now giving to his nephew the right to choose the best part of the inheritance for himself.

Lot was not only Abraham's nephew; he was also a righteous man and should have known better (2 Pet. 2:7-8). Lot was a man of faith and Abraham's spiritual brother. Surely Abraham found the grace to react the way he did because he was totally convinced that the Almighty rules in the affairs of men. He knew that God would right all the wrongs. He would receive from the Lord exactly what He wanted him to have. Yes, Abraham knew that if he pleased God, no one on earth could possibly do him harm or hinder his spiritual growth. He also knew that one day Lot would get what he deserved because God's judgment would fall upon him.

If you have been a Christian for more than a few days, you, too, have surely been greatly wronged by some self-centered, self-serving, inconsiderate brother in Christ; perhaps it was someone older than you in the Lord, or even your pastor. He should have known better. After spending so many years in the Church, he should have revealed more of the nature of Christ instead of being so carnal. Surely, if you have taken the low place in your dealings with this brother, as Abraham did with Lot, you have rested in the same assurance that was in the heart of Abraham. You know that God rules, and you also believe that God will right the wrongs. Vengeance belongs to Him. So you say to yourself, "Thank God! Like father Abraham, I have passed the test!"

But wait a minute—far from passing the test, the test (like Abraham's) has really only begun! You see, God is not pleased with the attitude that says, "God will make it right." If I want to be like Jesus, this attitude must be rooted out. I am so thankful that Jesus does not have this attitude. If the wrongs committed at Calvary against the Creator of Heaven and earth were ever made right, God would have to destroy humanity! Instead, the heart of the Lord cries from the cross, "Father, forgive them; for they know not what they do" (Lk. 23:34). Although it is likely that Abraham didn't start with an attitude of love and forgiveness, the next chapter of Genesis reveals through Abraham's actions that he had received the grace to love his brother Lot with unfeigned love.

Imagine the day Lot and all Sodom were carried away as slaves by the kings of the north (Gen. 14). That self-serving "brother" would now learn to serve others—as a slave! Abraham could have said, "Too bad for him. I knew this day would come. He just wouldn't listen. He deserves everything that's happening to him." Far from having that attitude, or considering Lot's plight to be a well-deserved judgment from God, Abraham rose up with only 318 trained servants and pursued those kings. He risked his life to save Lot. He could have justifiably said, "Well, I have an extremely important ministry that I just cannot jeopardize for the life of one rebellious brother. After all, the salvation of the world depends on the son I am called to bring forth; the Messiah will come through him. If I die in this impossible attempt to save Lot, the whole world could be lost; it might never be evangelized!"

Nevertheless, Abraham so loved Lot that he gave everything to try to save him, just as God "so loved the world that He gave His only begotten

Son" to save us (Jn. 3:16 NKJV). "Beloved, if God so loved us, we ought also to love one another" (1 Jn. 4:11). God did not give Himself to save people who were worthy of His kindness; nor did Abraham give himself to save a man who was worthy of his kindness. If I am not willing to love the brother or sister who has offended me, and even risk my all to save that person when he or she is still unworthy of my kindness, then I will never be conformed to the likeness of Christ—because *this* is His likeness.

Abraham's love for Lot was not just an outward pretense that hid the anger and resentment he still felt over what Lot had done to him. He loved Lot in the secret place of his heart to such a degree that he risked his life again for him in Genesis 18. There, God was about to destroy Lot's hometown with fire and brimstone. Abraham stood between a perverse Sodom and an angry God, not knowing what God might do to him as he "bargained" with God in intercession to save Sodom for the sake of Lot. God Himself testifies of the depths of Abraham's unfeigned love for Lot, a truly offensive brother, when He records in His Word, "And it came to pass, when God destroyed the cities of the plain, that God remembered Abraham, and sent Lot out of the midst of the overthrow..." (Gen. 19:29). God did not save Lot because of Lot's own merits. He saved Lot because of Abraham's love for him which became evident to God as He witnessed Abraham's intense intercession.

Could it be that Abraham's intercession for Lot over the years actually caused an unfeigned love for Lot to take root in his heart in place of bitterness? That much seems evident from other Scriptures. Certainly, this is one of the reasons the Lord exhorts us, "But I say unto you, love your enemies, bless them that curse you, do good to them that hate you, and pray for them which despitefully use you, and persecute you; that ye may be the children of your Father which is in heaven" (Mt. 5:44-45). It is highly unlikely that we will be able to love our enemies if we do not pray for them. If we do this, we will be not only children of our father Abraham but also of our Father which is in Heaven. Children are known to possess the characteristics of their fathers. We will be children of our heavenly Father because we will manifest His nature, which is to love those who have offended Him. Have you ever offended the Lord? If so, you must love those who have offended you, and God will do the same for you.

We will not be permitted to continue on to Day Two unless we also permit God to make a separation between light and darkness in the area of unfeigned love of the brethren. John, the Apostle of love, leaves no room for doubt: "He that saith he is in the light, and hateth his brother, is in darkness even until now. He that loveth his brother abideth in the light, and there is none occasion of stumbling in him" (1 Jn. 2:9-10). If we want to be people who walk in the light, we must receive grace to love our brethren. We are not called to love only the lovely; even from this first Day of Creation, God is calling us to love others as the Lord has loved us. He loved us while we were still offensive and unlovely sinners.

To conclude the first Day, consider what happened to Abraham, our spiritual father and example. On the very first Day of his walk with God, he experienced a separation between light and darkness in all three areas that we have been studying. In Abraham these three areas are as follows:

1. He experienced a separation from his worldly friends of Ur and Haran in Genesis 11–12.
2. In the same chapters, God began to separate Abraham's works of darkness from him, for example, his deception of saying that Sarah was his sister.
3. Then, in Genesis 13, God began to deal with Abraham concerning unfeigned love of the brethren. Of the three areas, this is probably the most costly in terms of commitment—but not too costly in the minds of all who long to go on to Day Two!

Chapter 7

Day Two—The Waters of the Word Are Separated

I cannot remember if I ever got back to mowing the grass that day, many years ago, after obeying the little voice and beginning to read Genesis 1 in a new way. I was amazed to see that the Bible does, in fact, use the earth as a symbol of man's spiritual life. As I eagerly read on to Day Two of Creation, my heart was filled with joy and expectation. Unfortunately, my joy turned to frustration as I came to Day Two because I just couldn't see what "separating the waters from the waters" could possibly mean in our spiritual lives. I prayed, "Lord, if You are the One who spoke to me to read Genesis 1 in this way, then only You can open my understanding." Almost immediately, the seven feasts of the Lord from Leviticus 23 came to mind, and they became a key to unlocking the message of the other Days of Creation. Some would call this type of experience mysticism, fanaticism, or just plain strange; I call it an example of the mercy of a God who wants His people to understand, even though we are deaf and blind! I suppose that in my case, He simply didn't have any other way to get through to me.

Day Two and the Second Feast

The second feast, the Feast of Unleavened Bread, was clearly the answer I needed to understand the second Day. Paul admonishes us, "Therefore let us keep the feast, not with old leaven, neither with the leaven of malice and wickedness; but with the *unleavened bread of sincerity and truth*" (1 Cor. 5:8). Paul is telling us, as New Testament Believers, to observe these feasts in a spiritual way; thus, we again find a solid biblical basis for applying the seven feasts to our spiritual lives. Paul likens unleavened bread to sincerity and truth. Jesus said that He is the bread of life we all must eat. Then He explains that He is referring to the word He speaks to us (Jn. 6:48,63). Therefore, from both Paul and Jesus we learn that the "bread" of this second feast refers to the Word of God or truth.

The Jewish people have observed this Feast of Unleavened Bread for the better part of 3,500 years. To this day they eat only unleavened bread for eight days each year—one day for the Passover, and seven additional days for the Feast of Unleavened Bread. They celebrate this second feast every year in commemoration of the first seven days of their journey from Egypt to Canaan because during those days, they ate only unleavened bread since they did not have time to leaven their bread with yeast and wait for it to raise (Ex. 13:6-8; Deut. 16:3). This celebration in the natural gives a symbolic message to His people year after year, just as partaking of the Lord's Supper with natural bread and wine gives a symbolic message to the New Testament Believer. A Christian can keep the Feast of Unleavened Bread in a spiritual way by eating the unadulterated bread of truth—spiritual bread that has no leaven.

The teachings of Christ further clarify the meaning of leaven. Jesus warned His disciples to "...beware of the leaven of the Pharisees and of the Sadducees" (Mt. 16:6). After His explanation, His disciples understood that He was not warning them about the yeast in bread, but about "the *doctrine* of the Pharisees and of the Sadducees" (Mt. 16:12). Therefore, bread that has leaven speaks of the Word of God mixed with false doctrine; unleavened bread, to the contrary, contains only pure doctrine. The Word of God tainted by false doctrine is easily recognized because it is constantly changing, just like bread that has leaven working in it.

The experience of a Bible school student demonstrates how leaven in our bread is characterized by a continual change in our doctrine or teaching. He wholeheartedly followed a teacher whose doctrine was not only questionable, but strongly rejected by many students and teachers. About two years after the student had graduated, he went back to the institute for a visit. While there, he joyfully shared with his spiritual mentor some verses of Scripture that he believed gave additional support to a doctrine the teacher had taught him. To the dismay of the former student, the teacher responded, "I'm sorry, but I don't believe it that way anymore." A word of caution: Bread with leaven never stays the same!

Part of the yearly commemoration of the Feast of Passover and the Feast of Unleavened Bread is that the Jewish family goes from room to room in their house searching for possible leaven. When they find it (as they always do, because a little leavened bread is customarily hidden somewhere in the house by the mother), they remove it and burn it. What a beautiful picture of what each one of us should continually do. We should continually search every room of our hearts to see if leaven has been hidden somewhere within us.

None of us were born again with pure doctrine, and we will never receive pure doctrine unless we are willing to humble ourselves and make many changes, as He graciously directs us in the removal of our leaven during Day Two! I know of one older minister who prides himself in the fact that he has never had to change a single doctrine that he has ever preached. Sadly, it is evident to many that he should have! When we find error in our doctrine, we must admit to it, remove it, and let the fire of the Spirit destroy it. Let's allow the Lord to set us free from a love of being right so that He can fill us with a sincere love of the truth!

Pure doctrine is not given to us just because we happen to belong to the right denomination. It is obvious that most denominations feel certain that they already have pure doctrine. That belief is often one reason they were formed in the first place. However, since there are approximately 1,300 denominations in the United States alone, and since there is only *one* truth—the Lord Himself—it is very probable that at least 1,299 of those denominations still have some degree of error. Our denomination cannot give us pure doctrine nor can it keep us from it if we humble ourselves. The Lord is willing to bring light to the humble soul who is seeking to be corrected!

An understanding of the second feast helps us understand the second Day of Creation and the work God wants to accomplish in our spiritual lives on that Day. As we have seen, water is a symbol of the Word of God. On this second Day, God "divided the waters...from the waters" (Gen. 1:7). In other words, He gives us grace to "rightly divide the word of truth" (2 Tim. 2:15). The Greek here means that we "dissect correctly" God's Word (*Strong's Greek Dictionary*, #3718). Doctrinal error most often results from not dividing the water of His Word correctly. How does this work?

Man, by nature, is an extremist. This is manifested by the fact that we almost always choose sides when we hear two people arguing. Rarely do we consider the possibility that both sides of the argument have merit. This is one reason why there have been heated doctrinal debates between opposite poles in the Body of Christ for 2,000 years. Often, it is simply a matter of each side seeing opposite sides of the same coin. Generally, neither side is willing or able to consider the possibility that the other side of the coin exists. Both sides seem to have valid Scriptures to back up their positions, and without a doubt, both sides have a measure of truth. The problem is, any truth carried to an extreme becomes error. Most of the age-old doctrinal disputes in the Body of Christ are the result of our tendency not to see the weight of scriptural evidence on *both* sides of a doctrinal issue. One example is the classical argument between divine predestination and man's free will. The first teaches that God alone decides who goes to Heaven and who goes to hell; the second affirms that man alone makes that decision. Who is right?

There have been honest, intelligent, and spiritual men in both doctrinal camps for centuries, and *both* sides have very strong arguments to support what they believe. Since God does not contradict Himself, this strongly indicates that His truth lies somewhere in between the two extremes. Both sides have been guilty of concentrating on verses that support their viewpoint without considering the balancing verses that support the other side. Almost certainly, neither group is rightly dividing or separating the Word of truth to clearly see both sides.

The Holy Spirit is well able to enlighten our eyes and bring us into divine balance between the extremes of any doctrinal position. However, we must humble ourselves for this to happen because pride blinds us (Obad. 3; Jn. 9:40-41). I would like to recommend one way to begin humbling ourselves so that we are permitted to see more clearly. Whichever side you choose in a doctrinal dispute, ask the Lord for the grace to gather as many verses as you can find that say the *opposite* of what you believe! Often this brings a healthy new openness with which the Spirit can work to bring us into proper doctrinal balance. On Day Two, the Lord grants us the grace to rightly divide the waters of His Word so that we obtain pure doctrine or the unleavened bread of the second feast. If, however, we are not willing to separate the light from the darkness in our lives on Day One, we can never properly divide or separate the Word of God on Day Two. As we noted, each Day forms the foundation for the next Day in our lives.

Why It Is Important to Have Pure Doctrine

1. Truth Is a Person

Jesus said that He is the truth (Jn. 14:6). Truth is a person, not simply an idea. Error is also more than just an idea, as we understand from the Apostle John's reference to "the spirit of error" (1 Jn. 4:6). Error is a spiritual being—Satan being the principal source. Therefore, the more truth we have within our hearts, the more of Christ we have formed in us. Conversely, the more error we have in our hearts, the more the influence of Satan is at work in us. As an extreme example, observe the tremendous influence of evil spirits that Hinduism has brought into the lives of its followers. It is easy to see how the enormous degree of error in these false religions has brought with it a tremendous manifestation of the power of the spirit of error. What we sometimes don't understand is that *every* doctrine brings to our lives the influence of a spiritual force—either the Spirit of truth or the spirit of error. If you long to be under the Lord's influence alone, then ask Him to purify your doctrine.

2. There Are No Lies in Heaven

Jesus said, "Whosoever therefore shall break one of these least commandments, and *shall teach men so,* he shall be called the least in the kingdom of heaven" (Mt. 5:19a). In Heaven, those who have led others into error will be called "least" or "small" because that is precisely what they are. No one will be calling them "least" if, in fact, they are great because there are no lies in Heaven! Consider then, the seriousness of allowing God to purify our doctrine. If we never come into pure doctrine, it will be proof that we have never gone beyond the second Day of the "redemptive week," or the second step in our walk with God. A person living in the first or second Day cannot be considered spiritually mature; he will be called "small."

3. Heresy Is a Work of the Flesh

Paul teaches that heresy, or doctrinal error, is one of the works of the flesh (Gal. 5:19-20).[1] People who have any works of the flesh operating in their lives **will not inherit** the Kingdom (Gal. 5:21). This does not mean that they will not be saved, but rather that they will not receive the inheritance. In other words, they will not enter Canaan, rest, or the seventh Day—our inheritance. Joseph, the seventh man in Genesis, is the man who is exalted to the throne and rulership of Egypt. We should keep in mind that inheriting the Kingdom of God and being saved from hell are two very different things. One who inherits a kingdom becomes the king of that kingdom—that is, the owner or the sovereign ruler over the kingdom.

We must conquer (overcome) all the works of the flesh if we are to reign with Christ (Rev. 2:26-27; 3:21). One of those works is heresy or false

---

1. The Greek word *hairesis* is translated as "heresy" in the KJV in this passage. Although some English versions translate this word differently in Galatians 5:20, those versions translate this same word as "heresy" in other passages. Since this Greek word means "differences of opinion," it definitely involves heresy because there is only one Truth.

doctrine. There are many scriptural reasons why ruling requires overcoming, but it should be self-evident that if we cannot rule over our own flesh, we are not qualified to rule over the world or others. Many Christians never get the victory over the flesh because they simply do not understand the way to arrive at that goal. The way is revealed throughout the Bible, beginning with God's "redemptive week." Sadly enough, the words of Hosea become the experience of many sincere saints, "*My people* [not the world] are destroyed for lack of knowledge: because thou hast rejected knowledge, I will also reject thee, that thou shalt be no priest to me" (Hos. 4:6a). If we are not permitted to be priests, neither shall we be kings.

4. Truth Sets Us Free, But Error Binds Us

We will be unshackled from certain bondages in our lives only when truth enters. Jesus declared, "You shall know the truth, and the truth shall make you free" (Jn. 8:32 NKJV). I have met people who are constantly looking for a greater deliverance ministry to set them free. Often, what they need is to be exposed to more light of the truth. Once this happens, the spiritual darkness that troubles them will be dispelled. Remember, just as the spirit of truth sets us free, so the spirit of error binds us.

5. We Are Called to Be Priests

We are called to be priests unto God. One of the important ministries of the priests is to **make a difference** between the holy and unholy, and to **teach** God's people all the statutes which the Lord has spoken to them (Lev. 10:10-11). How can a priest make a difference and teach what is right if he himself is not sure of what is truth? If a priest cannot accurately discern between right and wrong, making a difference between truth and error, he is not fulfilling his obligation as a biblical priest. I have heard leaders scoff at the idea that anyone could ever come into doctrinal purity and unity. If this is the case, no one can obey the biblical exhortation to eat the unleavened bread of truth without the leaven of false doctrine; likewise, no one can finish Day Two, and everyone will end up being called "little" in the Kingdom. Is not the God who revealed His mighty power in the Creation able to fulfill Day Two in *our* earth?

Chapter 8

Keys to Dividing the Waters

The problem of doctrinal confusion in the Church today is certainly not God's fault, nor is it His desire or plan. There must be some area or areas in which we, His people, are failing. The Bible gives some very clear instructions to those who are interested in finding the truth. I wholly believe that if we follow these instructions, "the Spirit of truth will guide us into all truth," just as the Lord has promised—and what a promise! (Jn. 16:13) This phrase "into all truth" obviously does not mean that He will cause us, as individuals, to know all the truth there is to know. The thought is that the Spirit will guide us "into all manner of truth," or "into any area of truth." In other words, there is no need to be deceived. The Lord does not say that the Spirit will lead us into a mixture of truth and error.

Keys to Obtaining the Unleavened Bread of Truth

Do we have a love for the truth? Proverbs exhorts us to, "Buy the truth, and sell it not" (Prov. 23:23a). The question is, Do we love the truth enough to pay the price? Let's now consider the keys to obtaining the unleavened bread of truth, and the price that is involved.

1. Only Heaven Can Make the Separation

The most important key is revealed right in the Creation account of the second Day, where we are told, "And God said, Let there be a firmament in the midst of the waters, and let it divide the waters from the waters...And God called the firmament Heaven" (Gen. 1:6,8a). That which maintains the proper division and balance between the waters of His Word in our earth is *Heaven*. In other words, *Heaven* decides who will have the truth and who will be deceived, so that our principal concern must be to please the Lord and not to be concerned about pleasing man. It is the Holy Spirit from Heaven who alone can lead us into all truth. Therefore, it is extremely important that we obtain His favor and do not grieve Him (Jn. 16:13; Eph. 4:30).

I have heard people say, "Well, *I* would never be deceived by the Antichrist, nor receive his mark in the last days because I understand what is going to happen." Unfortunately, they are already deceived into thinking that human understanding is sufficient for spiritual things. Consider the awesome warning we should receive from the fall of one-third of the angels who were originally in heaven (Rev. 12:4,9). At some time in the past, they were all created by God. We know that Lucifer, previously one of the mightiest angels, was originally perfect and sinless. He, like all the angels, lived in the manifest presence of God. We also know from Hebrews that angels are wiser and mightier than human beings (Heb. 2:7). We can only begin to imagine the tremendous power of Satan to deceive when we realize that one third of the angels of God were deceived into following Satan in his rebellion. If angels, living in the presence of God, could be misled by the spirit of deception, what hope is there for us mere mortals unless God grants us a miracle of grace to not be deceived? Certainly Heaven alone decides who receives that grace, and grace is given to the *humble*—to those who see their great need of God's mercy.

There are many Scriptures that confirm God's sovereignty in deciding who will receive truth and who will not. Let's consider just one. The disciples asked Jesus why He spoke only in parables to the people (Mt. 13:10). He answered, "Because it is given unto you to know the mysteries of the kingdom of heaven, but to them it is not given" (Mt. 13:11). Notice here that knowing the truth and the Lord's secrets is something that is either given or not given. Nevertheless, as men with free wills, we definitely have something to do with God's decision in this matter.

There was one major difference between the multitudes and the few who became Jesus' disciples. It is vitally important for us to understand that difference! Jesus considered their desire and attitude of heart. Imagine the different attitudes among the people after they had listened to hours of Christ's teaching. His words were captivating, anointed, and spoken with authority. The officers of the Temple sent to arrest Him were arrested *by* Him. They returned empty-handed and exclaimed to their angry superiors, whose orders had been disregarded, "No one has ever spoken like this man before" (Jn. 7:32,45-46). On at least one occasion, the multitudes were with Him for three days straight listening to Him (Mt. 15:32).

Imagine the crowds as they walked back to their homes after three days of teaching. Some probably said to their companions, "Weren't the things the teacher from Nazareth shared with us during these three days wonderful?" And others responded, "Well, yes, but if we analyze them, what have we learned that was new? He talked about fishing, sowing seed, making bread, pouring new wine in old wineskins, and a host of other things that we have all known and understood since we were children. So what's new?" Still others might have said to themselves, "It was so wonderful to have spent this time with the Lord. His words caused my heart to burn with a deeper love for God. Although it seems that He didn't say one thing that was new, in my spirit I feel that *everything* He said was somehow new—things that I have never understood or thought about before. I am sure there was a hidden message in what He was sharing." This last group of people, almost instinctively, very likely turned around and went back to where Jesus was, as though drawn by a huge magnet. Let's see what happened.

A seeker approaches the Lord and says to Him, "Lord, could I spend just a few more moments with You and ask You some questions?" (Of course, the Lord always has time for the hungry, but the lovers of this world rarely have time for Him.) The hungry heart continues, "Lord, I have a feeling that You were speaking about something much deeper than the natural world when you were talking about sowing the seed in the earth. Could You just explain these things to me?" The Lord, delighted to have found a heart that longs for His presence and truth, responds, "You are right, and I will gladly explain these things to you. You see, I was not speaking about natural seed—I was talking about My Word. I was not talking about just any sower, but I was speaking about the Son of Man, the husbandman. And the earth into which the seed is sown is really the heart of man..." (Mk. 4:14-20). Who would have guessed that Jesus used the **earth** as a symbol of **man's heart**, or that the **seed** represented the **Word of God**? How did the Lord ever come up with these symbols? Could it have been from His own Word, from Genesis 1?

Jesus continues to explain one parable after another to the hungry hearts who come away with Him and spend time in His presence. (Mark 4:34 tells us that this is what happened during His earthly ministry.) Today, as then, these people become known as His "disciples," or students. The difference, then, between those who understand His secrets and those who do not is simply that some love His presence and truth, and others do not. Truth is *given* to those who love His truth enough to spend time alone with Him seeking an understanding of His words that is deeper than the superficial meaning that satisfies the multitudes. As the psalmist declares, "In thy light shall we see light" (Ps. 36:9b). In other words, in the light of His presence, we receive the light of understanding. Those who are willing to pay the price to spend time with the Lord will understand His mysteries!

Most of God's people today, as was the case 2,000 years ago, are simply too busy with the cares and pleasures of this present world to be bothered with such trivial things as hidden truth or "hidden manna," as Revelation 2:17 calls it. Few see the value in sitting at the feet of Jesus, as Mary did, when there are so many things to be done in life. In fact, many people dismiss the whole idea that there are hidden meanings or gems of truth in His words. They go so far as to say that those who believe such things are heretical, or even dangerous to the Body of Christ. It is easier to call the hungry hearts "fanatics" than to pay the price to find those treasures by spending time with the teacher from Nazareth. The issue is, some "receive a love for the truth" and some do not. (See Second Thessalonians 2:9-11.)[1] Paul warns that those who do not love the truth will be deceived, because the Lord Himself "will send them strong delusion" (2 Thess. 2:11 NKJV). God shows no favoritism or partiality (Eph. 6:9). Rather, He simply gives us what we really want most in life (Ps. 145:16). Do you hunger for understanding of the mysteries of the Kingdom enough to spend time alone with Jesus? If you do, Heaven's grace will help you to rightly divide the waters of His Word.

2. Allow Our Hunger for Truth to Grow

On a number of occasions when people have heard that I am a pilot, they have asked me if I like to fly. That's like asking, "Is the pope Catholic?" I have yet to meet a person who has dedicated enough time and money to becoming a pilot who could say with a straight face, "I never could stand flying airplanes! I just did it because I didn't have anything else to do." Have you ever met a fisherman who hates to fish? Or a golfer who just can't stand golfing?

Most people find time to do what they most enjoy in life. Along life's way, I have met a number of corporate executives who carry enormous responsibilities and keep unbelievably demanding schedules. Yet every one

---

1.   The phrase "they received not the love of the truth," as translated by the KJV, NKJV, and ASV, is more accurate than "they refused to love the truth," as translated by the NIV and RSV. Of the 59 times this Greek word is used in the New Testament, the KJV translates it as "receive" 52 times. In fact, when this word appears in other Scriptures, "receive" is the most common translation given by all the major English versions.

of them manages to find time to do the one thing they enjoy most in life. I did *not* say that they find time to do *all* the things they would like to do—only what they enjoy *most*.

In spite of this fact, I have heard Christians declare that they simply do not have time to read and study the Word of God. Unwittingly, they are declaring that knowing the One who is the truth is simply not their top priority in life. According to Dr. Bruce Wilkinson of Walk Through the Bible Ministries, the average Christian business executive watches between 30 and 40 hours of television each week.[2] Regardless of whether or not this is totally accurate, this is enough time to read through the entire Bible every two to three weeks. We know this because the reading of the entire Bible is available on audio tapes, and it lasts 80 hours. What will we say to the just Judge at the end of our lives if we have unknowingly violated all the laws on life's highway during our journey through life? Will we tell Him that we simply did not have time to learn His laws? Would an earthly judge consider that a valid excuse if we were guilty of a traffic violation? As Christians, is it not our responsibility to learn the laws of the Kingdom of God to which we belong?

The issue is simply a matter of what we love most. If you would like to know what you love most, there is a simple test you can take to find out. Just make a mental note of the principal theme of your next 10 or 15 conversations with friends or acquaintances (conversations that are not work-related). You will soon discover what interest your heart continually gravitates to. We definitely talk *most* about what we love *most*.

"Then they that feared the Lord spake often one to another: and the Lord hearkened, and heard it, and a book of remembrance was written before him for them that feared the Lord, and that thought upon his name. And they shall be mine, saith the Lord of hosts, in that day when I make up my jewels" (Mal. 3:16-17a). The Lord has a very simple way of discerning who really loves Him! How often does our conversation center on the things of the Lord? Let's pray this simple prayer: "Lord, help me to receive from You a deep, genuine love for the truth!"

3. Obey the Truth We Already Have

Discerning between false doctrine and pure doctrine does not require natural ability; it is quite simple but requires a great price. Jesus declared, "If any man will do his [the Father's] will, he shall know of the doctrine, whether it be of God, or whether I speak of myself" (Jn. 7:17). If we do the

---

2.   Ramon Bennett, *Saga* (Jerusalem, Israel: Arm of Salvation, 1993), pp. 134-135.

Lord's will, we will be enabled to discern if a doctrine is true or false. Obedience is the price that must be paid for pure doctrine. Once again, the grace received on Day One forms the foundation for God's work in us on Day Two. If we do not respond in obedience on Day One to the separation between works of darkness and works of light, then we cannot obey to receive pure doctrine on Day Two.

What about the people who are following a false way? Does God not care about them? Can He not convince them? God certainly cares. The ones in error are the ones who do not care. Proof of this is found in the way they live. It has often been said that a man's morality determines his theology. When the Lord permits His light, or truth, to shine on our hearts, as He does to one degree or another for every human being who comes into the world (Jn. 1:9), what we do with that truth is of vital importance. If we choose to ignore it and disobey it, we prove to Him that we have no interest in following Him or the truth. So why should He give us more truth?

4. Some Things Can Be Understood Only by the Mature

There are many things in life that cannot be experienced without some degree of maturity. For example, it is impossible to fully understand all that is involved in a marriage relationship without ever being married. So it is with many of the wonderful truths in God's Word. We must grow up spiritually and experience God's truths before we can fully understand them.

This need for maturity is one reason most countries of the world require a person to be about 16 years of age before he can drive a vehicle. The lack of emotional maturity in a ten-year-old is sufficient cause to keep him out of the driver's seat—besides the more practical reason that he cannot yet reach the pedals! Isaiah asks a question that every hungry heart should ask: "Whom will he teach knowledge? And whom will he make to understand the message? Those just weaned from milk? Those just drawn from the breasts? For precept must be upon precept, precept upon precept, line upon line, line upon line, here a little, there a little" (Is. 28:9-10 NKJV). Clearly, newborns will not understand, and even those who are weaned must realize that we come into truth little by little and not all at once. Lord, cause us to grow up!

Day Two and the Tabernacle of Moses

We have compared the second Day with the second feast, but the similarity we find with the Tabernacle of Moses is even more striking. In the daily ministry of the priests in the Tabernacle, we know that they first came through the door, which is symbolic of our salvation experience. The second step for the priests was to approach the laver to wash their hands and feet *before* they drew near to the altar to offer the prescribed daily sacrifices (Ex. 30:17-21). What spiritual significance does the laver have for us? Spiritually speaking, what is it that washes us?

"Christ…loved the church, and gave himself for it; that he might sanctify and cleanse it with the washing of water by the word" (Eph. 5:25b-26). Therefore, this daily priestly ritual was symbolic of our daily washing, as New Testament priests, with the water of the Word of God. Isn't it amazing that the second Day of Creation deals with water, and the second step in the Tabernacle deals with water also? Jesus said, "Now ye are clean through the word which I have spoken unto you" (Jn. 15:3). His Word is what washes and cleanses us. Jesus declared this to His disciples just after He had washed their feet in John 13. Are we washing our spiritual hands (service) and feet (walk) each day by spending time at the laver—His Word? The psalmist also reveals what can cleanse our spiritual walk (or feet), when he writes, "How can a young man cleanse his way? By taking heed according to Your word" (Ps. 119:9 NKJV).

Scripture likens the laver to the Word of God in an even clearer way in James 1:22-24, where we are admonished, "But be ye doers of the word, and not hearers only, deceiving your own selves. For if any be a hearer of the word, and not a doer, he is like unto a man beholding his natural face in a glass: For he beholdeth himself, and goeth his way, and straightway forgetteth what manner of man he was." Here the Word of God is likened to a mirror that reveals what we are. It reveals our need and the defilement of our flesh that needs to be cleansed through washing. Since the laver represents the Word of God, it is little wonder that the entire laver was made from the mirrors of the women of Israel! (Ex. 38:8)

In the laver we find a wonderful revelation of the heart of God, as well as His provision for every one of us. Each morning and each evening the priests would draw near to this water-filled laver. As they looked into it, they could see themselves clearly in the reflection of the water and the brass. At the laver, they not only saw their spots and smudges, but in the water provided there they also received God's provision for removing them. When we read and study the Scriptures, they do for us what the laver did for the priests. As James tells us, the Scriptures serve as a mirror. In them we see what we are, with all our failures and shortcomings; at the same time, we receive the ministry of the Word, which is to wash, cleanse, and change us, giving us the answer to what we are. That is, the water of the Word removes our spots and smudges! What a wonderful God we serve, and what a merciful heart He continually reveals toward us, His people! How can we do other than worship and serve Him?

Day Two and the Second Man of Faith

The second man of faith in Genesis is Enoch. Is he a revelation of the second Day of Creation, where God purifies our doctrine, teaching us the difference between truth and error? Enoch's name in the Hebrew actually means "to teach," "to train," or "to narrow" (*Strong's Hebrew Dictionary*, #2585 and #2596). The Old Testament usage of this word is related to religious and moral training.[3] The concept is that a child's path is "narrowed" in order to direct him into the way of truth. Enoch's very name reminds us of the ministry of the priest—to teach and show God's people the right way.

Remember that "Heaven" is first mentioned in the Bible in the context of the separation of the waters on the second Day. Enoch was the man who was taken into heavenly places by a supernatural translation. Enoch "walked with God" (Gen. 5:24a). This is the only way to obtain pure doctrine and to have our own walk washed and purified. Enoch was the man who received the testimony that he pleased God (Heb. 11:5). To please the Lord we must know His commandments and keep them (Jn. 14:21). Therefore, we know that Enoch was a man who knew and obeyed the truth.

Years ago, a certain man of God wrote a mighty warning against false doctrine and the heretical teachers who promote it. He exhorted, "I urge you to struggle with all your hearts to preserve the doctrine you originally received, because certain men have crept in among you who have perverted the message of God's grace. They walk like Cain, their doctrine is like Balaam's, and they rebel like Korah. These men are like clouds that possess no water of the living Word. They are carried about by every wind of doctrine. They are like trees that the Father has plucked up by the roots because they are blind leaders of the blind who have not been rooted in the true faith. They are like wandering stars that give a sailor one message today and a different message tomorrow. Their doctrine and message is continually changing like bread that has been leavened."

Many students of the Word will immediately recognize that Jude wrote this message. I have paraphrased his principal message, which is against false teachers (Jude 3,4,11-13), and added words from Jesus and Paul (Mt. 15:13; Col. 2:7). Is it significant that Jude selected Enoch to contrast him with the false teachers and show us the difference between their

---

3.   Lawrence O. Richards, *Expository Dictionary of Bible Words*, Regency Reference Library (Grand Rapids, MI: Zondervan Publishing House, 1985), p. 601. (See "train.")

lies and God's truth? In verses 14 and 15, Jude declares that Enoch preached a convicting message under a powerful prophetic anointing that clearly separated the godly from the ungodly. In Enoch's life, as with all true men of faith, the message and the messenger were one and the same. Enoch was a man who learned the difference between truth and error in his own life, and then preached that message. God fulfilled Day Two in Enoch's life. Once He has done so for us, we will be permitted to move on to Day Three and another wonderful separation.

Chapter 9

Day Three—Do We Desire the Dry Land or the Waters?

A certain teacher began the first day of the new semester by saying, "Today students, we are going to begin our study of Genesis, but first let's just sing a chorus or two and spend a few minutes praising the Lord." After 45 minutes of singing and praying, the class ended, with all the students feeling very happy that they had spent their time wisely by seeking the Lord and His blessing. The next day the teacher explained again, "We are going to begin our study of Genesis today, but first let's just sing a chorus or two and pray." For the second time, the praise and worship lasted for the entire 45 minutes, and the students were again in agreement with the way things went. The third day, the same thing happened again. This pattern continued throughout the entire semester. In fact, by the end of that semester, the teacher had managed to mention only a few disjointed thoughts concerning the first six verses in Genesis. There was no other teaching whatsoever!

Why would any teacher do such a thing! In the case of this teacher, there were two reasons. First, he was so busy with other things at the school that he simply did not have time to prepare for his classes. The second reason was that he was reacting against the direction that the school's leadership was taking. They were leading the school toward more emphasis on an academic study of the Bible, doctrine, and theology. This teacher felt that the most important thing in life was the spiritual preparation of the students; therefore he almost totally ignored the study of God's Word during his class time. Who was right? At the time when I was a student in that teacher's class, I was not sure, but I believe that the answer is found in the truths of Day Three.

To help us understand the spiritual significance of Day Three, let's recall that in Genesis 1, *water speaks of the Word of God*. Now on the third Day, God gathered those waters that were covering the entire earth into one place, and the "dry land" appeared (Gen. 1:9). From that "dry land" the **first fruits** of the Lord's new creation sprang forth (Gen. 1:11-12). Once again, the seven feasts confirm for us that their seven-fold message reveals the same truths found in God's seven-step plan of Creation. The third feast, called the **Feast of Firstfruits**, reveals the firstfruits in our earth, as does Day Three of Creation.

On Day Three, one more divine separation is made. The Lord first separated the light from the darkness on Day One; then He separated the waters from the waters on Day Two. On the third Day He separated the dry land from the waters. In order for fruit to be produced, the Lord had to bring about this separation and then maintain an **extremely delicate balance** between the dry land and the water. Fruitfulness on the earth requires both dry land and water, but too much of either brings disaster. Too much dry land produces a desert, and too much water produces a flood. What is the practical lesson in this?

The water speaks of God's Word, but what does the "dry land" symbolize? As a first step toward the answer, let's recall that, biblically speaking, the fruits within us are called "the fruits of the Spirit"; they **spring from the Spirit of God** that is within us. On Day Three, the "fruits" **spring from the "dry land"** within our "earth;" they are not the product of the waters of His Word in us. So then, "dry land" seems to be related in some way to the Spirit of God, just as the waters are related to the Word of God. This concept is very much in keeping with the prompting I received that day while mowing the grass—that I should read Genesis 1 and replace "earth" with "the spirit of man." The "earth" is symbolic of the **spiritual life** of man that is being redeemed and made into a new creation in Christ. In Genesis 1:10, God called the dry land "Earth" (KJV, NKJV, RSV, NRSV, and ASV). This is the same Hebrew word used for "earth" throughout Genesis 1. The symbolism here is very interesting because we find an "Earth" (dry land) inside the "earth" (man's spirit). From that "Earth," fruits spring forth. Clearly it is the Spirit of God at work within the spirit of man that produces the fruits of the Spirit within us. In order for our earth to be fruitful, both the Word (waters) and the Spirit (dry land) must be present and active. We must allow God to develop in us a very delicate balance between a life dedicated to the water of the Word (reading, studying, searching, preaching, teaching), and a life given to spiritual exercises (prayer, intercession, praise, worship, and the operation of the gifts of the Spirit).

If a person or a church is out of balance in either of these two areas, serious consequences will result. The necessary balance is so delicate that only God Himself can accomplish the work of Day Three, or of any other Day for that matter! This is not to say that failure in man's life is ever God's fault. It is always man's. The Lord's plan is always to finish the work He has begun in us, but if we refuse to yield to the Creator at any stage, the work in our lives stops. Why would anyone want to hinder God from bringing a balance in this important area? Our problem on Day Three is very similar to our problem on Day Two: Man, by nature, is an extremist. We naturally tend to carry our viewpoints and our actions to an extreme. Anyone who wants to see how this part of man's nature operates from an early age need only turn a little child loose on a full cookie jar without supervision. In most cases, his actions will be carried to an extreme: He will not stop eating cookies until he is sick!

Life, including our physical bodies, depends upon many extremely delicate balances between opposite extremes. A lack of balance in our physical lives can quickly bring death. The Bible reveals that life in the Spirit is the same way. A lack of balance in our spiritual lives can also bring death! Our problem is that, by nature, we are like pendulums swinging from one side to the other, often carrying truths to an extreme. This is especially true when we first receive a new truth. Our tendency then is to focus all our attention on this truth to the exclusion of balancing truths. When God brings us into His true spiritual rest, the wild swings of our pendulum will no longer occur. Then we will find it easy to maintain a divine balance in many areas of truth. We will also find it easier to understand brethren who are promoting one side of a doctrinal coin to the exclusion of the other and to help them in a spirit of meekness.

Because of the human tendency to carry truth and revelation to an extreme, few people and few churches maintain a healthy balance between the Word and the Spirit—that is, between the "water" and the "dry land." Those who have seen the power and importance of the Scriptures tend to do more reading and studying than praying and praising; those who see the importance of life in the Spirit often tend to do more praying and praising than reading and studying. Lord, only You can bring us to the third Day!

The Result of Having All Word and No Spirit

If our earth continues to be totally given to the water of the Word, then we will end up having the wonderful truths and pure doctrines of Day

Two without the love and fruits of the Spirit found on Day Three. Not only is this possible, but the Bible and human experience confirm that it happens. The Apostle Paul indicates that it is possible to have great understanding of the mysteries of God's Word and tremendous knowledge without having love (1 Cor. 13:2). Paul also implies that it is possible to have the truth of Day Two without the love of Day Three. He exhorts us to grow in Christ until we have learned to "speak the truth in love" (Eph. 4:14-15). May we never be content merely to speak the truth of Day Two. Rather, let us go on toward perfection and learn to speak those wonderful truths from a heart filled with the fruits of **love** for others, **humility** before God, and **control** over our own flesh.

Many of us have heard astounding expositions of God's Word from men whose lives reveal little or nothing of the fruits of the Spirit called meekness, patience, and gentleness. Most of the world has known preaching ministries that have won literally thousands to Christ, but they lacked the fruit of the Spirit called "self-control," which is translated as "temperance" in Galatians 5:23. This Greek word is defined not only as "self-control" but also as "the virtue of one who masters his desires and passions, especially his sensual appetites."[1] Many effective ministries have been destroyed because their leaders were unable to rule over their own passions and sensual appetites. Could it be that they were content to remain on Day One or Day Two without going on to the fruits of the Spirit that our loving Lord wants to produce in us on Day Three?

Another lack manifests itself in us if we spend a disproportionate amount of our time in the study and exposition of the Word without developing the spiritual side of our lives. This lack is all too often observed in men who can amaze their hearers with deep, eloquent sermons, but who leave everyone with the feeling that it all came from the head, not the heart. If the message we preach (or share on a one-to-one basis as a witness for Christ) has not touched our hearts, then it probably will not touch the hearts of our listeners either. If it has not caused *us* to draw nearer to the Lord in the secret place, then it will not do so for others. And if our message has not been tempered, anointed, and given the fragrance of Heaven through time spent at the feet of Jesus, the truly hungry heart will go away feeling empty and unsatisfied by what we had to say.

The Lord Jesus Himself is a wonderful example of the importance of having both the Word and the Spirit flowing through our lives so that our earth produces fruit. No one has ever produced more fruit than He has!

---

1. *Logos Bible Study Software* (Oak Harbor, WA: Logos Research Systems, 1993), Greek Lexicon, #1466.

When He was 12 years old He amazed the best theologians of that day with His grasp of the Word (Lk. 2:46-47). Yet, He still needed to mature in His own spiritual walk (Lk. 2:52). Part of the process of maturing in Christ's life required that grace be poured into His lips (Ps. 45:2). Often what matters most is not *what* we say, but *how* we say it. One of the most amazing virtues in the Lord's life was that He had all the doctrinal and theological answers for many years, but never shared any of them, at least not publicly. We know this because the people from His home synagogue of Nazareth didn't even know how well He could speak, even though He had grown up there (Lk. 4:16-22). The first time Jesus publicly shared in Nazareth was His reading and teaching from the passage in Isaiah that declares, "The Spirit of the Lord God is upon me; because the Lord hath anointed me to preach..." (Is. 61:1). He then explained to those who heard Him read this passage, "Today this Scripture is fulfilled in your hearing" (Lk. 4:21b NKJV). They were actually hearing from the One whose heart not only knew the depths of the Word but also the anointing of the Spirit. This balance will cause our earth to produce fruit that remains.

The Result of Having All Spirit and No Word

"It was an amazing time in the presence of God. You should have been there!" our house guest declared, referring to a spiritual renewal convention where the Spirit of God had moved in a special way. He went on to tell of many other spiritual experiences and mighty visitations of the Spirit that he had witnessed. He told about the many great men of God he had personally met through the years. He shared in detail the spiritual sensations he had experienced while with them or while attending their meetings. Except for the time we spent sleeping, this man, previously unknown to my wife and me, continued to share such stories for most of the 24 hours he spent in our home. Someone had encouraged us to invite him to spend a day with us because they considered him to be a "spiritual giant." Undoubtedly, his stories were impressive. Therefore, we did all the listening and no talking almost to the very end of his visit. We were *almost* envious of his many spiritual experiences.

Just before it was time for him to leave, a truth from God's Word, related to the seven feasts of the Lord, came to my mind. At least a basic understanding of the feasts is essential if we are to really understand many passages from both the Old and New Testament. It is also essential if we are to observe the feasts in a spiritual way as Paul indicates we should (1 Cor. 5:7-8).

Our guest was so enthused by his own stories that he surely didn't notice that, for the first time in 24 hours, I had actually added something to the conversation. What he did notice was my reference to the word "feasts." Then he became quiet for the first time. He just sat there with a puzzled look on his face. I assumed that either he had not heard what I had said, or I had simply interrupted his endless train of thoughts. So I clearly repeated my comment about the feasts to him. The puzzled look remained. I said, "You know—the seven feasts that are so often referred to in the Scriptures. You probably teach about them yourself." For the first time, he was at a loss for words. With hesitation, and literally stammering, he responded, "The feasts? I *think* I have heard something about them somewhere, but the truth is, I don't know anything about them, and I have never studied them."

Upon hearing this answer, I was shocked—not because this brother just happened to be ignorant of this specific area of truth. My shock was not even the result of the clear evidence that he knew a lot about "moving in the Spirit" and very little about the Word of God. Rather, I was shocked because he happened to be one of the principal teachers at a fairly well-known Bible institute whose vision was to prepare ministers. Along with my shock, a new understanding began to dawn within me: The founder of the institute where he taught was the teacher I mentioned at the beginning of this chapter—the one who rarely taught anything from the Scriptures. This teacher had finally reacted so strongly against the "academic study of God's Word" in the institute I had attended, that he had left and founded his own institute. I could well understand why our guest would be a principal teacher there. As long as his only theme was "moving in the Spirit," and as long as that was what he practiced in his classes, I am sure he fit in very well at that institute.

Let me be quick to emphasize that we all desperately need to experience mighty meetings with the Lord as the early Church did. We definitely need genuine "movings of the Spirit." We also need to maintain the proper balance between the Word and the Spirit, which is so important to God's work on Day Three. However, one of the grave dangers of living without sufficient water of the Word falling on our earth is revealed in nature: "Give ear, O ye heavens, and I will speak; and *hear, O earth*, the *words* of my mouth. My *doctrine* shall drop as the *rain*, my speech shall distil as the dew, as the small *rain upon the tender herb*, and as the showers upon the grass" (Deut. 32:1-2). Note the key words I have italicized. He is speaking to an earth that can "hear," which is our earth. He tells us that His Word or doctrine is like rain that falls upon the tender herbs. On one hand, if our earth does not have areas where there is dry ground—symbolic of the spiritual realm—on which the rain of His Word falls, then it will be impossible for our earth to produce the fruit the husbandman labors to produce in us on Day Three. On the other hand, without the rain of His Word, everything on the dry land soon withers and dies.

I am aware of the fact that in the Church today rain is usually compared to the outpouring of the Holy Spirit, and in some biblical contexts this is proper. However, Deuteronomy 32:1-2 cannot be ignored. The Lord Himself tells us that His doctrine and Word are like the rain. It is also interesting that in Exodus 16:4 the Lord says, "...Behold, I will *rain bread* from heaven for you..." In our study of Day Two we saw that "bread" is a biblical symbol for God's Word or truth. Therefore, once again it is the Word that rains on us, not the Spirit. Many passages from the Old Testament make it clear that rain speaks primarily of His Word, *not* His Spirit. Consider Isaiah 55:10-11: "For as *the rain* cometh down, and...watereth the earth...*So shall my word be* that goeth forth out of my mouth: it shall not return unto me void...." Jeremiah tells us the same: "When he uttereth *his voice*, there is a multitude of waters in the heavens;...he maketh lightnings with *rain*..." (Jer. 51:16). Job used the same symbolism when he testified, "After my words they spake not again; and my speech dropped upon them. And they waited for me as for the rain; and they opened their mouth wide as for the latter rain" (Job 29:22-23).

Please note here an important principle that runs throughout the seven Days of the "redemptive week." The blessings of each Day can and *must* continue with us for the rest of our lives. For example, the water of the Word found on Day Two must come to our earth in the form of rain beginning with Day Three. We will forever need the water of that Word in our lives, but the Lord doesn't send a flood of water upon our newly formed garden. Rather, He sends the gentle rain that is produced from vapor that has been drawn from the vast store of water in the seas. This happens as our earth spends time in the presence of the One who is called "the Sun of righteousness" (Mal. 4:2). The heat and light of His presence draw out the portions from His Word that we need just as the sun draws vapors from the sea to form rain. Those specific truths are quickened to our spirits, and they turn into life-giving rain for our gardens, as well as for the gardens of others, becoming a living Word that falls upon us from Heaven.

May we always follow the example that the apostles in the early Church set before us. According to Acts 6:4, they gave their lives to two things: prayer and the ministry of the Word. They maintained the right balance between the Spirit and the Word. We must do the same, being sure that the gospel we share with others contains both the Word and the Spirit. The Apostle Paul was an example: "For our gospel did not come to you in word only, but also in power, and in the Holy Spirit..." (1 Thess. 1:5 NKJV). Once God has brought that balance in our lives, we will produce the fruit He seeks from our earth. Read on to discover what that fruit is.

Chapter 10

The Fruit He Seeks

Have you ever thought what it would be like to talk with some of the great men of faith from past ages and ask them questions? One of my questions would be, "What did you do that caused your life to be so honored and blessed by the Lord?" My great longing in life is to hear the Lord say to me someday, "Well done, thou good and faithful servant, enter thou into the joy of thy Lord." I earnestly want to know the secret to ending my life with that divine approbation. Those men of faith surely have the answers. They could cut through all the confusion that often exists in people's hearts because of the conflicting messages in this age of Christian radio, Christian television, Christian magazines, Christian books, and Christian tapes. Just imagine what it would be like talking with Abraham!

We might start off our interview, "Abraham, you are the father of faith and an example to us all; therefore, we would like to speak with you first. What were the great things you accomplished in life that caused you to experience so much of God's favor? Tell us about the greatest evangelistic crusades of your long ministry. How many were in attendance, and how many souls were saved?"

Abraham responds, "Well, I guess I can't tell you anything about that because I never had one single evangelistic campaign. I'm sorry—I can't help you there."

"Well then, Abraham," we continue, "tell us about some of the great miracles you performed. How many people did you see healed or raised from the dead?"

Abraham might answer this question almost sheepishly, "Well, child, the truth is, I was never used by God to do miracles. I really can't tell you any success stories there either."

As we begin to wonder about what kind of example father Abraham really is, we might ask in frustration, "Well, Abraham, what *did* you do? Surely you can tell us your own success story."

Abraham remembers well his life's story. Without hesitation, he begins, "Well, I journeyed from Ur of the Chaldees to Canaan, and I spent almost 100 years living in Canaan in a tent and as a stranger in a strange land. I never owned any land, therefore I had to keep moving about because someone was always claiming that I was living on their land. Even my nephew, Lot, fought with me about land rights; I just gave in because this world's goods never really mattered to me."

About then, with desperation, we interrupt him—"Abraham! Abraham! Listen! Please! Just tell us what you consider to be the greatest thing you ever accomplished in life!"

Abraham brightens up at this point and is very definite in his answer: "The greatest accomplishment in my whole life was undoubtedly to raise one son, the son of promise. Once he was born, I dedicated most of my time and energy to training him in the right way. You see, the Savior of all the world chose to come through him. If I had succeeded in evangelizing the whole world, but had failed to teach my son to follow the Lord with all his heart, neither you nor anyone else would have been saved! In fact, the Lord Himself said that He would only be able to fulfill His plan for my life and my family if I was faithful to raise Isaac the right way." (See Genesis 18:19.)

We begin to wonder whether our interview with Abraham has really been worthwhile, so we decide to wrap it up, saying, "Thank you, Abraham, for being willing to talk to us. We have just one final question: If the only important thing you did in life was to give birth to one son and raise him properly, could you explain to us how in the world you got to be such an important person in God's mind?"

It is as though Abraham has been waiting for this question. With a light on his face, he declares, "Oh, I can answer that. You see, the Lord is like you and me. He delights in showing His friends great favor and kindness. It doesn't really matter whether or not we amount to anything in man's eyes. Even though we never become anything more than a beggar on a dunghill, if we are God's friends, He just delights in sharing His throne with us. I never really amounted to much in man's eyes, nor did I accomplish anything important to man's way of thinking. I just spent my life being a friend of God, and here I am at His side!" (See First Samuel 2:8.)

We decide that there must be other great men in Heaven who can give us more insight into life than Abraham, so we move on. "Samuel, what about you? Can you tell us about your great ministry? What did you do during your lifetime?"

Samuel responds, "Well, I grew up in the house of the Lord, serving there as a porter. I opened and closed the doors of the Lord's house every day for Eli the priest."

"Yes, Samuel, we know all about that," we assure him, "but later, when you became the great prophet of Israel, tell us about the vastness of your national ministry and the tremendous influence you had among God's people. You must have had awesome national conferences every year!"

Samuel declares, "Oh, yes, I made one trip each year in a large circle, throughout my principal sphere of influence in Israel. During that annual trip, I always visited the same three cities—Bethel, Gilgal, and Mizpeh—and I judged the people there. It was about a 15-mile walk to Gilgal, the most distant city from my hometown of Ramah." (See First Samuel 7:16-17.)

We are now beginning to feel something of the disappointment we had experienced in our interview with Abraham. So we ask, "Samuel, how can it be that you spent most of the years of your life as a mighty prophet, never journeying more than 15 miles? How did you become great in God's eyes?"

"The only answer I can give you," Samuel replies, "is that I spent my life hearing the Lord's voice and obeying what He told me. He said that people who do this are those who really love Him (Jn. 14:21-23), and they will be loved by Him. I rarely traveled very far from home because He never told me to do so. I guess He enjoyed our friendship so much He just wanted me to have plenty of time to be with Him year after year, so that is exactly what I did! You see, my ministry was not really the central issue in my life. *He* was."

We could go on. We could talk to Enoch, who never seemed to do anything really important in man's eyes. Like Abraham, he just walked with God and became the Lord's friend. We could also talk to Jeremiah, who ministered under a mighty prophetic anointing for over 50 years. We would have to be careful not to embarrass him by asking how fruitful he had been. The truth is, other than his personal scribe, who at times seemed to have false motives, Jeremiah did not win one person to the Lord. Not even one person accepted his message. Some might say, "Yes, but let's talk to Moses. Now *he* was a man who really did great things!"

As earthly creatures, it is almost impossible for us to objectively evaluate Moses' life and accomplishments. This is true because something interesting happened to Moses' reputation *after* his death. During Moses' lifetime, God's people condemned and rejected Moses time and time again. They accused him of having brought them out of Egypt just so they would all die in the wilderness. After his death, however, he was elevated by God's people to become an unbelievably great historical figure. This romanticizing of Moses' life has fogged our current perspective. In our assessment of his accomplishments, we should keep in mind not only what his own people thought of him but also how the Gentile world of his generation evaluated his life from their point of view.

Moses spent 40 years learning the ways of Egypt. He was part of the royal family and a possible heir to the throne. After all those years of training, and having been brought by God into a tremendously influential position, it seems he could have stayed in the political arena and really brought extraordinary help to God's cause and His people. Instead, he threw it all away and lost his incredible opportunity to excel in life. After leaving the palace of the world's greatest empire, he spent the next 40 years pastoring someone else's sheep. His circumstances seemed to prove to Moses the foolishness of his decision—apparently, he was never able to secure a better paying job. After 40 years of labor, all he had was a wife, two sons, and a donkey. Moses then spent 40 years leading the Israelites around in a wilderness, after he had convinced them to leave Egypt and follow him to a promised land. Can we begin to imagine how his entire generation (Israel and the Gentiles alike) evaluated him as a man? He told Israel that they were on their way to a land that flowed with milk and honey. Far from taking them into that land, Moses took them into a wilderness that was much worse than living in Egypt. In that wilderness, Moses and that entire generation of Israelites died. The world would not call that success! Why then, is Moses remembered as a great man? Because he, too, walked with God and spent most of his last 40 years seeking the presence and friendship of God. *God* decides our end and our eternal position. Man's vote and evaluation have nothing whatsoever to do with it!

Of course, we can always resort to one last interview. We can turn to the Lord Himself, our example. The glory, power, anointing, and authority of the Lord's ministry were unparalleled by anyone else in history. He can obviously give us a clear example how to accomplish great things for God. Maybe the Lord's answers will rekindle our ambition for great things.

Our interview with Jesus would soon inform us that in the last hours of His life, after having poured out His life for others during three and a half years of ministry, He didn't have even one faithful disciple who stayed with Him to the end. In fact, of all the lepers, the blind, the lame, the demon possessed, and even the dead who were raised, there didn't seem to be one person who resisted the crowd when they cried, "Crucify

Him!" Jesus' own nation turned against Him and handed Him over to the Romans to be beaten (Lk. 18:32-33). When the world had finished beating Him, He was not even recognizable (Is. 52:14). Afterwards, when He was on the cross, Jesus' own people mocked Him, saying that He could save others but could not save Himself (Mt. 27:41-43).

One of the deepest agonies of the cross was not the shouts of the mockers who hurled insults in the face of the King. Rather, the agony that caused Jesus to die of a broken heart was the silence of others who stood at the cross—people who *should* have been shouting. They should have been shouting about how wonderful He was—about all the glorious things He had done for them! They should have been shouting that the sky darkened at noon that day because the sun refused to shine on humanity's darkest hour! (See Matthew 27:45.) Not only was His beloved John there but also Mary Magdalene. The night before, John had expressed so much love for the Lord that he had leaned on His breast. The Lord had delivered Mary from seven demons. (See Mark 16:9.) Many others who had been transformed by His ministry were also there. He surely looked at them from the cross, expecting that someone would at least say He was a good man, if nothing else. Sadly, not one of them lifted his voice to testify of Jesus' love, mercy, or kindness to him personally. (See Psalm 69:20-21.) Thus, Jesus died amidst the scorn, reproach, and mocking of a cruel world that concluded He was a total failure, and not one soul lifted his voice to declare otherwise! Are we also too ashamed of our crucified Lord to lift our voices and declare His goodness before sinful men?

Amid such total rejection, the Lord fought a tremendous battle with discouragement. At one point, He actually concluded, "I have labored in vain, I have spent my strength for nothing and in vain" (Is. 49:4a NKJV). After the cross, Jesus' own disciples said, "It is so sad. We thought He would be the Messiah, but now He's dead and it's all over" (Lk. 24:17-21 paraphrased). The Lord Jesus Christ departed from this world looking like a total failure in man's eyes. Today, He sits on the throne of glory as the King of all kings. Why? Since Jesus pleased the Father, the Father chose to place Him there; this was not subject to man's vote or opinion! (Phil. 2:5-10) If our goal is to leave this world looking like someone great in man's eyes, we are reading the wrong blueprint for success, and we are following the wrong examples.

With these hypothetical interviews, am I saying that evangelism is not important? that winning souls is a waste of time? that there is no need to see the miraculous manifested in our lives? or that the evidence of fruit in our spiritual lives is unnecessary? No, my message is just the opposite! I believe that the heart of the Lord is far more burdened for this world than we could ever be. He gave His life for it, something few of us are really willing to do, as proven by how little personal sacrifice we are disposed to make for Him and others daily. He knows that the world desperately needs to be won or it will face a hopeless eternity in hell. He is moved by that far more than we are! For 2,000 years the Church has basically failed in her great commission to take the gospel to the world. We are further from winning the world today than we were 2,000 years ago. Approximately 750,000 babies are born into the world each day, and the Church is winning approximately 17,000 souls per day to Christ.[1] Even if the Church is actually winning ten times this number, *this* cannot be termed "fruitful!" We are going backwards—and fast!

Something must change! I believe we must begin by examining our ways to find out why we are failing. In Genesis 1, the earth unmistakably begins to bring forth fruit on the third Day. Therefore, if we are not fruitful, it is certain that He has not yet finished the work of Day Three in us. Take heart, because this also means that when He *does* bring us into the third Day, we will *definitely* be fruitful. The only path to fruitfulness in winning the world is to do things *God's* way and not our own. If we examine the Scriptures, we can clearly see that our major problem today is that we are seeking to be fruitful as soul winners *before* we have developed the fruit of the Spirit, which is the primary fruit He seeks from our earth on Day Three. As we mentioned before, we want to *be* someone without *becoming* someone in Him.

The Fruit He Seeks From Our Earth on Day Three

Some may ask, "Why, then, does Jesus say that branches that do not bear fruit will be cut off and burned? Does He expect us to be fruitful today?" These are good questions in this context. We should remember, however, that the decision concerning whether or not a branch has borne fruit is made at the *end* of the season, not at the beginning. No husbandman will cut off a branch in the spring because it only has buds on it! If we *abide* in Him we *will* grow, and if we grow we *will* end up bearing fruit. Applying this to human life, no parent expects his newborn baby to be fruitful in any sense of the word. Is our heavenly Father any different?

Today, when Christians talk of being "fruitful," they invariably speak of winning souls or bringing forth spiritual children. We need to return to,

---

1.   Ramon Bennett, *When Day and Night Cease* (Jerusalem, Israel: Arm of Salvation, 1993), pp. 258-259.

and live by, the emphasis the New Testament gives to bearing fruit. The principal Greek word for *fruit* appears in the New Testament 56 times. Almost without exception, it refers to the fruits of the Spirit. Too often, we tend to put the cart before the horse. This tendency could be the result of our longing to reach the goal so much that we forget what is involved in getting there. How do we become spiritual fathers and birth children?

One of the most beautiful spiritual truths that can be found in marriage is that our children are a fruit of an intimate love relationship. God's unalterable plan for the Church is the same: that we bring forth spiritual children as an unavoidable fruit of having spent time alone with the King in His chambers of love. Abraham, our father and example, became an intimate lover of the Lord and, thereby, became a channel for the redemption of all mankind. **God will never ordain, authorize, or bless any other method to bear spiritual offspring.** It will only be when the Church returns to her first love, a love for *Him*, and knows the intimacy of the King's chambers, that this world will be won to Christ through love. In fact, any church or individual who does *not* return to his first love receives a very strong warning in Revelation 2:5, where the Lord says that He will remove his candlestick. This warning was given to the greatest soul-winning church in Asia—the Ephesian church (Rev. 2:1-7).

When I have reached the end of my life, my eternal destiny will not depend on how many souls I have won. Rather, it will depend on whether or not I am a lover and true friend of the Lamb! The Bible shows us that the Lord came seeking a wife—a lover who will give birth to children as a result of His intimacy with her (Rev. 21:9). Oh, how we have turned it around! Somehow we have come to the conclusion that He is seeking soul-winners. Let us heed the warning of Mark 8:36, "For what shall it profit a man, if he shall gain the whole world, and lose his own soul?" This verse is also tragic if we paraphrase it this way: "For what shall it profit a man, if he shall win millions of souls, and lose his own love relationship with the Bridegroom, and thus lose his place at Jesus' side?"

In John 13:35 and 15:8-10, Jesus gave us a clear revelation of how to win the world. When we have love one for another, and a genuine, fervent love for the Lord, then—and only then—will all the world know that we are disciples of the true and living God. This love will automatically begin to produce spiritual children! Jesus is not talking about love for ministerial success, love for the goals we have set for our ministry, love for our local church or denomination, or love for fame, money, or acceptance.

One of the most common mistakes people make when they come to the Lord is that they exchange a love of the things of this world for a love of spiritual things and the riches of Heaven. Many even consider it very

noble to seek after the riches of Heaven. Beware! Even as no earthly bridegroom likes to be sought for his riches, so the Lord will refuse to marry a
Bride who loves what He *has*, instead of loving what He *is*. From birth we
are filled with ambition. Even as Christians we have run after wealth and
many other vain goals. The Lord is seeking fruit from our lives that will remain. (See John 15:16.) Even though we may attain the fruit of a fulfilled
personal dream, it will never remain. As the Apostle Paul assures us, only
one class of fruit will definitely remain forever—the fruit of the Spirit.
"And now *abide* faith, hope, love, these three; but the greatest of these is
love" (1 Cor. 13:13 NKJV). "But the fruit of the Spirit is love" (Gal. 5:22a).
Love is the principal fruit the Father seeks in us. Long after there are no
more souls to win and no more churches to pastor, love for Him and for
others will remain! The depth of our love will determine our eternal position in His presence. Our relationship with Him today determines our position throughout eternity!

Chapter 11

How the Fruits Are Formed in Us

"Don't talk to me about God," growled our new acquaintance through clenched teeth. She had invited us to her house because we had the same last name, and we wanted to see if our family trees crossed anywhere. Bitterness just oozed from her as she continued, "After six million Jews died in Hitler's death camp, no one can convince me there is a God! My relatives have already gone through the only hell there will ever be. Hitler's plan for the Jews was nothing new in this world. For years, there were pogroms in Russia and Eastern Europe as Jews were isolated and were systematically persecuted and starved to death. Where was God then? Didn't He care, or was He asleep? Or didn't He know this was happening? What kind of a God do you believe in anyway? I wouldn't want to serve a God who allows things like this to happen!"

How it must break the heart of a loving God when souls are so embittered they cannot see His continual lovingkindness toward them! They cannot see the love of God in the beauty of the flowers, nor can they hear the heart of God in the singing of the birds. Man forsakes God, chooses Satan as his master, and then attributes Satan's wretched works and his blasphemous treatment of his subjects to a loving Creator. On every hand, there are people who say, "If there is a God, why does He allow wars, famine, disease, and horrible accidents?" It is not God's fault that man chooses to serve sin and the devil. When man places himself under Satan's dominion, all those things come with the package. Satan is so filled with hatred that his heart is consumed with an evil goal—to kill all his own subjects. (See Isaiah 14:12-16,20.)

Mankind needs to repent and recognize that one great proof of God's existence and of His infinite mercy is the fact that all humanity has not already perished at the hand of Satan. David praised the Lord saying, "O Lord, You preserve both man and beast" (Ps. 36:6b NKJV). God's mercy toward man moves Him to place limits on Satan; without those limits, the entire creation would have been destroyed long ago. On the other hand, divine justice demands that limits be placed on divine intervention in the kingdom of darkness. God has established not only the borders of national sovereignty but also the borders of spiritual sovereignty. God Himself established Adam's sovereignty and dominion over this world (Ps. 8:4-8; Gen. 1:28). Adam then chose to place himself and his family under Satan's dominion.

Since man is under the dominion of the desolator by his own choice, God can only do so much without violating *man's* own sovereignty and free will. God need not concern Himself with Satan's authority because Satan has no authority; but He does honor man's rights. Every human is given the opportunity to escape from the kingdom of destruction by repenting and voting in the Lord as the new King of his life. Not only Adam had the right to choose whom he would serve; so does every one of his children. When we choose the Lord as our King, He is free to intervene directly in our lives. Does this mean that all our trials and difficulties will now be over, as is sometimes taught in the Church?

There are times when even God sends affliction to His subjects (Ps. 88:7; Deut. 8:2-3). One of the many differences between God's ways and Satan's ways is that God brings tribulation to bless those who submit to Him, while Satan brings it to destroy his subjects. For example, Jesus Himself learned obedience through suffering. The psalmist experienced the same thing; he testifies, "Before I was afflicted I went astray: but now have I kept thy word" (Ps. 119:67). If we do not understand God's purposes for bringing us into affliction, we can fall into the trap that helped to destroy Israel's faith in the wilderness. In their afflictions, over and over they came to the conclusion that God was no longer with them, and that His favor was no longer resting upon them (Ex. 14:11; 17:7; Num 20:4).

I know many Believers who react in their trials just like Israel. Are we still so uncertain of God's love that we feel He loves us one day and not the next? How can we still doubt the love of the One who loved us so much that He gave His life on the cross to set us free? How many times have you heard a little voice telling you that your latest affliction is a result of your sin or rebellion? Have you ever been in a deep valley and felt that God had finally forsaken you or given up on you? The Lord has promised, "I will *never* leave thee, nor forsake thee" (Heb. 13:5b). Have you ever heard a voice saying to you, "You have sinned one time too many. The Lord is not going to forgive you this time. Now you are simply going to reap what you have sown. You are going to get what you deserve. The Lord is not going to rescue you from your problem again"? That is the voice of the enemy. The One who admonishes us to forgive others as He forgives—without measure—never talks that way! Why, then, does the Lord sometimes allow us to pass through long, dark valleys of affliction?

If we understand *what* the Lord desires to accomplish in our spiritual lives on Day Three, and if we understand *how* He accomplishes His goal, it will be much easier to submit to His dealings with a joyful and thankful heart. This is equally true for each of the seven Days. It is important then that we understand the truths of God's "redemptive week." When we have this understanding, it becomes very difficult for the enemy to bring us under the spirit of condemnation and fear—his main weapons against us. This was one of the main tactics Satan used against Israel in their wilderness journey. When we experience trials, it is a comfort to know that far from proving we are on the wrong path, our unpleasant experiences prove that the Lord still loves us. What a blessing to know that He disciplines and teaches those He loves! (Heb. 12:5-11) In the midst of our darkness, it is comforting to know that we are still on the right path, and that God still smiles on our lives.

God Works in Us to Produce the Fruits of the Spirit

The Bible reveals three main methods the Lord uses to produce the fruits of the Spirit in our earth on Day Three. We will consider them now. The process is not always pleasant to the flesh because, at times, affliction and suffering are involved. If, however, we understand what He is doing, we can more easily submit to the Creator's handiwork.

1. The Nine Spices Reveal the Process

God created the earth with a garden (Gen. 2:8). Since the natural earth is symbolic of our spiritual earth, we should expect to find references in the Bible to a garden within us, as Believers. One of those references is in the Song of Solomon 4:12: "A garden enclosed is my sister, my spouse, a spring shut up, a fountain sealed" (NKJV). The Scripture also tells us that the Lord is the husbandman of our garden, and He desires to find precious fruits in us (Heb. 6:7-10).

The Song of Solomon reveals the precious fruits the Lord desires to find in our garden. They are given as a list of nine spices or combinations of spices. "Thy plants are an orchard of pomegranates, **with pleasant fruits**; camphire, with spikenard, spikenard and saffron; calamus and cinnamon, with all trees of frankincense; myrrh and aloes, with all the chief spices" (Song 4:13-14). I have underlined the nine different spices, or combinations of spices, that are found in this list of "fruits." Any Israelite would have understood what the "chief spices" were because they were the spices used in the holy anointing oil, one of the most precious articles in the Temple. The "chief spices," (same as "principal spices" in KJV) which are enumerated in Exodus 30:23-24a, are myrrh, cinnamon, calamus, and cassia. Cassia, as one of the "chief spices," actually brings the number of individual spices in the Song of Solomon to nine.

Spices are mentioned extensively in the Scriptures. In addition to the anointing oil, they are also used to prepare incense, a figure of prayer (Ex. 30:34-38; Ps. 141:2). Something even more wonderful is that they produce the fragrance found upon the Lord (Ps. 45:8).

What is the spiritual significance of these spices? We have no way of knowing unless the Lord has given us a key somewhere in the Bible that explains them. He calls this list of nine spices in the Song of Solomon the "precious fruits" of our garden. He also gives us a list of the nine fruits of the Spirit in Galatians 5:22-23. By giving us these two lists, I believe that the Lord has provided the scriptural key to help us understand what each of these spices represents. For example, the first spice is camphire and the first fruit of the Spirit is love. Therefore, camphire should be a symbol of love. The second spice is spikenard, and the second fruit of the Spirit is joy. We can continue with the rest of the spices and fruits to understand the significance of each one.

A logical question here would be, "Are there any biblical confirmations that this is really what those spices represent?" Indeed, there are many confirmations. Since that study is outside the scope of this book, I will give just two. First, in the Song of Solomon 1:14, the Lord's bride compares Him to a cluster of camphire in the vineyards of Engedi. Camphire is a symbol of love. Therefore, the bride is saying that, to her, the Lord is like a cluster of love in the vineyards of Engedi. We know, of course, that He *is* love (1 Jn. 4:8), but what do vineyards and love have to do with one another? The answer is again found in the Song of Solomon: "Let us get up early to the vineyards...there will I give thee my loves" (Song 7:12). Therefore, the vineyards of Engedi are the place where the bride finds the love of her Lord, whom she likens to a "cluster of camphire." The vineyards are also the place where the bride enters into an intimate love relationship *with* Him.

To see that spikenard is a symbol of joy, consider the bride's declaration: "While the king sitteth at his table, my spikenard sendeth forth the smell thereof" (Song 1:12). While the King is eating from the table His bride has prepared for Him, the fragrance of spikenard fills the house. A record that this literally happened is found in the New Testament. The Apostle John tells us that Mary, Martha, and Lazarus hosted a supper for the Lord. While He was sitting at the table, Mary anointed the Lord with spikenard, and "the house was filled with the odour of the ointment" (Jn. 12:3). When one of Jesus' disciples was disturbed by this seeming waste, "Then said Jesus, Let her alone: against the day of my burying hath she kept this" (Jn. 12:7).

Why was the Lord anointed for His death with spikenard, a symbol of joy? Once again let's remember that the natural realm reveals spiritual truths. The Father anointed His Son with the oil of joy: "You love righteousness and hate wickedness; therefore God, your God, has set you above your companions by anointing you with the *oil of joy*" (Ps. 45:7 NIV). Therefore, Mary's simple act of love in the natural was a revelation of what the Father was doing in the spiritual realm. Jesus needed to be anointed with the oil of joy before His suffering and death because joy gives us strength (Neh. 8:10). Because of "the **joy** set before him," He was able to endure the cross (Heb. 12:2 NIV). Jesus' presence also brought the fullness of joy to Mary (Ps. 16:11b). Her natural house was filled with the fragrance of that spikenard, just as her spiritual house was filled with the joy she had found in His presence.

As sincere Believers, we all long for the fruits of the Spirit to be evident in our lives. Not all of us, however, are willing to go through the process required for this to happen. Consider how camphire and spikenard are obtained. **Leaves** of the plant are cut off, dried, and ground to a powder. Saffron is obtained by cutting off the **branches** of the plant, drying them, and grinding them. Cinnamon is **bark** that has been removed from a tree, dried, and ground to a fine powder. All the nine spices are obtained in one of these ways. According to the Bible, *we* are the plant that must suffer for these spices to be produced![1]

Suffering produces the fruits of the Spirit in us as few other things can. Consider several New Testament passages on this subject: "Now no chastening for the present seemeth to be joyous, but grievous: nevertheless afterward it yieldeth the peaceable *fruit* of righteousness..." (Heb. 12:11); "And every branch that beareth fruit, he purgeth it, that it may bring forth more fruit" (Jn. 15:2b); "...we glory in tribulations also: knowing that

---

1. See Isaiah 7:2; 55:12-13; 61:3; Ezekiel 15:6; 17:24; John 15:1-3.

tribulation worketh patience" (Rom. 5:3); "But the God of all *grace*, who hath called us unto his eternal glory by Christ Jesus, after that *ye have suffered* a while, make you *perfect*, stablish, strengthen, settle you" (1 Pet. 5:10). Finally, consider our Lord, who manifested the fullness of every fruit of the Spirit. The glory of His life and character was revealed more by the virtues of the *fruits* of the Spirit than by the *power* of the Spirit that He demonstrated. We too can share in the glory of His character *if* we are willing to choose the way He has ordained for us: "*if* so be that we *suffer* with him, that we may be also *glorified together*" (Rom. 8:17b).

When a person suffers affliction in any area of his life, it never leaves him the same. Suffering either softens our hearts or makes them harder. The determining factor is whether we turn *toward* God in the affliction or *away* from Him. It is amazing how gentle and patient a hard husband can become when he finds himself in a sickbed, dependent on the kindness of his wife! Sadly enough, there are many Christians today who have accepted the concept that we should not suffer—because supposedly Christ suffered everything for us. Paul did not understand or preach that gospel (Col. 1:24), and neither did Peter (1 Pet. 2:21).

The Lord enlarged my understanding of the spices and how they are obtained through an experience of affliction I had in the Philippines. (Let's remember that cinnamon is obtained by removing the bark or outer layer of the tree.) One day I noticed that a mosquito bite on the side of my face had become infected. I applied some strong topical ointment to it, thinking that it would respond quickly, as skin infections almost always do in the Philippines. Instead of healing, the sore started to spread. I applied even stronger ointments, all to no avail. I then started to take oral antibiotics. Finally, I ended up taking the strongest antibiotics available. Despite this treatment, the infection kept spreading, and the spot on my face kept growing, as more and more of the surrounding skin was affected.

I began to visualize the sore growing larger and larger until it covered my whole head, and then my whole body. I cried out to God, "Lord, what are You doing?" He must have been waiting for that question because He immediately spoke something I never would have thought of. He said, "I am just removing some of your bark." My response was, "Yes, Lord, I have a very hard and rough outer covering that needs to be removed. My hardness and impatience need to be removed and pulverized until Your gentleness and meekness are manifested in my life." Once I got the message, the Lord healed the sore as though it had been nothing at all.

What do leaves, bark, and branches symbolize in our spiritual lives? In many Scriptures, trees are likened to men. In fact, Isaiah 61:3 calls the redeemed "trees of righteousness, the planting of the Lord." (See also Song of Solomon 2:3 and Psalm 92:12.) It is significant that Adam and Eve, after their fall, tried to cover themselves by using leaves. From this revelation in the very beginning, we can understand the idea that, as spiritual trees, our leaves, bark, and branches are the things in our lives we use to clothe or cover ourselves—just as leaves, bark, and branches clothe or cover a natural tree. They are the outward manifestations of our natural man or what others see and experience when they get near us. For example, others may feel the hardness and harshness of our "bark." Therefore, our leaves, bark, and branches are symbolic of the fronts and pretenses, the evidence of our fallen nature, that we often manifest to others. Paul calls this natural man the "outward man" (2 Cor. 4:16). Although it is very unpleasant when the Lord begins to cut off the bark, branches, and leaves of our hard, proud, self-life, we all truly need to be tenderized and humbled. There is a certain quality of spiritual fruit, typified by spices, that cannot be produced in us any other way!

The Lord replaced Adam's fig leaves with a covering He had made from the skins of a slain animal (Gen. 3:21). He also wants to replace the coverings we use to hide our spiritual nakedness. Only the "Lamb slain from the foundation of the world" can cover our spiritual nakedness (Rev. 13:8).

Afterwards, when Adam and Eve looked at each other, they saw the covering of the slain animal instead of the false covering of their own making. The same possibility is available to all sincere Believers, who long in their hearts for the Lord to remove their covering of fig leaves and grant them the covering He has ordained for them. Oh, what rest will come to our spirits when we no longer have to pretend to be something we are not—when the Lord replaces our fronts and pretenses with the sincere, genuine nature of Christ. If all we are is hidden behind the covering of His nature, we can relax and simply be what we are in Him. We can always be at rest, continually allowing the Lord to be seen through our lives, instead of revealing the nakedness of what *we* are.

Anyone who has experienced the removal of at least some of his leaves, bark, and branches knows that this is a work only God can do. Just as a fallen tree is incapable of stripping itself of its covering, we also are incapable of doing so. Although the "outward man" must be removed and destroyed, we cannot accomplish this work through our own efforts. Paul declares, our outward man is in the process of dying: "Even though our outward man is perishing, yet the inward man is being renewed day by day" (2 Cor. 4:16b NKJV).

How does God accomplish this work? He uses other **members of the Body of Christ** to take away our covering of leaves and bark. God used

Joseph's **brothers** to **strip** him of his coat of many colors and send him to the "death" he experienced in Egypt. He also used the spiritual **brethren** of Jesus to deliver Him to the Romans to be **stripped** of His garments and crucified (experiencing the judgment *we* deserve, of course). God will do the same in our lives. The unsaved of the world will never be the principal tool God uses to deal with the deep pride and pretenses of our hearts. (We fully expect to receive persecution from the ungodly, and we bear it—sometimes even with pride!) Those closest to us will be the ones God uses to strip away our fronts and pretenses so that we can see our own nakedness and need. It is amazing how easily we become impatient with our spouse or children, but we can be so kind to others. We may even assume that a member of our family is the problem. The real problem is that we do not feel the need to hide our nakedness with fig leaves in the home. There, the "real us" can be clearly seen by all!

Unfortunately, most of us are troubled by a grave problem: We are deceived into believing that the "real us" is the one who is so kind and considerate—the one who manifests himself when we are outside the home. That is not the "real us." That is the man who is wearing fig leaves. If we desire more of the Lord, then He will have to show us just how easily a member of the church can rip off one of our fig leaves and expose our nakedness—the "real us." Sooner or later someone outside our home is going to "get under our skin," or should we say, "get under our fig leaves"? They are going to really offend us, and we are going to treat them like we treat our family. Then we will see what we *really* are, and we will need to seek God for the covering of the lambskins.

The fact that our brethren are used to crucify us is without doubt one of the most bitter aspects of the cross. Even the Lord was greatly affected by this tragic reality (Ps. 55:12-14). Unfortunately, many Believers withdraw from fellowship with others, and even stop attending church services, because they don't understand how so-called "Christians" could possibly mistreat others the way they do. However, we all help to crucify one another. Without even trying to do so, we all offend in many things (Jas. 3:2). That is our nature as fallen human beings. If you actually believe that you do not offend others just as others offend you, you do not yet know the man in the mirror. If you have any doubts, just ask a few of the people around you if you are really as wonderful toward them as you have thought! If we are not willing to continue submitting our lives to God's process of grinding us into fine spices, then God will not be able to finish His work in us. He uses the character of other people to accomplish this work of the cross in our lives so that the fruits of the Spirit come forth in us. For example, we will never learn patience unless we choose to continue walking with people who require patience from us. We will never learn to love as He loves unless we continue to love others even when they offend us. When difficult people really "get to us," sooner or later one of two things will happen. Either we will withdraw from fellowshipping with them, or we will be forced to draw near to the Lord with all our hearts to receive from Him the love and patience we need to continue walking with them. When we do the latter, His fruit begins to flourish in our lives.

When God uses another member in the church to strip away what we are, how do we react? Often it takes us quite some time before we can have a positive attitude toward that brother or sister. One thought that can do great spiritual damage to us and others is to believe that our brother has offended us on purpose. How many times have you gotten up in the morning thinking along this line, "I don't like brother so-and-so. Therefore, today I am going to do something that will really offend him"? Most of us would affirm that we *never* think or act that way; yet, when we are offended by someone, we assume that he acted that way on purpose! The truth is, few offenses are done on purpose. We are so good at offending everyone around us that we do it without even trying!

People who withdraw from fellowship with others when they are offended suffer the tragic results of that decision. They may end up being eternally lost. Jesus taught us to pray, "And forgive us our debts, *as* we forgive our debtors" (Mt. 6:12). If we do not receive the grace to forgive others, we cannot be forgiven; therefore, we cannot go to Heaven! Lord, please give us forgiving hearts!

Are you in a situation where the Lord is "removing some of your bark" through affliction? It helps immensely when you at least understand what is happening. We need to realize that we simply cannot continue past Day Three if we do not allow the Lord to form the fruits of the Spirit in us! Do not refuse this process by using the excuse that Jesus suffered everything for us. It is true that He paid the full price for our redemption so that we will not have to suffer in hell, but this does not mean that we do not need to suffer anything. His personal sufferings were not only to purchase redemption and healing but also to learn obedience to the Father (Heb. 5:8), and to give us an example that we should follow (1 Pet. 2:21). If the Son of God Himself had to learn obedience through suffering, who am I to conclude that I can learn it some other way? And if Jesus was a man of suffering, how can I be like Him if I refuse to live as He lived?

2. Fruits Are Produced as We See Our Own Need

Wouldn't it be tragic to pass through life thinking that we are really not too bad because we do not steal, kill, lie, cheat, commit adultery, and so on? How tragic it would be for us to stand before the judgment seat and have the Lord open our eyes for the first time to see ourselves as He sees us—in the light of His glory and perfection! How could we answer the Lord, at that moment, if He said to us, "...thou sayest, I am rich, and increased with goods, and have need of nothing; and knowest not that thou art wretched, and miserable, and poor, and blind, and naked"? (Rev. 3:17) It would then be too late to do anything about our condition, or to receive His grace to be changed. Something even more tragic would be to be sent from the presence of the One whose beauty we had just seen for the first time, never to be granted that privilege again. Besides this sorrow, it would be unbearable agony to be forced to live forever with ourselves, having seen just how vile we really are—and now with no hope of being changed! No wonder the Apostle Paul exhorts us, "For if we would judge ourselves, we should not be judged" (1 Cor. 11:31).

In addition to the cutting, drying, and grinding process used to produce spices, certain fruits of the Spirit can be produced in us through a revelation of our own need and spiritual condition. Jesus said, "And why do you look at the speck in your brother's eye, but do not consider the plank in your own eye? Or how can you say to your brother, 'Let me remove the speck from your eye'; and look, a plank is in your own eye? Hypocrite! First remove the plank from your own eye, and then you will see clearly to remove the speck from your brother's eye" (Mt. 7:3-5 NKJV).

If I really see my own need as He sees it, then I will consider *my* weakness to be a beam. I will be so overcome by my *own* spiritual condition that the weakness I might see in others will seem to be nothing more than a tiny speck! Conversely, the more critical I am of others, the less I am seeing my own condition and the more I need to follow the Lord's counsel and "anoint my eyes with eye salve" so that I might see my own spiritual poverty and wretchedness (Rev. 3:17-18).

If you think today that your neighbor or your brother in Christ has very serious problems, it is because you have not yet seen your own problems with clarity. No, Jesus is not telling us that we are the only ones with "beams" in our eyes, nor that everyone else's problems are less severe than our own. Rather, He is saying that once we have seen our own problems, and have struggled with them and cried out to God for His grace until we have actually conquered them, our attitude about the problems of others will be different. Some people have spent years weeping before the Lord because of their own failures, trying to get that "beam" out of their lives and conquer their weaknesses. Afterwards, when they hear a discouraged saint bewailing his own weaknesses, their attitude is, "Brother, you should see what the Lord had to do in *my* life, and the tremendous weakness He conquered in me by His grace, after I had failed for so many years. Your problem is *easy* for the Lord to change!" Yes, seeing our own need produces in our hearts the fruits of patience, longsuffering, compassion, kindness, mercy, and love toward others. The sooner we see our need, the quicker we will be changed!

3. Fruits Are Produced as We See the Lord's Beauty

It was already dark in the Philippines when I packed my suitcase for an all-night journey by boat. My mind was consumed with only one thought—a trial I knew would be facing me that night. The cargo boat of our mission was about 50 feet long, but it had only one cabin, with just one bed. I would be the only missionary on board that night, so the boat and its passengers would be my responsibility. I also knew that one or two Filipinos would be on board. I knew that their custom was to go straight to the captain's cabin and bed and make themselves at home, at least whenever they thought that they could get away with it. The Lord had already spoken to me and said that on this occasion, if I wanted to please Him and manifest His character of meekness, I would have to permit them to "get away with it." I knew that with one simple command from me, they would go scurrying out of the captain's cabin, but I also knew that I would not be able to give that command if I wanted to please the Lord.

Somehow I felt that this was not "just another test" on meekness, but rather the final exam to end one stage of the Lord's training in my life. I did not want to fail, regardless of the cost, but I was wrestling with the cost in my spirit. I said to myself, "There are numerous Filipino sleeping mats on that boat, and plenty of places to spread them out. Those Bible school students have slept on mats on the hard floor for their entire lives— they are completely used to it. They can still get a normal night's sleep if they sleep on the floor, but I am not accustomed to sleeping without a mattress. They really should have the courtesy to recognize that. If they don't, I'll just have to ask them to leave the cabin. I really need to get my rest because of what I must accomplish tomorrow. After all, I am the missionary who is giving his life to teach them; besides that, our mission organization owns the boat. Who do they think they are? I have every right to ask them to leave the cabin." After I thought like this for a while, another part of me would cry, "But Lord, I know that if I order them to leave the cabin, I will displease You. You would never act that way. You humbled Yourself and became a servant of servants!" On and on went the emotional struggle.

As departure time approached, I decided to ask the Lord for the grace to please Him. I prayed in my bedroom, and then started for the door. When I grasped the doorknob to leave the room, I felt the fire of my own spirit rising within me, a spirit that would definitely demand its rights. I turned around and decided to pray again for grace. After praying a little more fervently, I started out again. Once again, as I touched the doorknob, I knew that I would surely fail the test. My own lack of patience, longsuffering, and meekness would definitely win the battle. I turned around, and in desperation knelt at my bed to pray a third time. This time, I began to cry out to the Lord, pleading for grace and telling Him that I did not have the necessary meekness to pass the test.

In that instant, my spiritual eyes were opened and I saw the Lord Jesus hanging on the cross of Calvary. I could see the multitudes of mere mortals surrounding the cross and mocking Him. Some were spitting on Him and others were laughing, telling Him to come down from the cross if He was really the Son of God. There, in the midst of that crowd, the Creator of Heaven and earth hung, dying for them. He then spoke to me, "Marvin, do you see the multitudes and what they have done to Me? I *created* them, yet I allowed them to place Me on this cross. What rights do you have? Are you better than the Filipinos?" My heart broke before Him. I abhorred my pride that had blinded me into thinking that I was laying down my life for the Filipinos by coming to their country as a missionary. When I saw how our Creator humbled Himself to become a servant in order to save us, I realized what a great privilege it is to be permitted to serve in some small way. Finally, my concept of the "injustice" that it would be for the Filipinos to take the bed literally melted away.

Can anything we might be called to suffer be termed an injustice in the light of the injustice of *all* injustices—the sinless Lamb crucified on the cross? Yes, He had the nature of a meek Lamb and could, therefore, accept the cross without fighting back; but remember, He was also the Lion of Judah. He was the very Creator, the Almighty, being slain by scoffers and mockers whom He had formed! He could have destroyed the world had He chosen to do so. I am so thankful that His infinite meekness enabled Him to remain on that cross for me instead of demanding His rights or demanding justice! When we accept life's injustice, we and others are always blessed. The blessing that *we* receive is that we become more like Him and are more pleasing in His sight.

After the Lord had opened my eyes to see Him on the cross, I knew that the battle in my heart had finally been won. In fact, I looked forward to the *privilege* of sleeping on that floor! At least it would be an insignificant token of appreciation for what He had done for me. Maybe it would be an example to others—a manifestation of just one drop from the ocean of meekness that He demonstrated on Calvary's tree.

What was actually taking place in my heart as I saw His meekness revealed on the cross? Why did that little glimpse of His life give me sufficient grace to pass the test? The Apostle John explained it, "Beloved, now are we the sons of God, and it doth not yet appear what we shall be: but we know that, when he shall appear, *we shall be like him; for we shall see him as he is*" (1 Jn. 3:2). Of course, the greatest fulfillment of this verse will occur at the Rapture, when we see Him face to face. Nevertheless, He can "appear" to us today in a spiritual sense, in small ways. Every time He does so, we are changed by the revelation of what He is.

Obviously, one revelation of His beauty is not enough. We need to meet with Him daily to receive the grace we need to be like Him. How we need to spend more time beholding the glory and nature of Jesus Christ, beholding what He is! Second Corinthians 3:18 (NKJV) tells us what happens when we do—"But we all, with unveiled face, beholding as in a mirror the glory of the Lord, are being transformed into the same image from glory to glory, just as by the Spirit of the Lord." How do we behold His glory? That is one of the main purposes of worship. As we worship the Lord in Spirit and in truth, our spiritual man is beholding what He is, and something in our hearts is changed. Afterwards, we are never quite the same. We become more like Him, changed from glory to glory. That is why the meek One admonishes us, "**Come unto me**, all ye that labour and are heavy laden, and I will give you rest. **Take my yoke upon you**, and **learn of me**; for I am **meek** and lowly in heart: and ye shall find **rest** unto your souls. For my yoke is easy, and my burden is light" (Mt. 11:28-30). We will find **rest** as we **come** into His presence and labor under the **yoke** of **learning** what He is like, especially learning that He is **meek**. Looking upon the meek One with a hungry heart and learning about His meekness will always produce in us more meekness—one of those precious fruits of the Spirit. Do you have time in this world of cares and pleasures to do that? Do not allow the pursuit of the riches and joys of this world to rob you of the riches and joys of eternity!

Day Three and the Third Feast

As we have mentioned, the first fruits of the Lord's creation spring forth on the third Day of Genesis 1. It comes as no surprise, therefore, that the third feast is called the Feast of Firstfruits. Celebrated yearly by Israel up to the present day, this feast commemorates the Lord's acceptance of Israel as His firstfruits when they came out of Egypt and crossed the Red Sea into the wilderness. He declares, "Thus saith the Lord; I remember thee...the love of thine espousals, when thou wentest after me *in the wilderness*... Israel was holiness unto the Lord, and *the firstfruits* of his increase" (Jer. 2:2-3a). According to the Lord Himself, the purpose of that wilderness journey was to produce in Israel the spiritual fruit called "humility." The Lord exhorts them, "And thou shalt remember all the way which the Lord thy God led thee these forty years in the wilderness, to *humble* thee" (Deut. 8:2a). The Hebrew word translated here as "to humble" is exactly the same word used elsewhere in the King James Version as "to afflict" (*Strong's Hebrew Dictionary*, #6031). In fact, it is translated 50 times as "to afflict" and only 11 times as "to humble." This is the word found in Genesis 15:13: "And he [the Lord] said unto Abram, Know of a surety that thy seed shall be a stranger in a land that is not theirs, and shall serve them; and they shall *afflict* them four hundred years." Since this Hebrew word is the primary Old Testament word for both affliction and humility, we can understand that a person can not learn "humility" unless he experiences "affliction" in his life. This is precisely the thought of the psalmist when he declares: "They are not in trouble as other men; neither are they plagued like other men. Therefore pride compasseth them about as a chain" (Ps. 73:5-6a).

In light of this awesome truth, let us not choose the message heard in some sectors of the Church today that rejects affliction and suffering as though it were not the Lord's will for us. Those who want the Lord to finish the work of Day Three in their lives cannot accept that erroneous message! Since we have seen that the fruits of the Spirit are produced by affliction and suffering, we can easily understand now why the Lord would link the concept of "firstfruits" with Israel's entrance into the wilderness. As they suffered many hardships and great trials in the wilderness, their afflictions produced the firstfruits of humility. Thus they traveled on to Canaan, the Lord's rest.

Day Three and the Tabernacle of Moses

The third step in the Tabernacle of Moses is the brazen altar. We have seen that the third feast, the Feast of Firstfruits, and the third Day are linked in a very clear way. The Law of Moses also links the firstfruits with the altar because an offering of the firstfruits was offered yearly on the brazen altar. Amazingly enough, frankincense was offered on the altar along with the firstfruit offering (Lev. 2:14-16). Since the nine spices can only be obtained as a plant suffers, it is even more amazing to find that one of the spices is directly linked with the brazen altar, the third step in the Tabernacle of Moses. Obviously, the altar speaks to us all about the place of suffering and death. The sacrificial giving of our lives upon God's altar causes a sweet savor to ascend before Him, like the fragrance of His spices (Ex. 29:18).

For an Old Testament Israelite, the sacrifice of animals on the altar was symbolic of several things. First, it was a revelation of the sufferings and death of *the* Lamb of God who would come to die for them. Second, through the laying on of hands, the worshiper became identified with the animal they were about to offer (Lev. 1:4). This ritual revealed that we, too, are called to offer our lives as a living sacrifice unto God, as we take up our cross and follow the Lamb. The Apostle Paul said that he died daily; he also exhorted us to offer our bodies as living sacrifices (1 Cor. 15:31; Rom. 12:1). There is no other way to obtain those precious firstfruits of the Spirit!

Day Three and the Third Man of Faith

The life and experience of Noah, the third man of faith in Genesis, reveal, in an amazing way, the same message as the third Day of Creation. Just as the waters receded and the dry land appeared on the third Day of Creation, so, too, the same thing happened with Noah and the ark (Gen. 1:9; 8:3,13). The similarities do not stop here. We have seen that the only way to obtain spiritual fruit and the sweet savor of the Lord's spices is through the work of the altar in our lives, the third step in the Tabernacle. The first thing Noah did after the waters had receded was to build an altar and offer a "sweet savor" to the Lord (Gen. 8:18-21). Another clear scriptural link between the altar and Noah is that just as the altar deals with our flesh by killing it, so also the events in the life of Noah dealt with the flesh of man in the same way. The Lord literally destroyed all flesh "from off the face of the earth" (Gen. 6:12-13,17; 7:4). As God received Noah's sacrifice after the flood, He made a covenant with Noah and blessed him and his sons, speaking to them about being fruitful. In this way, God indeed confirmed that the altar brings us into fruitfulness (Gen. 9:1). In the same covenant, the Lord also promised Noah that there would always be **seed**time and **harvest**—that is, times of fruitfulness (Gen. 8:22). It is interesting to note that "seed" is first mentioned as part of Day Three in connection with fruit. Finally, Noah and the firstfruits are linked by Scripture in at least one other way. Immediately after Noah's sacrifice and the Lord's blessing on him, the Scriptures mention the first fruits that appeared on the earth after the flood. Noah became a husbandman, planted a vineyard, and partook of its fruit (Gen. 9:20-21).

Day Two Prepares Us for Day Three

As we have seen, the work accomplished on any given Day prepares us for the Day that follows. This is especially true for Days Two and Three. We all begin our walk with God as natural, earthly-minded people, who have strong survival instincts. What could possibly prepare our hearts to willingly and lovingly accept the suffering and death of the altar? Only the second step, which is the laver.

Remember: The laver was made from the mirrors of the Israelite women, and the water in the laver speaks of God's Word, which is our spiritual mirror. Therefore, as the Lord purifies our doctrine during the second Day, we spend much time looking into His Word, our spiritual mirror. In the Lord's mirror we see ourselves with all our spots, defilements, and spiritual leprosy. We also see the Lord Jesus Christ, our elder brother, with all His beauty and glory.

Jesus told His disciples that all who want to be His followers must deny themselves, take up the cross, and follow Him (Mt. 16:24). What could possibly motivate us to choose to die on a cross or at the altar? Jesus gave us the answer when He said, "If any man come to me, and hate not...his own life...he cannot be my disciple" (Lk. 14:26). To be His disciple we must choose the cross; but in order to choose the cross, we must hate what we are. Every sincere person who spends time looking into the mirror of God's Word, seeing the awfulness of his own condition, will come away hating his own life more and more. Nevertheless, *hating what we are is not enough*. People who come to hate what they are, without a living hope of being changed, often despair so much that they end up committing suicide. On the other hand, people who have also seen the Lord in the mirror have been filled with a love for His life and have hope for a better day.

On the second Day, when our hate for what we are and our love for what He is have both grown sufficiently, we will suddenly hear our elder brother and high priest saying to us, "Come with Me, My child, and I will show you the answer to your longing." He then leads us to the altar, which is the third step. There we see the knife, the fire, the blood, and the dying sacrifices. Our natural instincts tell us to run *from* the altar, but our heavenly instinct causes us to run *to* the altar. This is because we see that the altar is the way God has lovingly provided for us to be free of what we are and to receive what He is, revealed in the fruits of the Spirit. It is then that we understand in a deeper way the Proverb "...to the hungry soul every bitter thing is sweet" (Prov. 27:7). If we are hungry enough for what God is, the bitterness of death to what we are actually becomes sweet! Fortunately, our loving Lord does not plan for us to remain forever at the altar. There is a fourth step and a fourth Day awaiting us on our journey.

Chapter 12

Day Four—The Sun Appears

During my days as a student, a man was invited to come and share with the student body of the Bible institute that my wife and I were attending. The speaker was clearly a man who had met the Lord. He spoke from his heart as he shared with us a *revelation* of Christ, not just information *about* Christ. Since he had met truth, the Lord Himself, the speaker's words were not merely a dead doctrinal discourse. As he shared, we were being changed by the anointed, life-giving Word. As he testified of a personal experience with the Lord, it became clear why he could impart such a wonderful revelation of Christ to us.

This man told us how he and his wife, both Believers, had been on the verge of divorce. They argued with each other constantly. One morning while they were eating breakfast together, they became involved in one of their usual heated discussions. At one point, the husband looked up from his food and glanced across the table at his wife. He was awestruck when, instead of seeing his wife seated across from him at the table, he saw the Lord. With a broken spirit he told us, "From that day to the present we haven't had a problem getting along with each other. I now know with whom I am living, and I am careful how I speak to Him."

What would our lives be like today in the Church and in our own homes if we were all to receive such a clear revelation of Christ in His Body that we, too, would "know with whom we are living"? How would we treat others if we *really* took to heart the words of Jesus, "Assuredly, I say to you, inasmuch as you did it to one of the least of these My brethren, you did it to Me"? (Mt. 25:40b NKJV) An even better question is, how would we treat others if we truly understood the fact that we will definitely be judged according to what we have done to Him in others? (Mt. 25:31-46) At what stage in our spiritual walk will we truly discern the Lord's Body and see Him in others? Most Believers are well aware of the Scriptures I have just quoted. Unfortunately, our conduct often proves that understanding the truth with our heads, and living it from our hearts is never the same. Few of us would knowingly treat the Lord as we sometimes treat others. When will the gap between our heads and our hearts be closed so that this truth becomes a life-changing reality in us instead of being merely a doctrine? That will happen on the fourth Day of the "redemptive week."

As we progress from one Day to the next, we actually go "from glory to glory" (2 Cor. 3:18). Our life in Christ becomes more glorious, and His life in us becomes an ever deeper reality on each successive Day. Sadly enough, the spiritual life of most Believers stagnates on either Day One or Day Two. This happens primarily because they have not yet realized how much more of His presence and blessing is available to them if they would just continue their spiritual journey. Many are taught that they will just have to wait until they get to Heaven to experience more glorious things in God. I am so thankful that this is not what the Bible teaches! The Lord has great things ahead for you and for me *if* we desire them. Let's see what awaits us on Day Four if we have not yet arrived there. A glimpse of what lies ahead is often a great blessing because people with a clear vision usually run toward it, while those who do not have a vision perish (Hab. 2:2; Prov. 29:18).

What happened on the fourth Day of Creation? He began it by saying, "Let there be lights in the firmament of the heaven to divide the day from the night…" (Gen. 1:14). God began Day One in a similar way, saying, "Let there be light" (Gen. 1:3). He did not *create* light on either of these two Days, because God *is* light, and He has always existed (1 Jn. 1:5). Rather, as the Apostle Paul tells us, God commanded "the light to shine out of darkness" (2 Cor. 4:6).

Concerning the sun, moon, and stars, some believe that they were actually *created* on the fourth Day; others believe that they were created at the time of Genesis 1:1, "In the beginning God created the heaven and the earth." It is true that the Hebrew word "made" in Genesis 1:16 ("And God *made* two great lights…") and the word "create" are different. Since we know that the day and night cycle was in effect from Day One (Gen. 1:5,8,13), there are two possible explanations. Either the earth was already rotating around the sun, or God did an added miracle of causing the day and night cycle to exist on the first three Days without a solar system. There are arguments on both sides of this relatively common debate.

Regardless of exactly what happened on Day Four, one basic fact remains unchanged: The glory of the light of the sun is first seen in this fourth step of God's creative work (Gen. 1:14-19). Another fact also remains unchanged: The Lord Jesus Christ is the "Sun of righteousness" (Mal. 4:2). Therefore, the Sun of righteousness will become openly visible in our earth on the fourth Day. In other words, the glory and the beauty of the Lord will be seen by us as they visibly shine upon us as never before in our spiritual walk. At this point in our journey, we will actually see the Lord. He will appear to us.

Some will ask, "Do you mean that we will see Him in a dream or vision, or are you speaking about seeing Him in a physical way?" I am *not* speaking about "seeing" Him in a mental vision that could possibly be a product of our own imaginations, nor am I speaking about seeing Him only in a dream. Even the Apostle Paul could not determine whether this experience is physical or not. When he was caught up to the third heaven, he heard things that he was not permitted to tell (2 Cor. 12:1-4). Twice Paul declared during his testimony of this experience that he could not discern whether or not it had been physical ("in the body or out of the body"). However, he was certain of one thing: that it was very real. We, too, can be certain about one thing regarding Day Four: If we think we may have seen the Lord, but we are not completely sure, we have not yet experienced Day Four. Those who see the Sun of righteousness on Day Four have no doubt about what this experience involves!

Is there a longing in your heart to see the Lord as there was in the heart of the well-known hymn writer, Fanny Crosby? She was once asked if her blindness from infancy caused her great sorrow. Her surprising response was that she considered it to be one of her greatest blessings in life. She reasoned, "Because, when I get to heaven, the first face that shall ever gladden my sight will be that of my Savior!"[1] What about all of us who have been born blind in the spiritual realm, with our eyes covered by a spiritual veil that hides the Sun of righteousness? Do we have the living hope of seeing Him as He is, in all His glory? Maybe we would seek the Lord with greater fervor if we realized that there is a spiritual place in God where New Testament saints can see Him just as Old Testament saints did.

Some Christians have assumed that the Lord no longer appears openly to His people. The experience of many of God's saints, down through the

---

1. Kenneth W. Osbeck, *101 Hymns Stories* (Grand Rapids, MI: Kregel Publications, 1990), p. 167.

ages, has been quite the opposite. The Lord openly appeared to Abraham (Gen. 18:1), Isaac (Gen. 26:2), Jacob (Gen. 35:1-9), Moses (Ex. 4:1-5), the entire nation of Israel (Lev. 9:23), Gideon (Judg. 6:12), Samuel (1 Sam. 3:21), Solomon (1 Kings 3:5), Stephen (Acts 7:56), and Paul (Acts 9:17). About 60 years after the cross and 30 years after Paul had died, the Lord was still in the business of appearing to His friends. He appeared to John the Beloved on the isle of Patmos (Rev. 1:12-17). And oh, what glory John saw in that appearing! God's Word assures us that the Lord never changes (Heb. 13:8; Mal. 3:6). If the Lord's custom was to appear to His chosen ones in the Old and New Testament, then either it is still His custom or else He has changed. Besides this, do we not boast that the blessings and glory of the New Testament age are greater than those of the Old Testament age? Even Paul affirmed that this is so (2 Cor. 3:7-11).

Part of the confusion regarding this important matter is the result of a misunderstanding of one of the testimonies of the Apostle Paul. Speaking of the people to whom the Lord appeared after the cross, Paul said, "Then last of all He was seen by me also, as by one born out of due time" (1 Cor. 15:8 NKJV). Does Paul mean that the Lord granted to him one last divine appearing, making him the **last person** to see the Lord, as some teach? There are four clear reasons why this is not what Paul is saying in this verse.

1. The Lord's appearance to Paul on the road to Damascus in Acts 9 was the first time He appeared to Paul, but it was not the last time. If this had been the first and only time the Lord appeared to Paul, we might have some basis for concluding that the Lord stopped appearing to His people after this event. In reality, the Lord appeared to Paul on at least three other occasions (Acts 23:11; 2 Tim. 4:17; 2 Cor. 12:1-2). In fact, on the road to Damascus the Lord made it clear that His appearance to Paul at that time was the first appearance, with more to come. The Lord tells him, "...I have **appeared** unto thee for this purpose, to make thee a minister and a witness both of these things which thou hast seen, and of those things in the which **I will appear** unto thee" (Acts 26:16). Therefore, the Lord assured Paul, in His first appearance to him, that He would appear to him again in the future. Since Paul is an example for all Believers (1 Tim. 1:16), we can be sure that his personal walk and experience, as revealed in the Bible, are available to us all!

2. Since the Lord appeared to Paul several times, the Greek phrase "last of all" (1 Cor. 15:8) cannot mean that the Lord appeared "one last time" to men. This phrase can also be translated as

"last or lowest in rank,"[2] as it is translated in Mark 9:35 and Matthew 20:16. Paul's attitude of being the last or the least worthy of all is, in fact, the context of this verse as confirmed by the next verse, where Paul declares, "**For** I am the least of the apostles, who am not worthy to be called an apostle..." (1 Cor. 15:9 NKJV). Paul begins this verse with a word of clarification—"for"—which means "because." Therefore, what Paul is saying here could (and should) be translated as, "Then, least worthy of all, he was seen by me also...**because** I am the least of the apostles" (1 Cor. 15:8a and 9a).

3. Paul declares that the Lord was seen by him "as of one born out of due time." If being "born out of due time" means that Paul was born later than the other apostles, we might have justification to believe that the Lord stopped appearing to people after Paul. As several other English translations bring out, this is not so. The meaning of the Greek here is a "premature" or "abortive" birth. For example, the RSV translates it, "as to one untimely born." Paul is saying that the Lord appeared to him as though he had been born *before* the normal time. Genesis 1 shows that the normal sequence of events is for the Lord to appear to us on the fourth Day. But Paul experienced a measure of the blessing of Day Four prematurely. Putting this all together, then, we could paraphrase this passage in this way: "Then, as the least worthy of all, He also appeared unto me, as to a person who was receiving a blessing before the right time, for I am the least of the apostles...."

4. The last 2,000 years of Church history tell of a number of Christians who have seen the Lord. John the Beloved on the isle of Patmos is one example of someone who saw the Lord in the early Church, around A.D. 95, years after Paul had seen Him (Rev. 1:12-17). Sadhu Sundar Singh is another example,[3] and a good number of Chinese orphans in H.A. Baker's orphanage is another.[4] Unless *all* the Believers in the Church Age who have testified of seeing Him were deceived, then the Lord is still in the business of appearing to His people. If you have not yet seen Him, instead of assuming that it is impossible, please consider the possibility that you have a great

2. W.E. Vine, *An Expository Dictionary of New Testament Words* (Old Tappan, NJ: Fleming H. Revell Company, 1966), p. 310. (See "last.")
3. Cyril J. Davey, *The Story of Sadhu Sundar Singh*, (Chicago, IL: Moody Press, 1963), pp. 32-33.
4. H.A. Baker, *Visions Beyond the Veil* (Springdale, PA: Whitaker House, 1973), pp. 56-57.

hope and joy set before you as you continue to grow in the Lord. The fourth Day is just ahead! Paul tells Timothy that there is a crown of righteousness awaiting those "who have loved His appearing" (2 Tim. 4:8 NKJV). Yes, the Lord will appear at the Rapture of the Church, but is that enough for you? Do you long for Him to appear to you personally in this present life? Let's see if that fourth step really refers to the Lord appearing to us, His people.

Day Four and the Fourth Feast

The Feast of Pentecost, the fourth feast, is a commemoration of one of the most important events during the journey from Egypt to Canaan— Mount Sinai and the giving of the Law. Did the first Pentecost, at Mount Sinai, have anything to do with a literal appearance of the Lord to His people? When Israel came to Sinai (Ex. 19:1-3), the Lord told Moses to prepare the people for His appearing. He said, "And let them be ready for...the Lord will come down upon Mount Sinai in the sight of all the people" (Ex. 19:11 NKJV). His appearing was definitely a part of the fulfillment of this fourth feast.

Something almost unbelievable took place when the elders of Israel saw the Lord. We are told that after the manifest presence of God had descended on Sinai, "Then went up Moses, and Aaron, Nadab, and Abihu, and seventy of the elders of Israel: And they saw the God of Israel...they saw God, and did eat and drink" (Ex. 24:9-11). Could anyone imagine being in the literal presence of the Lord and having nothing better to do than to eat and drink? There must be a good reason for this detail to be recorded in His Word. We will come back to this thought later.

Day Four and the Fourth Man of Faith

The fourth Day of Creation is when the light of *the* Sun is clearly seen by our earth for the first time. It is, therefore, significant that there is no scriptural record of the Lord having appeared to any of the first three men of faith before He appeared to Abraham, the fourth man of faith in Genesis. Before Abraham's time, others "walked with God," but nowhere are we told that He "appeared" to them. I trust that we are all "walking with God," but His appearance is just ahead for us! The Lord did not appear to Abraham only once. Divine appearances are one of the outstanding characteristics of Abraham's life. He literally saw the Lord on several occasions (Gen. 12:7; 17:1; 18:1). The Lord was emphasizing that His appearings are to be expected on the fourth step of our spiritual walk. Notice that when the Lord appeared to Abraham in Genesis 18:1-8, eating and drinking were involved also, just as occurred during the first Pentecost. Keep in mind that father Abraham is a pattern for us (Gal. 3:7; Jn. 8:39). Therefore, we should expect to experience what he experienced.

Day Four and the Tabernacle of Moses

The fourth step for the priests in the Tabernacle of Moses was the candlestick in the Holy Place. They went into the Holy Place daily to trim the wicks of the candlestick and replenish the oil for the light. Again we see the amazing parallel that exists between the seven steps in the Tabernacle and the seven Days of Creation. The light of the sun, which is a symbol of the Sun of righteousness, is given on Day Four. Likewise, the light of the candlestick, the only source of light in the Tabernacle, is a symbol of the One who is the light of the world, and is the fourth step in the Tabernacle. It would have been extremely dark in that Tabernacle had it not been for the one source of light inside the entire tent—the candlestick.

Imagine the beauty and glory that was present inside the Tabernacle. Those who were not priests did not have the privilege of seeing it even once in their lifetime. The same is true today. If we do not learn to minister to the Lord as priests, offering "spiritual sacrifices" to Him (1 Pet. 2:5), we will never see His glory. The common people could enter the outer court, but only the priests could enter the Holy Place, and only the high priest could enter the Holy of Holies. The only thing that was visible to those outside the Tabernacle was the covering of badger skins, a material commonly used for making tents during Israel's journey. From the outside, the Lord's tent looked exactly like everyone else's tent, yet this deceptively common outer covering hid the untold riches and beauty found inside! It must have been a breathtaking experience to enter the Holy Place, where everything was made of gold or was covered with gold, including the walls that were made from large wooden planks that were covered with gold. The golden light of the candlestick made the gold appear even more brilliant. Just as light is a symbol of the Lord, so, too, gold is a symbol of the Lord (Job 22:25 NIV, NKJV, RSV, NRSV). His light and life filled the Tabernacle.

This Tabernacle, which was later replaced by the Temple, was the dwelling place of God. We understand that now the Church, which is the Body of Christ, is His eternal dwelling place, and therefore, is called the New Testament temple (1 Cor. 3:16; Eph. 1:22-23; 2:19-22; Jn. 2:19-21). The New Testament concept of Christ living within us is much more than mere mysticism, symbolism, or doctrine. The reality is that at the new birth, the very life of Christ Himself takes up residence within our physical bodies, just as much as the very life of fallen Adam resides within our bodies from our mother's womb. We all understand that if the life of Adam leaves the body, the body dies. In the same way, if the life of Christ leaves our bodies, our spiritual man dies. Tragically, the end of every human body that is not filled with Christ's spiritual life will be the second death (Rev. 20:14-15).

The unspeakable treasure of Christ's spiritual life literally resides in a human tent or tabernacle, and that is why Paul proclaims, "But we have this treasure in *earthen* vessels..." (2 Cor. 4:7). This reality is also seen in Peter's reference to his body as a tabernacle or tent (2 Pet. 1:13-14 KJV, NIV, ASV). The Lord's desire is not only to live *with* man but also *in and through* man. He will most surely reach that goal if we allow *our* life to decrease and *His* life to increase within us. In fact, we will see that the principal goal of the "redemptive week" is to make us into a dwelling place for the Lord. He will finally reach this goal in and through His people in the last days. A voice will be heard from Heaven declaring, "Behold, the tabernacle of God is with men..." (Rev. 21:3).

By comparing the fourth step in the Tabernacle with the fourth Day of Creation a clear message emerges. We receive a key from the fourth step in the Tabernacle that will help us bring together the fourth step in all the other groups of seven. The fourth Day of Creation in our lives involves a visible revelation of the One who is the light of the world—*the* Sun. However, the Tabernacle teaches us something deeper about this fourth step. There, we not only receive a revelation of the light of His life, as seen in the candlestick, but we also discover that the light of His life is filling the Tabernacle, a symbol of His Body, which is the Church. In other words, this fourth step involves two intimately related revelations: First, a very real meeting with the Lord where He literally appears to us, and second, a wonderful revelation of the light and glory of the Lord residing in others—in our brothers and sisters in Christ. We will see in a moment that it becomes very easy to see Christ in others once we have seen Him in the secret place.

He Appeared to Fulfill Pentecost in the New Testament Also

The first coming of Christ is definitely one of the clearest confirmations of what Day Four signifies for God's people. It is safe to say that the most important single event in the early Church, after the cross of Christ, was the spiritual fulfillment of Pentecost, the fourth feast. This outpouring in Acts 2 gave the Church the power it needed to be a witness of the risen Savior in all the world (Acts 1:8). Nevertheless, God's people would never have experienced the glory of this fourth feast without something far more basic and essential—the literal and physical manifestation and appearance of the Sun of righteousness to this earth. The Lord Jesus Christ actually came and dwelt among His people in a visible way. In fact, John 1:14 declares, "And the Word became flesh and dwelt among us, and we beheld His glory…" (NKJV). The literal Greek translation of this is, "The Word became flesh and *tabernacled* among us." God's glory was seen in a body of flesh. Fortunately for humanity, many of God's people recognized His glory in the fleshly tabernacle of Jesus, and therefore received the living Word. Peter saw something in Christ's tent of flesh that was far more than the son of a poor carpenter from Galilee. He saw the glory of the Christ, the Sun of righteousness. If Christ had not come literally, and physically revealed Himself to this earth 2,000 years ago, there would never have been a spiritual fulfillment of Pentecost in Acts 2. Furthermore, there would never have been a Pentecost for the added multitudes who have entered the Church since the initial outpouring in Acts 2 if those multitudes had not seen and recognized the glory of the Lord that dwells in His earthly Body, the Church. These two essential aspects—His literal appearance, and seeing Him in His Body—bring us into the blessing of our fourth step in the "redemptive week."

The New Testament Pentecost Also Involved Eating

As we mentioned before, Israel celebrated the Feast of Pentecost for the first time at Mount Sinai. We also noted that the Lord visibly appeared to all Israel at that time. The spiritual fulfillment of this fourth feast came to God's people in Acts 2 at the very time when the nation of Israel was involved in their yearly celebration of this feast. On that day, the Lord poured out His Spirit upon the Church in the upper room (Acts 2:1-4). Right after the Spirit had been poured out, 3,000 souls were added to the Church (Acts 2:41). Consider what happened next, in the context of this amazing visitation: "They *devoted themselves* to the apostles' teaching and to the fellowship, *to the breaking of bread* and to prayer" (Acts 2:42 NIV). They *devoted* themselves to these four things. That is a strong word. It seems even stronger when we see that one of the things they devoted themselves to was eating, "the breaking of bread!" Once again, the emphasis on eating that is related to this visitation of God is amazing.

Why Was Man Made With a Need to Eat?

If we take an objective look at our habit and need for eating, without thinking of the pleasure it brings, eating is really a very ridiculous exercise. After the food is prepared, which sometimes takes hours, we sit down at a table and place pieces of food in our mouths. We then spend a few seconds moving our jaws up and down, trying to keep it inside while we talk to one another, after which we swallow it. When we have finished eating, all the messy dishes must be gathered, washed, and put away. Then, we start the whole cycle again three or four hours later. Is there not a better way for man to get his energy? Plants seem far more "civilized." They get their energy directly from the sun. What a neat and tidy system! Obviously, the Creator could have made human beings with the capability to get energy directly from the sun—maybe with built-in solar batteries (these are relatively new to mankind, but God knew about them at the Creation). Why then did He make us with a need to eat? I believe there are at least five good reasons:

1. In our modern society, there is a tremendous lack of communication between husbands and wives, and between parents and children. Imagine what our lives would be like if we had solar batteries as our source of energy. We would never have to sit down and waste our time eating. We could work all day without a break because we would never get weak from hunger. Since most of the infrequent communication that *does* occur in many families is during mealtimes, solar batteries could have eliminated communication almost entirely! Therefore, man's need to eat, forces him to gather often with others for communion. The Lord made us with a need to eat because He wants us to engage in that ridiculous daily routine of sitting down together and trying to talk between bites. Food is an amazing catalyst to gather us all in one place and keep us there for a while. At least we get to know one another a little better!

2. I have never yet met a person who does not enjoy eating. In fact, man enjoys eating so much that Stoics (who seek to avoid physical pleasure) have tried to convince man to give it up as much as possible. They are a little like the farmer who was bewailing the death of his best horse. He said, "I can't believe it. Just when I had him trained to live on sawdust, he up and died on me!" Acts 14:17 gives us another reason God made us with the need to eat. "Nevertheless he left not himself without witness, in that he did good, and gave us rain from heaven, and fruitful seasons, filling our hearts with food and gladness." Food is a witness or testimony to God and His nature. He wants man to know that He is a good God who enjoys giving us legitimate pleasures and who wants us to be filled with joy. He is not trying to make life hard for us. Some may ask, "What about the millions of human beings who are starving today? That doesn't seem to give a positive testimony to His nature!" Actually, just the opposite is true. Starvation occurs when nations forsake

the only true God to serve other gods, who do not provide very well for their servants! I have never heard of people starving to death in a nation that is faithfully serving the only true God. The psalmist implies that this will never happen (Ps. 37:25). Therefore, famine may actually cause the starving soul to understand that the only true God *is* good and that He doesn't allow *His* servants to die of hunger.

In the last 50 years, the God of Israel has done an awesome work with the natural people of Israel that confirms these truths. When Israel was declared a nation in 1948, many scoffers laughed and said, "The Jews will starve to death. They don't know anything about farming. They are bankers and businessmen!" With most of their land being either desert or swamp, this prediction seemed all the more likely to be fulfilled. On the contrary, Israeli agricultural technology has today become some of the best in the world, and has become a great source of income for them. The income is not only derived from the enormous quantity of fruit that is being exported continually from Israel and that now fills the earth—as God promised would happen in the last days (Is. 27:6)—but the income is partly earned from nations that are willing to pay for Israelis to come and teach them how to farm! Israeli agronomists have developed such revolutionary farming techniques that their farms produce much more per acre than those of most other countries. Maybe because they had not learned the ways of the other nations, they were better students for the Lord to teach them some new secrets!

I can add to this a word of personal testimony. My wife and I have lived in a number of places in the world that are known for their tropical fruits. But we feel that the fresh fruit in Israel is by far the very best in the entire world. God enjoys blessing His people with the best!

3. Eating can give a tremendous object lesson three times a day. One of life's beautiful, as well as terrible, principles is that life comes forth out of death. That lesson is seen every time we plant a seed. Life springs from the death of the seed (Jn. 12:24). Likewise, Jesus' death on the cross produces life in those who believe (2 Cor. 4:12). Every time we eat, we are demonstrating and reliving that truth because almost everything we eat was once alive; it had to give its life so that we can live. Once we are conscious of this truth, eating can often remind us of the principle that life comes out of death.

4. Another very important lesson is that we become what we eat. With the exception of the oxygen we breathe, every atom that forms our bodies (after leaving the womb) had to pass through our mouths. In the spiritual realm, the same holds true—what we eat we become. If we feed our spirits on the Word of God and the Bread of His Presence, then we will find spiritual life and health. However, if we feed our spiritual man on the delicacies that the king of Babylon, Satan, wants to provide us, then we will perish. The spiritual delicacies of Satan come in many forms—magazines, books, television, video games, movies, music, radio, etc. Daniel 1 reveals the importance of this spiritual truth by means of a natural lesson in which Daniel determined not to defile himself with the king of Babylon's food. Just as many of the natural stories in the Old Testament do, this experience of Daniel gives us a spiritual lesson. Those who long to become men of the Kingdom, as Daniel and his friends did, must follow Daniel's example in their spiritual lives and determine not to defile themselves with the delicacies of Satan's spiritual food. An examination of not only the way of the world, but also the way of the Church confirms Jesus' statement that few will actually find the path that leads to life (Mt. 7:14).

5. Finally, from the very beginning in the Garden of Eden, eating was given to man as a test. The Lord has ordained eating to give us a way of knowing if we love the pleasures of this life more than we love Him. In Acts 17:18, not only the Stoics opposed Paul and the gospel but also the Epicureans, who promoted the extreme opposite from what the Stoics preached. They taught that the only worthy pursuit in life was fleshly pleasure because afterward we die and are no more.

The Lord wants us to maintain a balance between the extremes of the Stoics and the Epicureans. We must recognize that He wants us to enjoy legitimate pleasures, like eating, but without allowing our stomachs to rule us or to become our god (Phil. 3:19). In the garden, Eve allowed her stomach to influence her when she saw that the "tree was good for food" (Gen. 3:6). The Lord has ordained that we fast from time to time, at least in some measure, so that we maintain control of our fleshly appetites. The stomach was one of the factors in the fall of man. Sometimes denying our flesh by fasting is the only way to overcome spiritual strongholds and to win back the spiritual ground we have lost (Mt. 17:18-21).

Getting the Whole Picture

We have examined the evidence found in the fourth step of our spiritual life. With all the pieces of the jigsaw puzzle now in place, the picture becomes clear. On the fourth Day, the Lord Himself will appear to us in a clear way. Even though the details of how He manifests Himself to each one will be different, there will be certain aspects that will be the same. Let's consider the blessings of Day Four:

1. The Lord Promises to Manifest Himself to Us

We find an additional revelation of the first four steps of the "redemptive week" in the teachings of the Lord Jesus Himself. In John 14:16-20, Jesus promises His disciples that the Holy Spirit would be given to them and they would live because He lives. The entrance of the Spirit of Christ into our lives, bringing us eternal life, is the essential aspect of our spiritual experience at the door of the Tabernacle, which represents the salvation experience. We recall that the first step in the "redemptive week" was the moving of the Holy Spirit upon the face of the waters. After the cross, as recorded in John 20:22-23, Christ breathed upon the disciples, saying to them, "Receive ye the Holy Spirit" (Jn. 20:22b). He then began to speak to them concerning the forgiveness of sins. This was the disciples' new-birth experience. The essential ingredient of the new birth is the indwelling of the Spirit of Christ. As Paul says, "...if anyone does not have the Spirit of Christ, he does not belong to Christ" (Rom. 8:9 NIV). In addition to *receiving* the Holy Spirit, the disciples were then *baptized* in the Holy Spirit a few days later in Acts 2. We receive the Spirit to be born again, and we are baptized or immersed in the Spirit to be empowered to be witnesses (Acts 1:8).

After promising the disciples the gifts of eternal life and the indwelling of His Spirit in John 14:16-20—the experience of Day One—the Lord gave a one sentence summary of the grace of God that is found on Days Two, Three, and Four. He assured them and us, "He who has My commandments and keeps them [the truth and obedience of Day Two], it is he who loves Me [the one who progresses to the fruit of Day Three]. And he who loves Me will be loved by My Father, and I will love him and *manifest* Myself to him [the open revelation of Christ on Day Four]" (Jn. 14:21 NKJV). Without going into an exhaustive study of the Greek word translated as "manifest," let's consider the glory God is offering us when He uses this word. "Manifest" means "to show openly," and the root word means "to shine, to come to view, to appear, to be seen."[5] It is the word found in

---

5. *Logos Bible Study Software* (Oak Harbor, WA: Logos Research Systems, 1993), Greek Lexicon, #1718.

Revelation 1:16 where "...his countenance was as the sun *shineth* in his strength." It is also the word used in Mark 16:9 where we are told that He *"appeared* first to Mary Magdalene." *This* is "manifesting" Himself! If we long for the Sun of righteousness "to come to view" and "to show Himself openly" to our earth, then let us yield to His gracious work in our lives until He has brought us to Day Four.

2. We Will See the Lord in Our Brethren

Once the Lord has appeared to us, we will also be able to see and recognize Him in others. We will be able to discern Him in His Body or temple. At that time, we will be able to understand by experience what happened to Jacob when he met his brother Esau. Esau came out to meet him with 400 men, which is not the usual number in a welcoming committee! (Gen. 32:6) Not too many of us have ever faced a "brother" who is more difficult or dangerous than Esau! Jacob understood that Esau was coming as an enemy, planning to avenge himself of Jacob's past offenses. As Jacob cried out to God, the Lord appeared to him and Jacob wrestled with the Lord all night. He received the Lord's blessing just at the dawn of a new day (Gen. 32:24-29).

Like Jacob, each succeeding man of faith in Genesis progressed one step further than his father and also received all the blessings of the men of faith who had gone before. The same thing happens in our individual lives as we progress through the seven Days. As we progress, we do *not* leave behind the blessing and experience of the previous Day. In fact, it continues to grow and to become more blessed throughout the rest of our lives. We will see the details concerning Jacob's life in a later Chapter. For now, we want to discover from his life the dynamic change that will take place in our hearts when we see God's face, as Jacob did (Gen. 32:30).

The concept of a person's face is extremely interesting. A person's face reveals such clearly identifiable characteristics that, given sufficient time to become acquainted, we *rarely* confuse one person with another—usually not even identical twins! It is quite easy to disguise ourselves to look like someone else by changing our dress and our mannerisms. We can fool even our family and friends until they see our face. Even if a person is a total stranger, once we have had a good look at his face, we will recognize him anywhere. Science still does not understand why we are capable of this. In fact, this ability is so reliable that in our judicial system, many suspected criminals are pronounced guilty and sentenced to death based on the testimony of two or three eyewitnesses who caught only one glimpse of the accused person's face at the scene of the crime.

Jacob had just seen the face of God. He had seen enough of the identifiable characteristics of God that he would be able to recognize Him anywhere, under any circumstances. The next day, as Jacob met his brother Esau, he told him, "I have seen your face as though I had seen the face of God" (Gen. 33:10 NKJV). Was Jacob flattering him just to win his favor and possibly save his own life? Was this simply a diplomatic thing to say to an extremely difficult brother? The Scriptures never recorded anything that is meaningless or vain. There is a beautiful truth revealed here.

Jacob could actually recognize the face of God in his brother because he had seen the face of God the night before. In our earthly life, once we have met a man, we can almost always pick out his son from a group, although we have never personally met the son. We easily recognize many of the characteristics in the son that we saw in the father. The face is the principal source we use to establish this link between father and son. He is usually very different from his father—but because he has enough similar facial characteristics, we can recognize him as his father's son. Jacob had seen *the* Father the night before. He had seen many identifiable characteristics in the face of God. Even though Esau was very different from his heavenly Father, Jacob was still able to see in him at least a few of the characteristics he had seen in his Father the night before.

Once the Lord has openly revealed to us the glory of the Sun of righteousness on the fourth Day, and we have seen Him as He is, we will find it very easy to recognize Him in His children. Yes, they may be totally unlike Him in most ways, but there will always be at least something of their Father that we will be able to recognize in them if they are indeed true sons, born of the Spirit. There will be enough of God in them for us to understand "with whom we are living," as the man at the breakfast table understood. Once we have seen the Lord, we will be able to recognize Him *anywhere* and under *any* circumstances, even when we see Him in a brother as difficult as Esau. Oh, how the Church needs the blessing of Day Four today, so that we may stop biting and devouring one another! (See Galatians 5:15.)

3. We Will Break Bread With Our Brethren

As we have seen, time after time the Scriptures link the fourth step with eating. The hungry soul longs to eat from the table the Lord prepares for His people. Unfortunately, we often ignore the Bread of Life when it is offered to us. How could a starving soul be offered the finest bread in the universe and simply refuse it? The truth is, we often disdain the package it comes in. Unless we can look past the covering of common badger skins and see the glory that fills His tabernacle (His Body), we may go through life passing up many wonderful spiritual meals.

Paul tells us that corporately the Body of Christ is as a loaf of bread that should be broken together. He writes, "The bread which we break, is it not the communion of the body of Christ? For we being many are one bread, and one body: for we are all partakers of that one bread" (1 Cor. 10:16b-17). Sure, we all want to eat the bread of life—that is, to hear a living word from the Lord. But how many times has the Lord tried to give us that word through another member of His Body, and we have failed to recognize and receive it? We didn't even look beyond the wrapper it came in to see the glory!

We often attend church, hoping that the pastor will have the word of God we desperately need. As we approach the Lord's loaf of living bread (the Body), it is crucial that we understand a simple fact. The precise word we need might be given to us before we ever get through the door of the church building. If we discern the Lord's Body and the heavenly treasure that dwells in earthly tents, we might hear His voice through a brother in Christ that greets us as we approach the place of meeting. Of course, we might not accept or even hear that bread of life because the wrapper on the bread is very unappetizing. Instead of embracing the word of God, we might say to ourselves, "I know this brother only too well. After all, last week he revealed what he is really like when he offended me. I saw those badger skin coverings for what they are. I know what kind of a person he is. I now can easily discern his condition." Yes, but can you discern the Lord's Body? Can you see the glory of the Lord that is hidden behind those dirty badger skins? Can you recognize the face of God in your brother?

If we have not yet come to Day Four, we may not have the maturity or grace to see the Lord's face in an Esau. Nevertheless, we do not have to wait until the fourth Day to understand that the Lord can speak to us through other members of the Body of Christ. Since we fail to discern the Lord's Body, many of us are spiritually sick, weak, and even dying. This is Paul's warning to us in the context of partaking of the bread and wine of the Lord's supper. He gave this warning just after explaining that we are the loaf broken to feed others (1 Cor. 10:16-17; 11:23-30). Surely, this is the reason eating together is so often linked with our fourth step: The Lord wants us to eat together in both the natural and the spiritual realms. He longs for us to have communion with Him *and* communion with His Body. Communion only with Him in our prayer closet is not enough. Both communions are essential for our spiritual health and for the health of His Body.

Once again, the natural realm was ordained to give a revelation of something that happens in the spiritual realm. Our churches should encourage and promote times of fellowship around natural meals. Not only is this fellowship a wonderful way to draw closer to others, to hear of their victories and sorrows, to become friends, and to learn to carry one another's burdens, but these times are also opportunities to break spiritual bread together. We should expect to receive something wonderful from the Lord through our brethren as we discern Him in His Body and hear His voice. We can also fully expect the Lord to use us to speak to others and feed them during our times of natural fellowship. One caution here: We should *never* gather around a meal with other Christians prepared to preach to them or give them what *they* need. We should go with the scriptural attitude of being quick to hear and slow to speak (Jas. 1:19). In the course of sincere, unfeigned fellowship, the Lord will be faithful to use us, often when we are not even aware that He is doing so. What we thought was a wonderful revelation might fall on deaf ears, but something else, just mentioned in passing, may be the key a broken or needy heart requires.

We must also recognize that the Church is not a social club. Christians do not gather because they have a common interest in some earthly activity or hobby. If we draw near to a local church with the idea of meeting a lot of nice people, we will leave wounded, offended, and disillusioned. The fact is, David's motley crew in Adullam's cave is a more accurate picture of what we will meet in the true Church—those who are in distress, in debt, and discontented (1 Sam. 22:1-2). This kind gathered to David in that day, and still gather to our heavenly David today. We will discover that, in some ways, people in the Church are even worse than people in the world. This is an accusation frequently leveled against Christians. Instead of denying it or justifying ourselves, we should understand what is happening in the Church.

When a person chooses to follow the Lord, the forces of hell are unleashed against him. He is swimming upstream, against all odds. He faces spiritual battles that people in the world who are going downstream never face. Spirits of pride, immorality, hatred, strife, envy, lying, stealing, and every other foul thing, come against a Believer in a way they never come against Satan's hell-bound followers in the world. Although we will never lose the war, there will be times when every one of us will lose a battle. The scene of spiritual defeat and spiritual carnage is not a pleasant one. Onlookers from the world get the idea that Christians are worse than they are. Maybe we are, but at least we are on our way to Heaven!

Considering that our weaknesses are amplified by spiritual attacks, it is certain that many things are ready to blow churches apart. Ultimately, there will be nothing that can keep us together—nothing, that is, except the presence of the Lord Himself. If your reason for being part of a church today is to recognize the Lord who lives in His Body and to receive something from Him through that Body, then you will never regret having belonged to His people. Woe to you if you are part of a church for any other motive. It will definitely *not* be a comfortable place for you!

The Weight of Evidence

At this point, there could very well be uncertainty in the hearts of some readers about whether or not the Lord still does appear to His people. I am conscious of the fact that a personal revelation of the Lord in each of our lives is not generally considered to be part of the normal spiritual growth process. Therefore, it is important to firmly establish the biblical basis for believing that the Lord desires to give this blessing to each one of us. How can we be sure that this is so?

1. Paul assures us that the New Testament age is **much more glorious** than the Old Testament age (2 Cor. 3:7-11). This declaration was actually made in the context of Paul's reference to the glory that Moses experienced when he spent time in the visible presence of the Lord, and when he asked the Lord to show him His glory (Ex. 33:18-23). Are we to assume that the New Testament age is more glorious than the Old Testament age, but that somehow the *greatest* glory God revealed to any man in the Old Testament (the privilege of seeing Him) is no longer available?

The glory of God is the only real glory there is, and Moses longed to *see* it. Do you? If the New Testament age is more glorious than the Old Testament age, God has a measure of glory to show us that not even Moses saw. This is part of what is revealed in the New Testament in the lives of Paul and John. They were taken into God's presence and heard things that could not be told (2 Cor. 12:1-4; Rev. 10:1-4). This was clearly a greater glory than what Moses witnessed because there is no indication Moses heard things he was not permitted to share. In fact, it appears that "all" God spoke to Moses he declared to the people (Deut. 5:26-27).

2. Paul assures us that **all** the things that happened to Israel on their journey from Egypt to Canaan are examples for us in the last days (1 Cor. 10:11). If the Lord no longer appears, then **all** the things they experienced are examples for us **except** one of the most important events of all—the visible appearance of God in the "sight of all the people" at Mount Sinai during the fourth feast, the Feast of Pentecost (Ex. 19:11).

3. Paul is an example for all Believers (1 Tim. 1:16). Again, if God no longer appears to His people, then Paul is an example in everything **except** for one of the most glorious aspects of his life—the repeated appearances of the Lord to him.

4. Jesus is an example for all Believers. We are being conformed to His likeness in "all things" (Rom. 8:29; Heb. 2:17). Jesus testified that He could see and hear the Father as He ministered on the earth. Therefore, once again, if the Lord no longer grants that kind of relationship, we can be conformed to the likeness of our example in everything **except** this extremely important detail! Oh, how we *need* to do and to say only what we see and hear from the Lord instead of being led by our own ideas and desires!

5. Not only is Jesus our example in this area but He also promised that He would, in fact, "manifest" Himself to His people. This Greek word is very powerful. As already mentioned, this word means "to show one's self, come to view, appear." Although it may be possible to "interpret" this to mean something other than His visible appearance, the scriptural usage of this word should serve as the basis for our interpretation. He has "come to view" in the lives of His people throughout the entire Bible. Also, after Christ's resurrection, many holy people who had died were resurrected and they **"appeared** to many people" (the same word as "manifest") (Mt. 27:52-53 NKJV). There is little doubt about the meaning of the word "manifest" in this context. In Hebrews 9:24 we are told that Christ "appeared [was "manifested"] in the presence of God for us." He also "appeared" (manifested Himself) first to Mary Magdalene after His resurrection (Mk. 16:9). The meaning of the word "manifest" is clear from these New Testament usages of this word.

6. The entire Bible shows, by example, how the servant of God should live and what his relationship with the Lord should be like. In both the Old and New Testament, the Lord appeared to many men and women of faith. *If* the Lord no longer appears to His people, then we can expect to follow their example with the exception of His appearing. It would not be considered sound doctrine to treat other areas of their lives this way, so why should we do so with respect to His appearing?

7. In Malachi 3:6, the Lord assures us that He never changes. It is significant that He makes this declaration at the end of the Old Testament Scriptures, just before the New Testament begins. This tells us that there is continuity between His ways as revealed in the Old Testament and His ways as revealed in the New Testament. In

Hebrews 13:8 we are also assured that Jesus Christ is the same yesterday, today, and forever. If the Lord appeared to His people in the past, He still appears to them today. It is also significant that Malachi 3:6 is in the context of the Lord's appearance in His Temple! (Mal. 3:1-5)

8. The Lord appeared visibly to fulfill Pentecost in both the Old and New Testament. Should we not expect the same type of fulfillment in our own lives?

9. Abraham is presented throughout the Bible as our father and example. One of the outstanding characteristics of his life was that God appeared to him on several occasions. Will God allow us to follow his example and experience what he experienced?

10. John the Beloved saw the Lord on the Isle of Patmos about 60 years after the cross (Rev. 1:13-17). Does not the Lord still appear to those who are "beloved," or should we conclude that *this* was really the last time He appeared to His disciples?

Are There Any Questions?

The Lord's appearing on Day Four may be a revolutionary truth for some readers. Therefore, I will pause to answer some questions before we go on to Day Five. Included here are some of the most common questions regarding the fourth Day:

1. *Should I seek the experience of seeing the Lord?* In general, this experience will not be granted before we come into the maturity of Day Four. When the Lord brings us to this point, it will be His faithfulness that grants us this experience and not our own seeking. Of course, there should be a longing in our hearts to see the glory of the Lord, just as there was in Moses' heart. Seeing the Lord should be part of the "joy set before us" that gives us strength to continue on in our journey (Heb. 12:1-2). We should ask God to bring us to this place, recognizing, however, that our prayer will only be answered after the work of Day Three is completed in us.

2. *Is seeing the Lord a prerequisite for going on to Day Five?* The prerequisite for going on to Day Five is that the work of Day Four be completed within us, which includes a revelation of His glory. Therefore, no one will go on to Day Five without seeing the Lord. But who would want to miss this most glorious blessing anyway?

3. *Does this mean that no one should be a pastor or leader if he has not seen the Lord?* In the New Testament, the Apostle Paul placed

the most mature Believers that were available over the churches he established (Tit. 1:5). Certainly these men had not yet finished their spiritual journey to maturity, yet God used them to lead others. In the realm of leadership, what we call "maturity" is, in **some** ways, relative. For example, a two-year-old usually thinks that his seven-year-old brother is the greatest and can do no wrong. To the contrary, a ten-year-old thinks that his seven-year-old brother is still just a little boy, whereas he considers himself to be almost a man! As God visits the Church in these last days and brings us into maturity, God's people will no longer be led by children, as is often the case (Is. 3:4). Until then, if you are a spiritual five-year-old, you can be sure that your ten-year-old brother can teach you a lot; so humbly follow him if you want to learn! On the other hand, for all of us who are leading others when we are not yet mature ourselves, we can be sure that the Lord will lead us in sure paths if we walk humbly before Him and before those we are leading. When a spiritual ten-year-old leads others who are even less mature than himself, it is quite difficult for him to become puffed up in pride as long as he continues to see himself from God's viewpoint and not from his follower's viewpoint. Surely the humility in young King Solomon pleased the Lord when Solomon prayed, "I am but a little child: I know not how to go out or come in...give therefore thy servant an understanding heart to judge thy people" (1 Kings 3:7b,9a).

Come Back Here Later

For some readers, the concept of actually seeing the Lord in our day has already brought new joy and zeal into their Christian life. Others may still be having difficulty accepting or digesting such a possibility. However, as we move on to Days Five, Six, and Seven, two things will occur. First, the reader will see that the amazing similarities between the various seven-step lists will be even more striking than they were in the first four Days, thereby confirming the validity of the whole study. Second, the reader will see in the following Days that the things God has prepared for them that love Him are even far more wonderful than a personal appearance of the Lord Jesus Christ on Day Four. Most of us know that Paul said, "Eye has not seen, nor ear heard, nor have entered into the heart of man the things which God has prepared for those who love Him" (1 Cor. 2:9 NKJV). On the other hand, few people can quote the next verse, which is clearly the most important declaration in this passage: "But **God has revealed them to us through His Spirit**. For the Spirit searches all things, yes, the deep things of God" (1 Cor. 2:10 NKJV). After you have seen a few more of the glorious things God has prepared for those who love Him, I suggest you come back to Day Four and read it again. You will probably find it much easier to understand, accept, and digest!

Chapter 13

Day Five—His Word Is Fulfilled

We were standing together on a taxiway at the international airport. We had been friends for several years; we were both pilots. We just happened to meet at the airport that day. Little did either of us know that this would be our last time together. It would not be because of a tragic accident. Something far worse happened to him. He was "killed" by success. His success was the fruit of ambition, which was Eve's first sin, mixed with tremendous natural ability, which is often a great liability in life. As we stood on the taxiway, talking, I had no way of knowing that this would be my last opportunity to speak to him from my heart before his rise to success.

We had ministered together for some years in the same church. Many had called him a prophet. On one hand, it is devastating to the human heart to believe the negative opinions of others about ourselves. However, it is even *more* devastating to believe their praises! Either way, we will end up in a ditch when we judge ourselves by what man thinks of us—a ditch of either despair or pride. When we judge ourselves by God's opinion— the only opinion in the universe that matters—all our pride will melt away, and we will be greatly humbled. Then, we will discover that He delights to lift us from the low place into eternal success.

My friend's "vision," as he called it, was utterly unworthy of anyone who is a true prophet. I tried in vain to convince him that his vision was not *God's* vision for his life. My heart told me that God had a tremendous purpose for this very capable man, but I knew that the only way for God's purposes to be realized in his life would be through the school of the Spirit. If he was to follow the Lord, he would face crushing defeats. There he would learn that human abilities are never the foundation to true spiritual success. He would also learn that *only* when we are weak are we really strong. To build His Kingdom, the Lord mightily uses those who see their great need of *His* abilities in every area. That way, no flesh will ever glory in His presence, and we will become eternal testimonies to His grace and goodness rather than to our wonderful natural abilities.

My words fell on deaf ears, and my friend continued his headlong rush toward fame and greatness. He finally reached his goal. He became very famous and very powerful—not that being famous and powerful is wrong. On the contrary, this is something that every truly spiritual person will experience sooner or later—*if* he never makes it his goal, and *if* he reaches it in and through God. The Lord promised this to David. He said, "[I] have made thee a great name, like unto the name of the great men that are in the earth" (2 Sam. 7:9b). God created man to be great and powerful and to be set over all His creation (Heb. 2:6-7). As long as our greatness comes from a humble relationship with Him, there is no danger. Far from trying to keep man from being great, part of the promise the Lord made to Abraham was, "And I will make of thee a great nation, and I will bless thee, and **make thy name great**" (Gen. 12:2a). If you and I are sons of Abraham, we, too, have inherited this promise (Gal. 3:29; Rom. 4:16). God wants to make us kings and priests unto Himself as David was. Every servant whose longing is to exalt the Lord and to do His will, will sooner or later be exalted himself. The history of God's people shows that for some this happens in this present life; for others it is reserved for God's eternal Kingdom.

During Jesus' 40-day trial in the wilderness, Satan offered Him all the kingdoms of the world if He would simply take a shortcut. Satan continues to use this tactic on people. Many people do not pass this test because they accept the enemy's shortcut to the throne. In reality, very, very few pass this test. Very few pass it because very few are even given the opportunity to take the test. God knows that our choice would lead to disaster. Therefore, in His mercy, He never allows us to be offered the kingdoms of this world. Few of us would choose, on our own, the long and trying path to the throne that the Lord has ordained for us. For this reason, I am not critical of my friend. He was faced with a test that most of us will never be ready to face. Unfortunately, he took the shortcut. He became a powerful political figure in his nation. Sadly, his later departure from politics brought great reproach to the name of Christ.

My friend had actually come to believe what others said about him. He concluded that he was a prophet, called to be a political leader. I tried to explain to him that instead of having a God-given spiritual vision, he had only carnal ambition. In the beginning of our spiritual lives, carnal ambition fills the heart of every son of Adam. It also fills the Church today. Very few discern the difference between this ambition and God-given spiritual vision.

My hope is that the last chapter of my friend's life has not yet been written. Since our God is the God of restoration, some day my friend may very well fulfill the great things God had planned for him from the beginning. I am so thankful that the Lord has often given me many opportunities to finally pass a test I had repeatedly failed. Have you ever thanked Him for giving you sufficient opportunities to finally pass your tests? Maybe you believe that you have squandered your last chance to pass some test you have failed over and over. Do you honestly think that any normal earthly father would refuse to give his son another chance to succeed where he has failed, as long as the son wants to keep on trying? How much more will your heavenly Father do the same for you!

I also shared with my friend that there is a huge difference between being *called to be* a prophet and actually *being* a prophet. *Being* a prophet implies that we have spiritual maturity, authority, and most of all, the character of *the* Prophet, Christ Jesus. The difference is very easy to define—just five Days of God's dealings. We are speaking about the first five Days of God's "redemptive week" in our lives. On the fifth Day we are finally made to be what God called us to be from the first Day. On Day Five, God fulfills His promises regarding our lives.

The transition from carnal ambition to spiritual vision is a slow process that requires the work of God in our lives, the work of five consecutive Days. Finally, when we have spiritual vision, we suddenly *no longer want to be the leader*. The life of Moses reveals that. At age 40, he considered himself quite capable of leading God's people. At age 80, he felt he wasn't capable even to be considered to lead Israel. God Himself had a difficult time convincing Moses to accept the position. Is Moses a revelation of a rare type of person, or is he a revelation of the outcome of God's crushing and humbling process in our lives? If we seek position, it is because we are not yet ready for the position. We may very well have the call to the position we seek, as did Moses, but let us first submit to the Lord's preparation.

Day Five

"And God said, Let the waters bring forth abundantly the moving creature that hath life, and fowl that may fly above the earth in the open firmament of heaven. And God created great whales, and every living creature that moveth, which the waters brought forth abundantly..."

(Gen. 1:20-21). We already know water is a symbol of the Word of God. Here, on the fifth Day, the waters bring forth life. The Word is fruitful in us on this Day as it becomes life in us; no longer is it only light or vision. Indeed, the Word of God in our earth is fulfilled in the fullest sense, producing life. In the Creation account, the height and depth of this fulfillment is symbolized by the life produced in the birds that fly in the height of heaven and the creatures in the depths of the seas. God's promise to make us into something specific for His Kingdom is finally fulfilled on Day Five.

When the Lord first works on us as the heavenly potter, He already knows what He wants to make when He takes the ball of clay into His hands. From the very beginning of our life in Him, the creative word He speaks over us goes forth from His lips as He calls things that are not as though they were (Rom 4:17 NIV). By His Word, the Lord destines each of our lives to a certain ministry or office in His Body, the Church. On Day Five, the heights and the depths of that Word will be fruitful and will be fulfilled in us. Some people hear that creative word on Day One and, therefore, know what God plans to do with their lives. Other people neither hear nor understand His purposes for them until those purposes finally become a reality in them. In either case, the Lord knows what He is making. He has spoken a creative word that will accomplish His will in us. He will watch over His Word to fulfill it (Jer. 1:12 NIV). It is not essential for us to understand what He is making with us. Sometimes it is a blessing to know; other times it is better not to know.

Paul the apostle heard the word of God and knew what God was planning to do with him from the time of his conversion (Acts 9:6,11-16). The word of the Lord went forth over Noah at his birth (Gen. 5:29). The same thing happened in Jeremiah's life (Jer. 1:5). This was also the experience of Christ Jesus (Is. 49:1-2). At Peter's first meeting with the Lord, he received a revelation of what the Lord wanted to do with him (Jn. 1:40-42).

For some people, knowing what the Lord is calling them to becomes a hindrance. Many years ago the Lord spoke to a young man, through older ministers, that he was being called to a prophetic ministry. Part of the message that was given to him came from Jeremiah 1:7, where the Lord exhorted Jeremiah, "Say not, I am a child: for thou shalt go to all that I shall send thee, and whatsoever I command thee thou shalt speak." The young man was being encouraged to place his immediate attention on God's purpose for his life. Later, while talking to him, I casually mentioned to him about how wonderful it was that he had been called to a prophetic ministry. His very forceful answer was, "You heard what was said! I am not *called* to a prophetic ministry. I already *have* a prophetic ministry." For this young man, knowing God's purpose became a definite hindrance in his life because that knowledge exalted him in pride and actually delayed the fulfillment of that purpose.

Few of us remain humble after we understand the fullness of what God graciously plans to do with us. Fortunately, the Lord is very wise to hide from our understanding His complete plan for us. I am sure that even Paul could never have begun to imagine the full importance of his conversion on the road to Damascus. He could not have foreseen the honor his name would carry 2,000 years later in the Church. If he had seen this clearly, he probably would have needed several more thorns in the flesh to keep him humble. Since he could not see all the glory, one thorn was sufficient! (2 Cor. 12:7)

Revelation Versus Reality

Regardless of how much understanding we have of God's purposes for our lives, we urgently need to understand the enormous difference there is between revelation and reality, or between light and life. It is one thing to know that we are *called* to be a prophet. It is an entirely different thing to actually *be* a prophet. This was the knowledge my friend was lacking when he sought to become a political leader in his country. I believe that God's desire to teach us this difference is part of the reason for the amazing redundancy we find in the latter part of the Book of Exodus. Exodus 25–30 is dedicated to all the intricate details of how God wanted Moses to make the Tabernacle. Now if *I* had been writing the Bible, after this I simply would have said, "And Moses went down from the mountain and made the Tabernacle exactly as the Lord had shown him in the mount." Instead, the Spirit of God dedicated Exodus 35–40 to repeating all those details as each piece of the Tabernacle was actually made. The Lord seems to be shouting to us that there is a huge difference between receiving a revelation and having that revelation become reality in us. Not only was the Tabernacle designed to show us the seven steps into God's glory but also to give us the message that a mere vision or revelation of those steps is not enough. That vision must be fulfilled within us, step by step, until we *become* a tabernacle with all seven steps fully formed within us.

Most of us make the mistake in our walk with God of confusing revelation and light, concerning what God wants to do in our lives, with reality and life. This was also the mistake of the young man who believed that he already had a prophetic ministry. He was ignoring the fact that God often "calls those things which do not exist as though they did" (Rom. 4:17 NKJV). On Day Five, the word of God that went forth over us on Day One, promising to make us a vessel of honor, becomes the reality of life in us, and we become on Day Five what God had ordained for us to be.

Day Five and the Fifth Man of Faith

Is there any doubt that Isaac, the fifth man of faith, speaks to us of God's word or promise being fulfilled? He was the son of promise that Abraham waited so long to bring forth. His very life stands as a monument to the faithfulness of God to fulfill His word in the lives of His servants. The process was long, but the promise of God was finally fulfilled.

Day Five and the Fifth Feast

The fifth feast is the "memorial of blowing of trumpets" (Lev. 23:24). This feast commemorates the use of silver trumpets during the wilderness journey of Israel. During that journey, the trumpets were used for several purposes, as is explained in Numbers 10:1-10. One of these purposes was to sound an alarm for war so that the people could prepare themselves for battle. Paul compares God's servants with trumpets that sound an alarm for war: "For if the trumpet give an uncertain sound, who shall prepare himself to the battle? *So likewise ye*, except ye utter by the tongue words easy to be understood, how shall it be known what is spoken..." (1 Cor. 14:8-9). A trumpet symbolizes a man with a message, which is seen in Isaiah's exhortation: "Cry aloud, spare not, lift up thy voice like a trumpet, and shew my people their transgression, and the house of Jacob their sins" (Is. 58:1). Therefore, servants of the Lord who have a message from God actually become the trumpets God uses to accomplish the very same purposes for which trumpets were used in the wilderness journey.

What do trumpets, or people with a message, have to do with Day Five? We have seen that on Day Five we actually become the ministry, voice, or trumpet the Lord has decided to make us. Also, we become people with a message because, on Day Five, the word within us is no longer merely **doctrine**; it is **experience**. Neither is it only a promise because it has produced life in us. People can tell the difference between a parrot that has learned to repeat a message and a prophetic voice that speaks from personal experience.

Day Five and the Tabernacle of Moses

The fifth step in the Tabernacle is the table of showbread. Just as the emphasis on the candlestick is the light that it gave, so the emphasis on the table is the bread that was upon it (Lev. 24:5-9). From John 6 we know that bread is symbolic of the living Word, the Lord Jesus Christ, who is the bread of life. The extreme importance of being fed daily with that living bread from Heaven was discussed at the end of Chapter 2. Could it be that there comes a time in our spiritual lives when we, too, become bread that can nourish others with the living Word? The table of showbread symbolically speaks to this question.

There were 12 loaves of bread on the table of showbread, one for each of the tribes of Israel. These loaves were symbolic of all Israel not only because of their number but also because the loaves were prepared from ingredients that had been provided by *all Israel*, as described in Leviticus 24:8. One message that resounds from this table is that the Lord wants to make every member of His holy nation bread for others. The Lord Jesus is not only the **living bread,** He is also the **pattern** to which we are being conformed (Rom. 8:29; Heb. 2:17). Therefore, we should fully expect to be conformed to His likeness until we, too, become living bread to feed others with the living Word from Heaven.

The 12 loaves on the table of showbread served as food for the priests in the Tabernacle (Lev. 24:9). Each week the priest would place fresh bread on the table and remove the old, which then became food for the priests (Lev. 24:8-9). From several Old Testament references, the Hebrew word for "showbread" can actually be translated as "the bread of the Presence" (Ex. 25:30 NIV).

What a beautiful picture! This ritual shows us the *source* of that bread or spiritual food in our own lives. The priests continually ate bread that had been seasoned in the presence of the Lord for a whole week in the Holy Place. The spiritual "bread" or truths that God gives us as spiritual food should also be exposed to His presence day after day, as we spend time before Him. During our daily devotional time, we should meditate on the new truths He is showing us and express them to the Lord as we worship Him in spirit and in *truth*. The showbread in the Holy Place was also exposed day after day to the fragrance of the incense, a symbol of prayer, that was offered there daily. We, too, should expose the new truths God speaks to us to the influence of prayer, humbly asking Him for greater understanding of what He is showing us. In addition, the showbread was exposed to the light of the candlestick, the light that allowed the bread to be seen. Only as God's light shines on the truth (the "bread") can we see it clearly for what it is. The psalmist summarized this beautifully when he wrote, "In thy light shall we see light" (Ps. 36:9b). In conclusion, before our spiritual bread is ready for consumption it needs to be exposed to God's presence, to prayer, and to God's light. Too often, we indulge in the tendency to share with others fresh truths that we have not yet bathed with these influences.

If we expose our new "bread" to the divine influences found in the Holy Place, we will be following the example the Old Testament priesthood gives us. The very priests who placed the showbread before the

Lord were the ones who ate it. Both spiritually and naturally we become what we eat. Therefore, as we partake of our spiritual showbread, our very lives will soon become an expression of the bread that comes from His presence, from the place of prayer, and from the place of His light or revelation. For all who want to become living bread for the nations, the table of showbread reveals the way. If our bread or truth has first been placed before the Lord, what we share will become for our listeners much more than "ordinary bread" (1 Sam. 21:4 NIV). They, too, will become conscious of His presence as they partake of it! We must be careful to remember, however, that the bread of God's presence, or His living word, *must* first be assimilated by us. It must become life in us before it can become life for others as we share with them.

There is an amazing link between the showbread and the fifth Day of Creation. We saw that the spiritual fulfillment of the fifth Day is that the water of the Word actually produces *life* in us, that life being represented by birds and fishes. In a similar manner, on the fifth step God actually makes us to become bread of *life* for others. Through the intervention of the Spirit of God in our lives, the word moves from the realm of doctrinal beliefs to a living reality in us. This is an inward, personal work, but it also becomes evident outwardly as we become an expression of the living Word for others. On Day Five, in a new way, we can share the living Word that descends from Heaven because it is *a message we have become*, not merely a sermon we preach. People can tell the difference. He wants us to *be* the message, not just to *preach it*. Then we truly become a mighty trumpet that speaks to God's people and the world.

God's Needlework

To this point, we have considered each aspect of the series of sevens separately. We have seen over and over how much they are interrelated. In our study of Day Six and Day Seven we will not treat them separately. Instead, we will interweave them so we can see the beautiful pattern that is produced. Like most of us, the Lord appreciates needlework. He ordained that it be included in the door of the Tabernacle: "And thou shalt make an hanging for the door of the tent, of blue, and purple, and scarlet, and fine twined linen, wrought with needlework" (Ex. 26:36). I trust that the needlework created by the interweaving of the threads of truth found in Day Six and Day Seven will somehow become part of a new door of understanding for you. May that door invite you into His presence and life in a way you have never before experienced, and may we all respond to the invitation He has extended to us to be in Him and He in us!

Chapter 14

Day Six—The Man in God's Likeness

The following story actually took place. I trust that it will bring a new understanding of God's ways to many hearts.

The sheep had waited a very long time for God to send them a true shepherd. Just a few years before, they had been at the point of spiritual death as they faced fierce enemies in battles that were insurmountable. They had become so famished and weak from a lack of spiritual food that they were never sure if they would win the next battle or not. Sadder still, sometimes they didn't even care. To add to this, countless false shepherds had passed through their congregation and fleeced them time and time again. The top leaders of their denomination had continually laid heavier and heavier burdens on them, not the least of which were the financial sacrifices they were required to make. Those leaders knew how to receive, but they knew nothing of giving. They were completely useless as a source of spiritual food, protection, or counsel. They were unable to provide for the flock even one shepherd who would care for the sheep. These people were truly sheep without a shepherd.

How well they can remember the day all that changed. As their new shepherd shared with them a message from Heaven, instead of a canned sermon, their hearts burned with a new love for the Lord and a new longing to run the race with everything that was within them. In their opinion, no congregation ever had a better shepherd than theirs. All those years of sorrow had become distant memories—and yet they again drew strangely near because their pastor was sharing with them some heartrending news. He was telling them, "We have had some wonderful years together. Many tremendous blessings have been granted to us, and mighty things have been accomplished in this flock. However, my time with you is drawing to a close. God has spoken to me that my ministry here is finished. There is no need for you to fear because I will place the flock in the hands of an extremely capable leader."

In an instant, the memory of those many years of suffering as sheep without a shepherd came rushing in upon the startled congregation. How they feared that their future would be something they already knew all too well—a revisiting of the past! If ever there was a real "back to the future," this was it! The shock of once again feeling alone and uncared for overwhelmed them. Some interrupted the pastor with an explosive mixture of sorrow, love, loyalty, appreciation, and deep fear. Others, with tears and a dedication to eternal values, declared, "Pastor, we don't care where you are going in this world. We will quit our jobs, sell our homes and businesses, and move, as long as we can be with you! We are your sheep, and no other person will ever be able to pastor us as you have!"

The pastor's response only caused more thoughts and emotions to well up within them. He continued, "I know that every one of you loves me dearly. I am very sorry, but the path I am called to walk I must walk alone. Nevertheless, I do have a word of encouragement for you. While it is true that within a few days we will no longer be together, after a little while, when you have felt the full weight of our separation, we will know the great joy of seeing each other again. This can be true only because I am leaving you."

Although they were heartened by his encouraging words, yet the people continued to be confused and disappointed. How could the pastor's leaving be the reason they would one day see him again? That made no sense to them at all. Soon, the pastor left and the people were devastated. They knew that they would never again be happy being pastored by a hireling or a stranger; so, they made a decision that cost them their reputation. They stopped looking to men for help. They started seeking the Lord as they never had before. The tears, the groanings, and the intercession were truly awesome. At times the spiritual travail of many of them resembled literal birth pains. Something was being born in them—the very life their pastor had manifested before them!

A very short time later, they finally understood what the pastor had been trying to tell them. They understood why he had said that his leaving would be the reason they would see him again. One day, a leader who had been with the congregation from the beginning was sharing the Word. They *thought* they knew him well. But as they listened to one of the most wonderful messages from God's Word they had ever heard, their eyes were suddenly opened. It was their beloved pastor speaking to them again! No, he had not secretly returned to them disguised as one of the sheep; rather, the life their pastor had imparted to them was now being revealed through one of his spiritual sons! That life had been reproduced in this son—the exact same vision, anointing, revelation, miracles, and character they had seen in their spiritual father. In fact, this son, and a number of others just like him, were doing things that were even more wonderful than their beloved shepherd had once done.

By now you may have realized that the son was Peter, and his pastor was Jesus. The congregation was the early Church, and their denomination was The Legalistic Union of Pharisees and Sadducees. When the Lord returned to Heaven, after the cross, He committed the lives of His sheep into the hands of a very capable leader, the Holy Spirit, who revealed the things of Christ to the Church and also conformed them to the likeness of the Son. Jesus was referring to this process when He told His disciples that they would soon see Him again because He was going to the Father (Jn. 16:16). John the Beloved testified about how his own life had been used to reveal Christ when he declared, "That which was from the beginning, which we have heard, which we have seen with our eyes, which we have looked upon, and our hands have handled, of the Word of life…That which we have seen and heard declare we unto you, that ye also may have fellowship with us: and truly our fellowship is with the Father, and with his Son Jesus Christ" (1 Jn. 1:1,3). Peter and John, along with many other spiritual sons of the Lord Jesus, could say that they were manifesting before others exactly the same message, miracles, and character they had personally witnessed in Christ for several years. They were doing this so others could have the same fellowship they had enjoyed with their wonderful Shepherd.[1]

Why, then, did the Lord withdraw his physical presence from the disciples? He did so because **He no longer wanted to walk with them**. The experience of walking with Him is glorious, but this is not the Lord's ultimate goal. He wanted to bring an end to walking *with* the disciples in order to bring them to the place where He walked *in and through* them! His goal for us is the same. After meeting with us in wonderful ways, the Lord brings us to the place where it seems that His presence has been withdrawn from us. This is not because He has forsaken us. His purpose is to produce the deep cry of spiritual travail in our hearts so that His life might be formed in us. He wants to walk in and through us also! This is what happens on Day Six.

If we understand that the natural earth and the Garden of Eden within it are a revelation of our spiritual lives, it is very easy to understand the

---

1. To see that every detail of the above story actually took place, read John 13–16. Read especially, the following Scriptures, in the order listed, to see what the Lord told His disciples—John 13:33,36-37; 16:16-23; 14:12,16,21-23, and 16:7-15.

significance of God's work in us on Day Six. On the sixth Day, God formed a man in His own likeness and image and placed him in the garden (Gen. 1:26; 2:8). There in only one Man in the universe who is in God's likeness and image. This Man, who is capable of dwelling in the garden of our hearts as a husbandman, is the Lord Jesus Christ.

Romans 5:14 declares that the first Adam was a "pattern of the one to come" (NIV). The word *pattern* is also translated as "figure" or "type" (KJV, NKJV, RSV). This word is defined as "the pattern in conformity to which a thing must be made."[2] In this passage, Paul is comparing Adam with Christ. Paul also refers to Christ as "the last Adam" (1 Cor. 15:45). Since the first Adam is a God-given pattern for the last Adam, the details God revealed in the first Adam, **before he fell**, must be fulfilled by the last Adam, Christ.

How did Christ fulfill the pattern found in the first Adam? Both Adams are called "the son of God" because God was the Father and source of both (Lk. 3:38). They were both brought forth by the Father as sinless men. They both became the father and source of life for a new generation (1 Cor. 15:45-49). The life of Adam's wife was taken from his wounded side, as was the life of the Church, Christ's wife (Jn. 19:34-35). Adam bore God's image and likeness. Christ is the only other man who has fully borne that image. He is called the "express image" of God (Heb. 1:3).

Consider the most glorious aspect of the first Adam in relationship to each of us, individually. He was formed and placed on the earth in a garden to care for the garden (Gen. 2:8,15). We know that Christ is also called a "husbandman" (Jas. 5:7; Heb. 6:7), and the garden He cares for is within us (Song 4:12; 6:1-2; Heb. 6:7-9). Is it possible that Christ's very life is being formed within our "earth" to be placed, by an act of God, into the garden of our hearts?[3] Remember, the garden into which Adam was placed had been in the process of preparation for five previous Days of God's creative work. (Every jot and tittle of God's Word is very significant.) Is it possible

---

2. *Logos Bible Study Software* (Oak Harbor, WA: Logos Research Systems, 1993), Greek Lexicon, #5179.

3. The Apostle Paul actually refers to this "placing" of a mature son several times in the New Testament when he speaks about "adoption." This word does not refer to becoming God's children through adoption as we know it. We are His children by birth because the life of Christ Himself is birthed within us. Christ is never called a son by adoption, even when He lives within us! The Greek word "adoption" that Paul uses refers to the placing of a mature son into his position. See W.E. Vine, *An Expository Dictionary of New Testament Words* (Old Tappan, NJ: Fleming H. Revell Company, 1966). See "adoption" and "son."

that long after the new-birth experience there is a spiritual place in God where Christ, the man in God's image, enters our earth in a way He never did before? Paul told Believers who were already born again, "My little children, of whom I travail in birth again until Christ be *formed* in you" (Gal 4:19). Although Paul's spiritual children were born-again Christians, they did not yet have Christ "formed" within them.

Some may question, "If I have been born again, can I not rightly say that the very life of Christ has been placed within my heart?" Yes, His life definitely enters our spirits at the new birth when the Holy Spirit, the third Person of the Trinity, takes up residence in our hearts. However, there was a huge difference between the babe born in Bethlehem's manger and the mature Christ who was manifested in the Jordan River. He grew from a little baby to a full-grown man. He also grew spiritually in wisdom and in favor with God and man (Lk. 2:52). Since He is our example, we, too, must experience the same growth in our spiritual lives. The *fullness* of His life must be "formed" in us through spiritual growth. The Scriptures clearly state that His life within us has three basic stages: 1) little children, 2) young men, and 3) fathers (1 Jn. 2:13). Our heavenly Father longs for the full stature of the mature Christ to live within us and to be revealed through us. Our growth should not stop with the babe in the manger, nor even with the young man of the carpenter shop; the Lord wants to reveal the Anointed One of the Jordan River in us!

After Jesus had been in preparation for 30 years, He came to the Jordan River where the anointing of the Son (Jn. 3:34b) descended from Heaven and remained upon Him. At that moment, Christ was revealed to Israel for the first time. In the Greek, "Christ" means "the Anointed One." Only after His anointing in the Jordan did Jesus begin to preach the gospel, because only after that could He say, "The Spirit of the Lord God is upon me; because *the Lord hath anointed me* to preach good tidings unto the meek" (Is. 61:1a). Even John the Baptist, His own cousin, did not know who the Anointed One was before this (Jn. 1:31). How could the Anointed One have been revealed to Israel if He had not yet been anointed? John said that he was sent to baptize with water because through baptism the Father was going to both anoint and reveal the Son (Jn. 1:31-33 NKJV). Although the Son was alive and being prepared on the earth, His glory was not seen in the earth until He came to the Jordan River. An awareness of these truths should help in understanding how new-born Christians can have Christ living within them from their new birth onward, even though they do not yet have the fullness of the Christ of the Jordan formed in their lives. They have the life of the One who was born into their mangers (hearts), but that life within them is under the creative hand of the Father: He is preparing them for the experience of the Jordan River, the sixth Day, and for the life and walk of the Anointed One. Since Jesus is our pattern and example, is it not reasonable to expect that every disciple who follows Him will fully experience the same things He experienced?

According to Paul, the glorious New Testament hope is precisely the fullness of Christ's life within us. "Christ in you, the hope of glory" (Col. 1:27b) is one of the principal themes in the writings of Paul. Furthermore, Paul explains to us that we hope only for those things we do not yet possess (Rom 8:24). If we already have Christ within us to the *degree* Paul refers to, then why should we still "hope" for it? In Ephesians we find two prayers of Paul, which originated from the Holy Spirit, that help us understand these truths. **The Spirit's prayers are always answered.** First, Paul prays that we would be granted a tremendous spiritual experience for a seemingly simple reason: that we might know the hope to which we have been called (Eph 1:16-18). I wonder how many Believers have actually experienced the fulfillment of Paul's prayer? His cry is this: "That…the Father of glory, may give unto you the spirit of wisdom and revelation in the knowledge of him: the eyes of your understanding being enlightened; that ye may know what is the hope of his calling…" (Eph. 1:17-18).

Maybe we are tempted to respond, "Paul, we don't really need the Lord to go to the bother of doing all these things you ask, just so we may know what our hope is. We already know what our hope is. Have you forgotten that you already told us in Colossians 1:27 that Christ in us is our hope?" This is certainly true, but too often, on every level of our spiritual lives, there is an enormous chasm between head knowledge and heartfelt conviction. Only a spiritual experience such as the one Paul prays for can bridge that chasm and change our spiritual vision and the way we walk. Head knowledge changes our doctrine and puffs us up. Spiritual understanding changes our walk and humbles us (1 Cor. 8:1).

Before we continue, I believe that a word of caution is in order here. If we have not yet experienced the fulfillment of Paul's first prayer, it will be very difficult for us to accept the things we are about to consider regarding his second prayer. Even if we accept them, we will not understand them in our spiritual man unless the eyes of our understanding have been opened, as Paul asks. Some will be tempted to compare what we are saying with their present experience, the experience of others around them, tradition, or even the experiences of past generations of wonderful saints. This is dangerous because we will be standing on a very shaky foundation if we base our doctrine and hope on man's experience or man's tradition. We *must* base our doctrine, vision, and hope on the Word of God and declare with Paul, "...let God be true, but every man a liar..." (Rom. 3:4).

I am aware that the vision I am sharing in this book is not our everyday Christian experience. Furthermore, it is possible that through the ages very few have fully entered the "rest" of God. If I allow human experience or tradition to determine my vision, I will make the same mistake God's people made when Christ came the first time. They could correctly discern that no one in their long history of wonderful saints had ever experienced the things Christ was offering them. In fact, no one had ever really entered the true rest of God (Heb. 3:10-11; 4:8; 11:39-40). Two thousand years ago, most of Israel missed the day of their visitation partly because of their tradition. Will we do the same? It seems that few have entered rest in the past, and few are entering today. That *must not* affect my doctrine. What *should* affect me directly, however, are the answers to two questions: "Will I enter that rest?" and "Will those I am responsible for enter that rest?"

Peter declares that something glorious awaits us at the end of this present age. He says that we "...are kept by the power of God through faith unto salvation ready to be revealed in the last time" (1 Pet. 1:5). Although what Peter is referring to here could include the Rapture of the Church, let's consider the possibility that it involves much more than that. The word "revealed" here is the verb of the word "apokalupsis," or "apocalypse" in English. This is the word used in Revelation 1:1 to refer to the "unveiling" of Christ's glory in the earth in the last days. Paul confirms that Christ's glory will be "revealed" *in us* (Rom. 8:18b), and that "the creation waits in eager expectation for the sons of God to be revealed" (Rom. 8:19 NIV). In these passages, Paul uses the Greek noun "apokalupsis" as well as its corresponding verb form. Linking this with Peter's declaration, we come to understand that a tremendous glory, never before seen by man, will be unveiled in *the* earth, as well as in *our* earth, "in the last time." Whatever that involves, I long to be a part of that visitation.

Few would be content to stay on Day One or Day Two if they had a revelation of the tremendous hope that awaits Believers on Day Six. If we do not receive this *revelation*, it is doubtful we will experience the *reality* of that life within us. We seldom reach a goal that we do not even know exists.

The theme of Paul's second prayer in the Book of Ephesians is that the revelation of our hope (Christ in us) would become reality in our lives. He writes, "I pray that out of his glorious riches he may strengthen you with power through his Spirit in your inner being, so that Christ may dwell in your hearts through faith" (Eph. 3:16-17a NIV). Notice the two-step process revealed here by the words "so that." If I say, "I am packing my suitcases *so that* I will be able to leave on time," it is understood that if the first action is not accomplished, I will not be able to accomplish the second. Further, the first action is done with a goal in mind. This is precisely what Paul's prayer reveals.

First the Holy Spirit must work within us to prepare Christ's dwelling place. There is a goal and purpose to His work: "*so that* Christ may dwell" within us. If we do not permit the Holy Spirit to prepare Christ's dwelling place in our earth during the first five Days, then we will never experience the glory and hope of the sixth Day—Christ in us. In our study of Day One, we found that God's work in us begins with the moving of the Holy Spirit. His work in us ends the same way; only the Spirit can bring us into the glory of the sixth Day.

In his second prayer, Paul goes on to explain what it means for Christ to dwell in our earth. This is one of the most powerful passages in the entire Bible—something that awes and humbles me every time I read it. Unfortunately, unless we have received a spiritual revelation, as Paul asks for in his first prayer, we will have scales on our eyes when we read this passage. Paul's longing is that Christ would dwell in our hearts so that we would be "filled with all the fullness of God" (Eph. 3:19 NKJV). This is an unbelievably powerful prayer, that will most surely be answered in and through the Body of Christ. We must personally believe, however, that this is possible if we are to be personally part of the fulfillment and one of the members of that glorious Church through which the fullness of God will be revealed ("unveiled") in the earth in "the last time." Few people would claim that the Church today is really filled with *all the fullness of God*. The tragedy, however, is that few people even believe that it is possible for the Body of Christ to reach that spiritual position, and fewer still are pressing toward that mark of God's high calling! Is it any wonder that we need the "eyes of our understanding" to be opened through a tremendous spiritual experience to "know what is the hope of our calling"? (Eph. 1:18)

Following his second prayer, Paul explains to the Ephesians how the Lord will accomplish His goal of bringing us into spiritual maturity. Through five God-given ministries, the Lord will bring us to the spiritual stature or height of Christ in His fullness. Paul explains that those five ministries will continue to function in the Church "till we all come...to the *measure of the stature of the fullness of Christ*; that we should no longer be children…" (Eph. 4:13-14 NKJV). So the goal is to grow out of our spiritual childhood into the maturity of Christ. The next verse confirms this goal by saying that we can actually "…grow up into him in all things, which is the head, even Christ" (Eph. 4:15). What a glorious end awaits us since fallen humanity has been given the opportunity to grow up into Christ in *all things*, not only in some things!

We need a mighty moving of the Holy Spirit in our hearts to bring us to Day Six. Jesus, as well as Paul, shows us that the Holy Spirit is sent to us *before* the fullness of the Son is placed within us. The Holy Spirit first comes to prepare us to be Christ's temple or dwelling. Jesus explains that the Holy Spirit leads us into all truth, revealing His commandments to us (Jn. 16:13). The Spirit is also the source of grace to enable us to keep those commandments (Heb. 10:29). As we have seen in our study of Day Four, if we receive and obey His commandments on Day Two (Jn. 14:21a), we then experience the love of Day Three (Jn. 14:21b) and the manifestation of the Sun (Son) during Day Four (Jn. 14:21c). Christ goes on to promise us that after this process, He will actually come and dwell within us (Jn. 14:23). Since reaching Day Six depends on the work of the Holy Spirit in us, it is no wonder that Paul exhorts us, "And do not grieve the Holy Spirit of God, by whom you were sealed for the day of redemption" (Eph. 4:30 NKJV). We desperately need His favor and approval!

The Bridegroom Awaits Our Redemption

What is Paul referring to when he says that we were "sealed" by the Holy Spirit for the day of **redemption**? (Eph. 4:30) Earlier in the same Epistle, Paul writes that we "were *sealed* with the Holy Spirit of promise, who is the guarantee [down payment] of our inheritance *until **the redemption** of the purchased possession*…" (Eph. 1:13b-14 NKJV). Surely Paul is speaking about the same Holy Spirit, the same "sealing," and the same "redemption" in both places. As several English versions bring out in their translation of this verse, *we*—God's people—are the "purchased possession" that He is redeeming.[4] For example, the New International Version translates this phrase as, "until the redemption of those who are God's possession." Therefore, the Holy Spirit is the down payment of our inheritance until God has finished His work of redemption in us.

---

4. This rendering is correct because in First Peter 2:9 (NIV) Peter tells us that we are a "people belonging to God." Here, Peter uses the same Greek word that is translated as "purchased possession" in Ephesians 1:14. Also, Paul tells us that we were "bought with a price" (1 Cor. 6:19-20). We were definitely "purchased."

For those who thought they were already redeemed, this verse may bring fresh understanding. God's redemption is a progressive work. Our total redemption will be completed only as the Holy Spirit finishes the work of all six Days of the "redemptive week" and we enter God's rest. On Day Six, we will receive the entire inheritance, which is Christ Himself formed within us. We will no longer have only the "down payment" of our inheritance—the Holy Spirit—but we will then possess the fullness of our inheritance—Christ Himself dwelling within us. Does Ephesians confirm this? Let's continue.

The inheritance that *we* have in Christ and the inheritance that *He* has in us are principal themes of Ephesians. This is the context of Ephesians 1:13-14, where Paul writes that the Holy Spirit is our down payment *until we are redeemed*. This becomes clear by comparing the verses just before and after this passage. Two verses earlier Paul explains that *we* have an inheritance in Christ (Eph. 1:11). Then, five verses later, we are told that *Christ* has an inheritance in us (Eph. 1:18b). As we have learned, this dual inheritance occurs in the marriage contract where the husband becomes the property of the wife and the wife becomes the property of the husband (1 Cor. 7:4 NIV). For this reason, Canaan (our inheritance) will be called "married" (Is. 62:4). Christ has already unconditionally given His body for His bride; now He asks us if we are willing to do the same for Him. The cross must be permitted to finish its work as we give Him our bodies as living sacrifices (Rom. 12:1). Is He worth it?

After two people become one flesh through marriage, they live in the same house. Just as Hegai prepared Esther for her wedding with the king, giving her everything she needed to be ready, so the Holy Spirit is preparing us to become one flesh with the King of kings (Esther 2:8-9,12). This is precisely the desire that Paul expresses in his second prayer in Ephesians. He prays that the Holy Spirit would prepare the Lord's dwelling place by spiritually strengthening our inner man, with the goal that Christ would dwell within us (Eph. 3:16-17). Paul is not asking that a little of what Christ is would dwell within us. No, he asks that we would be "filled with all the fullness of God" (Eph. 3:19 NKJV). The final result is found in Ephesians 5:29-32, where we become bone of His bone and flesh of His flesh. This marriage will occur only when we, the "purchased possession," have been fully redeemed. The cross brings redemption to every area of fallen man—spirit, soul, and body. The Bridegroom awaits the full redemption of His Bride!

Let us remember, however, that Christ will never marry the old sinful nature that lives within us. That nature must die. There must be a death and a resurrection in our lives. For that reason, Paul, in his first prayer in

Ephesians, requests that we understand two things: 1) that our hope is Christ in us, and 2) that this hope will be fulfilled in us through the same power of God that raised Christ from the dead and will also raise us from the dead (Eph. 1:19-20; 2:4-6). Neither will Christ marry children. We must grow up in Him, as Ephesians 4:11-15 explains. This spiritual growth takes place throughout the "redemptive week" when what we are continually decreases and what He is increases within us.

The Apostle Paul expresses this same thought with different words in Romans 8:19, "The creation waits in eager expectation for the sons of God to be revealed" (NIV). These sons are children who have grown up. The Greek word Paul uses in Romans 8:19 is "huios"; it refers to mature sons.[5] They are no longer "little children" for whom Paul travails until Christ be formed in them. Paul goes on to explain that they are sons who have been "...conformed to the likeness of his Son, that he might be the firstborn among many brothers" (Rom. 8:29 NIV). This is an awesome truth. Achieving spiritual maturity, or the fullness of Christ's life being formed in our earth, was precisely Paul's desire and burden for the entire Church. He expressed that desire to the Galatians for whom he was travailing (Gal. 4:19). This was God's goal from the beginning as seen in the sixth Day. The Creator desires to place the man in God's image—the last Adam—in our spiritual earth just as He placed the first Adam in the natural earth. What, then, does travail have to do with reaching that goal? We will find that answer in the next chapter.

---

5. Note that Jesus uses *huios* in Matthew 5:9,44-45. He tells us that we will be "sons" (*huios*) of **our Father** (NIV, NKJV, ASV, RSV) if we are peacemakers and if we pray for those who despitefully use us. If He is already "our Father," then we are already His children (*teknones* in the Greek); but we will only be **mature** sons or "huios" if we have the character to pray for those who mistreat us. This is not the nature or character of little children. For further insights on the New Testament usage of "huios," refer to Vine, *An Expository Dictionary of New Testament Words.* See "son."

Chapter 15

Spiritual Travail

Let's return to the story about the early Church with which we began the last Chapter so that we can get the rest of the story. The following conversation cannot be documented, but something very similar was surely spoken.

"Peter, what are we going to do?"

Peter responds, "I don't know, John, but do you remember how we all argued among ourselves about who was the greatest? I will never forget how our beloved Master was the only One who was willing to stoop and wash the feet of everyone. He had nothing to lose. He was the King. He knew His calling, and He knew that no one's opinion could affect that. We were all struggling to be something we weren't, so we couldn't afford to humble ourselves and serve. He not only washed our feet, but He humbled Himself beyond comprehension and went to the cross for us. John, wasn't it wonderful how our hearts burned when we were with Him?"

"Yes," John answers, through tears, "and I also remember how many times we wept with joy when He gave hope to the hopeless, sight to the blind, strength to the weak, and even life to the dead. Wasn't that a glorious day when we just happened to arrive at Nain in time to stop the funeral procession of the only son of that poor old widow? What compassion our Lord revealed to her by raising him from the dead! Now those glorious days are forever past—just a wonderful memory. No one else will ever see or hear what we have witnessed. Imagine, Peter, how many hurting hearts there are in this world that will never receive a touch from that gentle hand? But maybe now that hope is gone, it's better that they never even find out that there once was hope. What are we going to do, Peter?"

Almost unconsciously, Peter turns and looks toward Jerusalem. From the heights of the Mount of Olives, he can see where the upper room is. A few moments ago, his Lord and Master ascended into Heaven in a cloud. It seems that there is nothing more to live for. How can he possibly be happy fishing again? How can he forget the Lord's glory? And, how can he forget the multitudes of hopeless faces that he had seen filled with joy by the light of the Savior's countenance? An ever greater agony—how can he blot out the far greater multitude of hopeless faces that now would never be touched by that glory? Peter, lost in his thoughts, murmurs to himself, "Only a short time ago, the Greeks came and implored, 'Sir, we would see Jesus.' How tragic! They will *never* see Him now. Only *we* know what they have missed!"

Realizing that John is behind him waiting for an answer to his question, Peter looks again toward the upper room and whispers with a broken heart, "I don't know, John. But I *do* know that it no longer matters to me who is the greatest. In fact, I only wish that *someone*, maybe even *you*, could reveal just a few drops of the glory we have bathed in daily. I would so gladly wash that person's feet. I would so gladly be a servant to *anyone* for the joy of once again seeing a little of the fullness we have witnessed. I don't know what to do, but I have a longing to return to that upper room and pour out my heart before Him in prayer...and to serve."

That is exactly what they did. The same disciples who couldn't pray with Jesus in the garden for one hour spent the next ten days praying, weeping, waiting, and meditating—meditating on what their master had told them. Jesus had said that it was best for them that He was going away (Jn. 16:7), but they couldn't understand how His leaving to go to the Father would help them see Him again in a little while (Jn. 16:16). When they had asked Jesus to explain this mystery, He had told them that they would experience travail like that of a woman giving birth. He had also assured them that a travailing woman ends up with great joy because of the life that is birthed, and that the same thing would happen to them (Jn. 16:20-22).

At least they could now understand what He had meant by "sorrow." In fact, they even began to understand what He had meant by "travail." There were times when their burden for the lost, the sick, the dying, and the hopeless multitudes caused them to intercede with such fervency that it was actually like the travail of a woman giving birth. The travail was even more acute when they remembered how glorious *He* was and how carnal *they* were, and when they compared the spiritual riches He shared so freely with others with their own spiritual poverty. This caused groanings that could not be uttered. Some time passed before they fully understood Jesus' riddle—that they, just like a woman, were in fact giving birth to a new life! Yes, they had been born again themselves; but now, as they entered spiritual maturity, they were birthing into the world a spiritual life they never thought could possibly be revealed through them. It was the very life of their beloved Shepherd! Indeed, they were seeing Him again—in His Body of Believers. Finally, they could understand what He had meant when He said that they would not see Him again until they would see and recognize Him in those who would be sent by Him (Mt. 23:39).

Paul referred to this travail of the early Church when he wrote to the Galatian Christians, "My little children, of whom I travail in birth again until Christ be formed in you" (Gal. 4:19). The phrase "travail in birth" is really only one Greek word, which means to feel the pains of childbirth. Obviously, Paul was referring to a spiritual travail that is frequently referred to throughout the Old and New Testament. We know that **travail involves great pain and suffering**. Paul experienced an abundance of this travail for God's people. As a result, he also became the channel through which God answered the cry of the Greeks: "Sir, we would see Jesus" (Jn. 12:21b). A few years after the cross, the Greeks did, in fact, see the Lord—through Paul!

Besides involving pain and affliction, there is an additional aspect to spiritual travail. In Romans 8:22-27, we discover the nature of this spiritual travail: "For we know that *the whole creation groaneth and travaileth in pain* together until now. And not only they, but ourselves also, which have the firstfruits of the Spirit, even *we ourselves groan within ourselves*, waiting for the adoption, to wit, the redemption of our body. For we are saved by hope: but hope that is seen is not hope: for what a man seeth, why doth he yet hope for? But if we hope for that we see not, then do we with patience wait for it. *Likewise the Spirit* also helpeth our infirmities: for we know not what we should *pray* for as we ought: but the Spirit itself *maketh intercession* for us *with groanings* which cannot be uttered...**because he maketh intercession for the saints** according to the will of God."[1]

This is truly an amazing passage of Scripture. Once again, the context of this passage is the "hope" of Christ being formed in us. Here, as in Galatians 4:19, Paul links the fulfillment of this hope with travail. In this passage from Romans, however, we learn what spiritual travail involves.

---

1. Note here that once again the New Testament Scriptures compare the earth of the Creation with our earth or spiritual life. Paul says that just as the "whole creation" groans in travail, so we also groan in travail.

Travail in our natural lives is generally accompanied by groanings. Paul refers to this travail and groanings and declares that we are groaning for the fulfillment of our hope if we have the "firstfruits of the Spirit." Then, to clarify what this means, he tells us that the Spirit likewise makes *intercession* for us, along with those same *groanings*. Thus, Paul links *travail with intercession*. Many saints have experienced the spiritual birth pains of deep prayer and intercession accompanied by unutterable groanings. These pains may become so intense that they almost become physical as the heart cries out to God under a burden of intercession that only the Spirit of God Himself can produce in us.

Facts Concerning Travail

Four important facts regarding natural travail should be understood here, since they find a direct correlation to spiritual travail.

1. No woman has yet travailed for herself. The agony and extreme cost of her travail are experienced for another—for the little one who is being born.

2. In the normal course of events, travail is the only way to bring forth new life to the world (Gen. 3:16).

3. Travail is not something a woman *chooses* to have. It *comes* upon her (1 Thess. 5:3b). Often it comes at a very inconvenient time and with surprising rapidity. Travail is actually induced in a pregnant woman as a result of a complex relationship between chemical agents that are injected into her bloodstream by both the baby and the mother when it is time for the baby to be birthed.[2]

4. Travail is inescapable (1 Thess. 5:3c). The new life within her *must* come forth, and the cost will definitely involve pain and groanings. If a woman could escape travail by stopping it, many women would understandably do so when the pain became unbearable. This, of course, would produce death for both her and the new life within her.

1. Travail Is Never for Ourselves

During the Lord's last week on earth, He surely was more aware than ever that He was facing the greatest battle that any human being had ever faced. His battle was not with the religious leaders of Israel, but with all the forces of hell that were arrayed against Him. He was fighting for the

---

2.   Niels Lauersen, M.D., Ph.D., *It's Your Pregnancy* (New York: Simon and Schuster, 1987), p. 364.

eternal destiny of mankind, not for His own life. We cannot begin to imagine the spiritual and emotional pressures He felt as the last few days of His life slipped away.

What would we have done if we had been in His place? We probably would have gathered the disciples around us and pleaded, "In a few days my life on earth will be over. I will be beaten and crucified. I will feel the full weight of the world's sins and will bear the punishment for sins that each of you deserves. Would you brethren just lay your hands on me and pray for me? I am really feeling the pressure of what I am facing, and I need you to stand with me." Far from doing that, the Lord spent His last days encouraging them, instructing them, praying for them, and counseling them. His travail was for others, not for Himself. So it is today, as He continually intercedes for *us*, just as the Holy Spirit does (Heb. 7:25; Rom. 8:26-27).

Paul also travailed for Israel with total selflessness and such an unbearable agony in his spirit that he actually "wished" he be separated from Christ and accursed if that would result in the salvation of Israel (Rom. 9:2-3). The word translated as "accursed" in the King James Version actually means both "separated" and "accursed." Paul testified that he had "great heaviness and continual sorrow" in his heart for them. Sorrow here means "consuming grief or pain;" in the Greek it is closely related to the word travail (*Strong's Greek Dictionary*, #3601, #5605, and #5604). Imagine the supernatural spiritual travail for others that Paul experienced here. The love of God so consumed him that he would have willingly laid down his own spiritual life for them! If that seems foreign to us, maybe we are still too involved in our own struggle to get ahead, too wrapped up in "number one," too centered in ourselves, to be able to comprehend the travail of the Spirit.

Moses came to this same place of total selflessness that Paul knew. He travailed (interceded) for Israel, "Lord, please forgive their sin—but if for any reason You are unwilling or unable to forgive this great sin, and if punishment must be meted out and a sentence executed, then let that punishment fall on me—let my name be blotted out of the book of life" (Ex. 32:31-32 paraphrased).

Did not Christ die in our place? Does not Moses reveal a heart that has been filled with the love of Christ? Is it not possible to love as Christ loved when He gave His life? If it is possible for the fullness of Christ's life to be formed within us, then it is possible for Him to love through us with the depths of love that only He knows. The Spirit-inspired prayer of Paul for the Body of Christ is that we would "know the love of Christ which passes knowledge" and "be filled with all the fullness of God" (Eph. 3:19 NKJV).

It is possible to love as He loved if we can *really* be "conformed to the likeness of [the] Son" as the Scripture promises us (Rom. 8:29 NIV). Oh, the rest that will be ours when our strength is no longer spent on concern and love for ourselves! This sixth step is essential for us to enter that rest.

2. New Life Can Come Only Through Travail

When it is time for the Lord to bring new life and a new day to His people, He does so through spiritual travail or intercession. Many biblical examples bear this out, of which Abraham is one. Right after the Lord announced to him that the long awaited son, Isaac, would be born, Abraham experienced a powerful ministry of intercession (or spiritual travail) for the sake of another—Lot. Abraham interceded before the Lord that the righteous would be spared in the overthrow of Sodom and Gomorrah (Gen. 18:10,20-33). God spared Lot because of Abraham's love for others (Gen. 19:29).

What if Abraham had not interceded for Lot? A new life for Lot and his children probably would not have been granted. An even greater tragedy may have befallen Abraham and the world. Most likely he would still have given birth to the new life he named "Isaac," but he may have missed the higher calling of God. For the sake of Abraham's eternal destiny and that of all mankind, God wanted Abraham to become more than the source of Isaac's life. God also wanted Abraham to become the source and channel for another life—the life of the Christ from Heaven, the One who so loves others that He continually gives Himself for them. What if the selfless life of Christ had not been birthed in Abraham through intercession for Lot? He might still have birthed Isaac, but would he have been capable of birthing the spiritual life and values in his son that would qualify Isaac to become a patriarch in the messianic line?

Abraham's intercession was for something far greater than the salvation of Lot. Surely, without his being aware of it at the time, Abraham interceded for the salvation of the world because his intercession prepared him to become a channel for the love and life of Christ in the earth. He not only imparted natural life to his son, Isaac, but also spiritual life. That life continued to flow through his descendants until they gave birth to the Savior who saved us all from our spiritual Sodom and Gomorrah. As in the life of Abraham, Christ's life can be formed in us only as we learn to intercede for others. The nature of the great intercessor is to give Himself to intercession for His people. Therefore, God can fill us with the fullness of what He is only when we allow Him to do in and through us what He loves to do—carry the burdens of others.

Later in Israel's history when it was time for God to send a fresh visitation and usher in a new era, spiritual travail or intercession also birthed that era. The time came when Israel was not to be ruled by judges any longer, but rather by kings. Samuel, a man who experienced God's mighty anointing on his own life, was the vessel God used to bring about that change and to anoint the first two kings. We must remember Samuel's origin. His mother was Hannah, a woman who interceded mightily with a heavy spiritual burden. We are told that "she was in bitterness of soul, and prayed unto the Lord, and wept sore" (1 Sam. 1:10). Hannah had wept for years over her barrenness. Finally, the Lord heard the cry of her spiritual travail and gave her a son, Samuel, through whom she became a channel for the new life that would usher in a new day for God's people.

How concerned are you about the spiritual barrenness around you and within you? Does the lack of Christ's fullness in your life, in the Church, and in the world, concern you enough to weep as Hannah wept? Maybe you are expending great effort to be fruitful in God's Kingdom by bringing souls to Christ. Clearly, that is an important work, but what kind of an atmosphere will your spiritual children encounter in the Church? Will their hearts be moved to run after God as they are immersed in the unselfish and loving care of people who manifest the meekness and humility of the Lamb? Or will they find themselves embroiled in division, strife, envy, carnal ambition, and many other manifestations of the flesh? Is it not safe to say that, in many ways with regard to the fruits of the Spirit, we are an unfruitful and barren people? Are we concerned enough about the condition of the Body of Christ to travail before the Lord, pleading that His life would be revealed in the earth? Let's pray individually, "Lord, let that travail come upon me!"

More than 1,000 years after Hannah's travail and the new day it brought, Israel's spiritual condition was such that she was in desperate need of another visitation from Heaven. Four hundred years had passed since the days of Malachi when the last prophetic message had been recorded in Israel. Suddenly, the greatest prophet of all time came crying in the wilderness, "Prepare ye the way of the Lord, make His paths straight" (Mt. 3:3; see also verses 1-5). John the Baptist was speaking under such a powerful anointing that the entire nation went out into the wilderness to hear him preach. Once again it was a new day. Few in Israel had any idea just how new this day really was. They were privileged to witness not only another visitation of God, but *the* visitation that men of faith had awaited for many years. The Messiah was coming, and the New Testament age was beginning! Did this new day, and the new life it brought, also begin with the travail of prayer and intercession?

Yes. The New Testament age began at the altar of incense, the sixth step in the Tabernacle of Moses. Incense was placed upon the fire of that altar daily. This incense was symbolic of the prayer of intercession offered by the power of the Spirit of God (Ps. 141:2; Rev. 8:3). When it was time for Christ, the last Adam, to come, the first event that led up to His coming is recorded in Luke 1. The priest Zacharias was in the Temple burning incense while the people were praying (Lk. 1:5-10).[3] There is nothing surprising about this biblical detail because new life is always brought forth by the same means—travail, which is prayer or intercession. Gabriel appeared at the altar and announced that John the Baptist's ministry would prepare Israel for the glory of the Messiah and thereby usher in a new age—the age of grace. It all started at the altar of incense, to where we, too, must come today. Are we hungry enough to travail? Do we so long for Him to fill our earth with His glory that we are willing to spend time burning spiritual incense on the spiritual altar of our temples so that He will be manifested in a mighty way in our spiritual earth?

Through her spiritual travail, Mary also became a channel through which the fullness of Christ was revealed in the earth. The angel Gabriel also appeared to her in preparation for the coming of the last Adam to this earth. When he announced to her that the Messiah would be born through her, she asked, "How shall this be, seeing I know not a man?" (Lk. 1:34) She did not understand what would cause the conception and travail needed to birth the Son.

The angel answered her question by turning her vision toward the heavenly Bridegroom who awaited her in the chambers of the King. She would most definitely conceive and experience travail, but not through natural means, nor would her travail be only natural. Mary was destined to experience spiritual travail before the travail of her natural delivery. Gabriel explains, "The **Holy Spirit** will come upon you, and **the power of the Highest will overshadow you**; therefore, also, that Holy One who is to be born will be called the Son of God" (Lk. 1:35 NKJV). In other words, Mary was going to enter God's secret place and find herself under the shadow of the Almighty, the place the psalmist discovered: "He that dwelleth in the *secret place* of the most High shall abide under *the shadow of the Almighty*" (Ps. 91:1). From the Song of Solomon, a book that reveals the details of an intimate love relationship, we discover what happened to Mary when the Highest *overshadowed* her. There, the bride declares to her

---

3.   At the time of Zacharias, the altar of incense was in the Temple in Jerusalem. This does not change the significance of this altar because the same seven steps are found in the Temple that are found in the Tabernacle of Moses. See footnote #1 in Chapter 3.

lover, "As the apple-tree among the trees of the wood, so is my beloved among the sons. I sat down under his *shadow* with great delight, and his fruit was sweet to my taste" (Song 2:3 ASV). Later, in this love story, when the marriage has been consummated, a voice declares, "Under the apple-tree I awakened thee: there thy mother was in travail with thee. There was she in travail that brought thee forth" (Song 8:5b ASV). Spiritual travail or intercession takes place as we come under the shadow of the apple tree—under the shadow of God's presence. On each occasion that Mary spent time in the chambers of love with the King, she became more aware that something of the divine life had been deposited within her, and she would never again be the same. In the secret place with Him, His life is deposited within us and brought forth through us as we travail under the burden of intercession that only the Holy Spirit can give. She had surely interceded that new life would come to her people, and it did—through her! We can only speculate concerning the glorious times of intercession that Mary experienced as the shadow of the apple tree covered her. Speculation will be replaced by personal testimony when the Lord allows us to experience the same intimacy in our own lives as we come to Day Six. Lord, grant us that place in Your presence!

A few years after Mary had travailed to bring Christ to the earth in a physical way, a group of people experienced travail to bring Him to the earth in a spiritual way. Mary was one of them. She knew what was needed. The outpouring of the Holy Spirit in Acts 2 sprang out of the intercessory travail of the upper room: "Then they returned to Jerusalem from the mount called Olivet...And when they had entered [Jerusalem], they went up into the upper room where they were staying: Peter, James, John, and Andrew; Philip and Thomas; Bartholomew and Matthew; James the son of Alphaeus and Simon the Zealot; and Judas the son of James. These all continued with one accord **in prayer and supplication**, with the women and Mary the mother of Jesus, and with His brothers" (Acts 1:12-14 NKJV).

Today, it is time for new life to come forth once again in the earth. Joel 2 and Acts 2 both promise that in the last days there will be a mighty manifestation of God's glory in the earth. As we have seen, Peter refers to it as an "unveiling in the last time" (1 Pet. 1:5). As in past visitations, we can be sure that travail will precede God's last-day visitation and actually cause it to be brought forth. This fact might give us a clue to why a woman is seen travailing in the last days in Revelation 12:1-2.[4] How else do we expect new life to be brought forth in our day?

---

4. For the Scriptural reasons why we know she is the Church in the last days, see Marvin Byers, *The Final Victory: The Year 2000*, Second Edition, (Shippensburg, PA: Treasure House, 1994), pp. 96-99.

Regardless of what we believe about the woman of Revelation 12, Isaiah and Paul assure us that the Church will most certainly travail in these last days. Isaiah reveals a woman whose husband is "the Lord of hosts" (Is. 54:5). Paul and the New Testament interpret this woman to be the Church or heavenly Jerusalem.[5] Isaiah 54:13-14 tells us that the day will come when this woman will be "far from oppression" and her children will experience great peace. We know that this day is near at hand. Only the coming of the Lord can totally fulfill this promise. Just before this occurs, the woman will pass through a time of great suffering and pain when the Lord hides His face from her. The Lord likens this experience of the last days to what happened in the days of Noah (Is. 54:6-9; Mt. 24:37-39). Therefore, Isaiah is assuring us that a time of anguish and the pain of travail is at hand for the Church.

Just as the Church began with the deep sorrow associated with great spiritual travail, so the Church will end. That travail will cause the light of God's glory to shine through the Church (Is. 62:1-3). That same travail will cause Jerusalem to bring forth many mature sons (Is. 66:8-10). In the last days, the Church will travail neither for its own benefit nor to be saved from tribulation. Like the early Church, the last-day Church will also travail to bring forth the life of Christ that will meet the great spiritual need in the lives of men. Like Abraham, the Church will travail in intercession so that others, not itself, will be saved from the city of destruction. Again, like Paul, Moses, and Christ, the Church will be willing to give its very life so that others might be saved. Do you long for that purity of heart and motives in your own life? God offers it to those who will believe and receive.

3. Travail Is Induced

Often the world mocks and ridicules the Church for its lack of uprightness and purity. We have witnessed the tragic fall of some of the Church's mighty men, and the world has concluded that the Church preaches one message but secretly lives another. Sadly, the world is a witness to the fact that many of the Church's leaders manifest more interest in the money of their listeners than in their eternal souls. These leaders plead for finances like some of the great preachers of past generations pleaded with people about their souls. Is it possible that we are in many ways suffering the reproach of our own fleshly ways, and not the reproach of Christ? The fleshly life is ugly and it leaves a stench; the Spirit-filled, Spirit-led life brings a sweet fragrance to all who are touched by it. Isaiah speaks about the judgment God will bring upon the leaders of His own people

---

5. Compare Isaiah 54:1 with Galatians 4:26-27 and Hebrews 12:22-23.

because they crush and plunder God's people for their own financial gain (Is. 3:14-15 NKJV). He laments that the leaders are spiritual children who lead God's people into error and destroy the divine path for their lives (Is. 3:12). Undaunted by the destruction they are causing, the leaders walk in pride, certain that they are God's answer for the world, and draw attention to their supposedly beautiful spiritual walk (Is. 3:16). Precisely because of these things Isaiah forewarns, "And so it shall be: Instead of a sweet smell there will be a stench" (Is. 3:24a NKJV). The whole world can smell that stench today, and they therefore reject the Church.

The spiritual travail that can change all this by bringing forth the Lord's life will definitely come upon us in God's divine time, whether it is convenient for us or not. We cannot choose to have this experience when it suits us, or when it best fits into our schedule. However, both the mother and the new life within her play a role for travail to be induced. This happens when the new life in her has been fully formed, and she is unable to keep it within, limiting its manifestation and expression.

In the same way, the Church needs to experience the injection of a mighty motivating agent from Christ Himself into its spiritual bloodstream. However, the Church has a role to play to bring on travail. We desperately need to come before God and ask Him to help us feel the same urgency that is in His heart to bring new life to the earth. We need to plead, "Lord, pour upon us 'the spirit of grace and of supplications' " (Zech. 12:10). We cannot continue to keep His life to ourselves. Have we heard the cry of the Gentiles, "Sir, we would see Jesus"? If we really hear that cry in the depths of our spirits, it will become a mighty motivation to travail. We will find ourselves weeping before the Lord for others, whether it fits into our schedule or not!

In many cases, the world has not rejected the Lord. They have not yet had the opportunity to reject Him because they have not yet seen or heard from Him. They have only heard from lukewarm Christians who preach a watered-down message that comes from a half-hearted commitment. Some of us may believe that our lives are better than this evaluation. If we feel this way, we need to compare ourselves with the life and commitment of the Lord Jesus Christ instead of comparing ourselves with Christians who are less committed than we are! I am not pointing the finger; I am including myself in this sickly body of Believers. I recognize that, in many ways, we are all the spiritual product of the Church that exists today. However, God *can* and *will* bring a change to those who long for it enough to seek it.

Multitudes have rejected a so-called "gospel" message that is based on head knowledge rather than on a relationship with the living Lord. They have rejected the preaching of theology and theory. Oh, how they need to hear a word that comes directly from the heart of God through messengers who dwell in the secret place of the Most High, travailing in the closet of prayer. They need to hear a word that is so saturated with His presence that it causes their hearts to burn and their spirits to cry out, "Men and brethren, what shall we do [to be saved]?" (Acts 2:37c) They urgently need to see Jesus living in the lives of men and women who are so consumed with holy conviction and holy living that those around them become convinced of their need of a Savior. Until this happens, we cannot accuse the world of having rejected the Lord. They have only rejected *us*!

Does your heart break with a burden of spiritual travail because of the cry of the Gentiles? Can you hear its echo throughout the earth, coming from millions of searching, hungry hearts? Will you allow God to open your ears to hear that cry and to open your eyes to see your own condition and inability to answer that cry? The world will be drawn to the Lord through a life that reveals the reality of the cross through selflessness and self-denial. If we *live and preach* Christ crucified, all men will be drawn to Him (Jn. 12:32-33; 1 Cor. 2:2). Is this message too costly? The cost of saving souls has always been very high. In fact, for the Father, the price was infinite. He gave the pearl of greatest price—His own Son. For Jesus, it cost Him His own life. Paul, too, suffered the loss of everything (2 Cor. 11:23-28; Phil. 2:17; 3:8). In your estimation, is the eternal reward worth the price?

4. Travail Is Inescapable

The odds of survival were infinitesimal for the four women, a few young children, and some servants. They were facing 400 armed men led by a very angry and vindictive man. That man had waited a long time for this opportunity. His day had finally come. He would kill every one of them just to get even. Jacob didn't have much of a choice. It was either wrestle with God until God heard his cry and intervened, or watch everyone around him die at the hand of Esau. Whether or not it would require a whole night of travail for Jacob to become a channel for God's salvation didn't matter in light of the stakes that were involved and the options that were left to him. For Jacob, spiritual travail was totally inescapable that night.

A few years later Jacob's family faced odds that were even less favorable for survival than what they had confronted with Esau. Through subtlety, Levi and Simeon had just managed to kill all the men of an entire town in the land of Canaan. They had wrought this brutal vengeance for the moral defilement of their sister, Dinah, by one of the young men of that town (Gen. 34). Jacob and his family were strangers in Canaan. No one knew them very well. Through this event, they earned a reputation of being such dangerous men that no other city or village of Canaan would be safe as long as they were permitted to live. This presented no great problem for the inhabitants of Canaan. All they had to do was send out a small army, search for Jacob and his family, and kill them all. For Jacob, spiritual travail was once again inescapable. The only hope of survival was to go to Bethel and intercede for God's protection and mercy on the family.

Have your eyes been opened to see what the chances of survival are for the people around you? Does it matter to you that many of them will almost certainly spend eternity in the lake of fire, the second death? For those whose spiritual vision is capable of seeing this reality, spiritual travail is inescapable. As happened to Jacob, we will experience times when the burden is so great, and the concern for others so overwhelming, that sleep will elude us. We will find ourselves wrestling with God for the sake of others. Inescapable travail is part of the message we receive from the life of Jacob. Jacob discovered that something happens within us as we travail. Chapter 16 reveals Jacob's discovery.

Chapter 16

Jacob Travails and Receives a New Name

Jacob's life reveals the glory of the sixth Day of Creation and shows us how to enter it. We should expect this since he is the sixth man of faith in Genesis. As we have seen, on the sixth Day a man in God's own likeness and image is manifested in our earth. Consider how this actually happened in Jacob's life. During Jacob's wrestlings with God, his name was changed from Jacob, "supplanter," to Israel, "prince of God" (Gen. 32:24-28). Throughout the Scriptures, names have been used to reveal the character of the people who bore those names. When Jacob's name was changed to Israel, we understand that his new name revealed a new character that had been formed in him. Does this mean that Jacob himself had been changed? Is God in the business of changing us? If your answer is yes, you need to carefully consider the following point. It may bring you a new freedom from condemnation. God has no interest whatsoever in changing *what we are*. He wants to kill, or crucify, what we are so that *what He is* can live in and through us. Let me share an experience with you that taught me this lesson.

Some years ago, I was filled with remorse as I reflected back on how hard I had been on my young wife during the early years of our marriage. By reason of God's grace on her life, she endured and the marriage survived. A few years later, I began to rejoice before the Lord knowing that He had made major changes in my life, changes that had greatly improved our marriage. I rejoiced even more when I began to think how our home would be after another 20 years of changes. As I thanked Him for that wonderful hope, He spoke to me very clearly, "There is no hope for you." I was devastated. I asked, "Lord, do You mean that I will not finish my life with Your blessing? Do You mean that I will become a spiritual shipwreck and not finish my course?" In His kindness the Lord explained, "Your old man is the very body of sin. I am not trying to improve sin. I am trying to kill it so that My life, which is perfect, can live in and through you" (Rom. 6:6-9; Gal. 2:20).

This understanding brought even more joy than I had known before. I suddenly understood that what *I* am will never change, but there is a glorious hope that I will decrease so He can increase! (Jn. 3:30) I need not make excuses for what I am or what I do. I need only to repent and recognize that I must receive more grace to deny myself, embrace the cross, and die.

When we fail in some area, we often begin to make excuses for ourselves. We think in our hearts, or even express with our mouths, something like this: "But you don't understand. I am not that way. I don't know why I did what I did, but I am simply not that kind of a person. It was just a one-time slip. If you knew me better, you would know that I am not that way." On and on we go. The truth is, if we knew ourselves better, we would realize that we are capable of far worse! What we call a "one-time slip" is, in fact, exactly what our old nature is like. If we don't repeat the same thing, or something worse, it is only because of God's mercy. When we fail in any way, the correct reaction should be, "Lord, You see what I am. I ask You to forgive me and give me the grace I need to crucify my flesh with its affections and lusts. Thank You for being willing to live Your life in and through me" (Gal. 5:24). This understanding can set us free both from condemnation when we fail and from pride when we succeed. Anything good in me comes from Him (Rom. 7:18).

No, Jacob's character had not been **changed**; the man who was living in Jacob's tabernacle (body) had been **replaced**. The old man, Jacob, had decreased, and the new man, Christ, had increased within Jacob and had taken control of his life. We know that this really happened in Jacob's life for two reasons. First, his name became "Israel." Israel is one of more than 700 names of the Lord that are found in the Bible. "When Israel was a child, then I loved him, and called my son out of Egypt" (Hos. 11:1). Matthew 2:15 tells us that this Son, whose name is Israel, is really the Lord Himself. In Isaiah 49:1-3,6, "Israel" is the name of the servant who glorifies God and becomes the salvation of the nations. In this passage we discover that "Israel" is both a nation and one of the names of the Lord. With this understanding, we can appreciate what the Lord means when He speaks directly to "Israel," promising to gather them from among the nations of the earth. He assures them, "I will say to the north, Give up; and to the south, Keep not back: bring my sons from far, and my daughters from the ends of the earth; **even every one that is called by my name**" (Is. 43:6-7a). Should it seem strange that we are called by the Lord's name, when, in fact, the wife traditionally carries her husband's name? Jacob was now called by the Lord's name because the Lord lived within him.

There is a second reason we know Jacob had been filled with the life of Christ. Jacob's experience the morning after he had wrestled with God all night in spiritual travail hints at what had really taken place in Jacob's spiritual earth. There are no unimportant details in God's Word; therefore, it is extremely significant that, concerning the dawn of that new day, we are told, "And as he passed over Penuel the sun rose upon him, and he halted upon his thigh" (Gen. 32:31). The Sun of righteousness, Christ, was shining on Jacob's face because the Lord had been formed in his life. Also, Jacob's thigh had been weakened—he now limped. Jacob could no longer trust his own thigh, the strongest part in the human body. Jacob's strength had been replaced by the strength of the Lord, in whom he had learned to trust. Afterwards, we find Jacob leaning on his staff because he needed support (Heb. 11:21). This is also what happened to the one who travailed under the shadow of the apple tree in the Song of Solomon—she came out of the wilderness "leaning upon her Beloved" (Song 8:5). We will not come out of our spiritual wilderness and finish the journey from Egypt to Canaan unless we, too, learn to lean on the Lord instead of leaning on our own strength and understanding.

Jacob, the sixth man, not only reveals what is involved on the sixth Day—a new man is formed in us—but he also reveals the path that leads us into that sixth Day. One of the outstanding characteristics of Jacob's life is spiritual travail or intercessory prayer. His spiritual struggle with the Lord was what the Prophet Hosea recalled 1,100 years after Jacob's death: "Yes, he struggled with the Angel and prevailed; he wept, and sought favor from Him. *He found Him in Bethel...*" (Hos. 12:4 NKJV). We remember Jacob for this even today. Jacob knew how to wrestle with God; he knew how to intercede. His intercession identifies him, the sixth man of faith, with the altar of incense, the sixth step in the Tabernacle.

Jacob found God in Bethel. Of the ten times that Bethel is mentioned in Genesis, eight of them have to do with Jacob. Bethel is definitely one of the most important places in Jacob's life story. On his journey to Uncle Laban's, Jacob met with God in Bethel when he saw the ladder that reached to Heaven. When the Lord told him to leave Laban's, the Lord called Himself "the God of Bethel" (Gen. 31:13), in other words, the God who had met with him at Bethel. Later, the Lord commanded him to return to Bethel and dwell there after two of his sons had killed the Shechemites (Gen. 35:1).

What does "Bethel" have to do with the sixth man of faith and the sixth step? *Bethel* means the "house of God" in Hebrew, and God's house is called "a house of prayer" (Is. 56:7). Jacob's wrestling in prayer and intercession is clearly a key truth in his life, intimately linking him with the altar of incense, the sixth step. He was a man of spiritual travail who brought forth a new life.

Consider the Lord's Needlework

Spiritual travail, affliction, the embracing of the cross, and the price that must be paid for Christ's life to be formed in us are all interrelated like threads in needlework. The way the Spirit has interwoven these glorious, but costly, threads of truth into the sixth step of the "redemptive week" is awesome. This tapestry provides us with a beautiful and clear message from God's heart. We already saw that the sixth step in the Tabernacle is the altar of incense, a symbol of the *travail of intercession* that causes Christ's life to be formed in us. A second aspect of spiritual travail is the *travail of affliction*, which is also unavoidable if we are ever to be *fully* conformed to the image and likeness of Christ. For those who have seen the glory of the Beloved and who love what He is, the price is not too high. What is that price?

The price of being like Christ is simply to be like Christ. If we want to live like He lived and do the things He did, we cannot be selective in deciding which facets of His life we want to imitate. Yes, Christ came with a mighty revelation of divine power and authority to raise the dead, cleanse the leper, and preach the gospel, but He also came as "a man of sorrows, and *familiar with suffering*" (Is. 53:3 NIV). Being conformed to Christ's image and having His glory in our earth on the sixth Day are blessings that will cost us something—the sorrow and suffering of many bitter experiences. Without the travail of affliction, His life will not come forth in and through us. Let's keep in mind, "to the hungry soul, every bitter thing is sweet" (Prov. 27:7b). If we are hungry for the Lord, our bitter experiences become "sweet" because they cause more of His life to be formed in us! No one is born with such hunger for the glory of Christ's life to be formed in him that he considers the bitter aspects of Christ's life to be sweet or, as Paul considered them, "light afflictions" (2 Cor. 4:17). Ask the Lord to create in you more hunger for Him so that you will be privileged to reach the sixth Day and the "exceeding and eternal weight of glory" that Paul declares those "light afflictions" will produce.

The flesh considers the suffering and afflictions of Christ to be an extremely high price to pay because, like Israel's flesh during their wilderness journey, it does not want to die. Yet, the old generation in the wilderness *did* die, and a new generation symbolic of the new man in us *did* come forth during that 40-year journey. In fact, Israel experienced so much suffering and affliction in the wilderness as God *lovingly* dealt death-blows to their fleshly ways that God gave them a sixth feast precisely to commemorate their affliction during those years. He commands them, "And thou shalt remember all the way which the Lord thy God led thee these forty years in the wilderness, to humble thee...he humbled thee, and suffered thee to hunger..." (Deut. 8:2-3). In Chapter 11, we noted that the Hebrew word translated here as "humbled" actually means "afflicted."

How did God plan for Israel to "remember" the affliction and hunger of those 40 years? In the same way He caused them to remember the other major aspects of that journey—through a feast. The sixth feast in Israel, or the sixth divinely established yearly holiday, is called the Day of Atonement (Lev. 23:27-32). There were several requirements for Israel to properly observe the feast. First, they had to "afflict their souls" (Lev. 23:27). From the time of their wilderness journey to the present day, Israel has understood that this involves fasting (Zech. 7:5; Ps. 35:13 ASV, RSV). In other words, the Israelites were commanded to remember the affliction and hunger of the wilderness journey by afflicting themselves with hunger once each year.

Once again, the similarity between the seven steps in our spiritual walk and the seven feasts is amazing. We have already observed that our sixth step involves the travail of intercession and suffering; now we see that Israel's sixth feast was given to remember their affliction in the wilderness! Why do we need affliction during the sixth step of our walk to enter the "rest" of the seventh Day? Peter reveals one of the blessed results of suffering: "Forasmuch then as Christ hath suffered for us in the flesh, arm yourselves likewise with the same mind: for *he that hath suffered in the flesh hath ceased from sin*" (1 Pet. 4:1). We will never be at rest in our spiritual man as long as we continue living in sin; and we will never cease from sin unless we accept the suffering or spiritual travail of Christ.

It will now be easy for us to understand the importance of another aspect of Israel's annual observance of the sixth feast, the Day of Atonement. Once each year, only on the Day of Atonement, the high priest would enter the Holy of Holies to make an atonement for sin on behalf of the entire nation (Lev. 16:2,17,29-30). This cleansing from sin, or atonement, was the most important moment of the year in the spiritual lives of the Israelites. It is extremely significant that the only way into the Holy of Holies, which is the **seventh step** in Moses' Tabernacle, was through the **sixth feast**. This is what we have been seeing from the beginning. The completion of the six

steps brings us into the rest of the seventh step. It is also extremely significant that the high priest was permitted to enter the Holy of Holies only as
long as he carried with him incense from the altar of incense, which is the
sixth step in the Tabernacle of Moses. He did this so that he would not die
in the Lord's presence (Lev. 16:12-13). If we do not experience the death of
the flesh (our self-life) that the sixth step symbolizes, and if we do not experience the spiritual travail for others symbolized by incense, we cannot
enter the Holy of Holies. No trace of the flesh or of selfishness can live in
God's manifest presence there, and would never be given access to that
glory. Thank Him for this second altar in the Tabernacle that prepares us
for the glory that is just ahead!

The amazing way in which the sixth feast interweaves the truths of all
the other groups of seven steps does not stop here. Each year on the Day
of Atonement, the high priest made an atonement for himself and for all
Israel (Lev. 16:2,17,29-30). The phrase "to make an atonement" is actually
all one Hebrew word; it means "to cover" (*Strong's Hebrew Dictionary*,
#3722). This "covering" was not only essential for the high priest who was
to enter the Holy of Holies but also for all who wish to enter that seventh
step. The Lord instructed the priest to make this atonement or "covering"
for himself once he had "**put on**" linen garments (Lev. 16:32-33). Why does
the Lord establish a connection between the "covering" of the Day of
Atonement and the need for the priest to "**put on**" linen garments? The
answer is found in the New Testament. Linen garments are associated
with righteousness (Rev. 19:8), and Christ is our righteousness (1 Cor. 1:30;
Phil. 3:9). Paul exhorts us to "**put on Christ**" (Rom. 13:14), which in the
Greek means to "put on" in the way that a person puts on a garment.

Christ is the *only* covering that can totally cover our spiritual nakedness. Fig leaves cannot cover us; only the skins of the Lamb will do so. At
the **beginning** of our journey from Egypt to Canaan, our sinful life is
"covered" or atoned for through the shed blood of the Passover Lamb.
This brings us the blessing of forgiveness for our sins. At the **end** of our
journey, as we are about to enter our inheritance, we find a covering that
is much, much deeper and far more wonderful than the covering we enjoyed throughout the journey. What we do is covered in the first feast. But
this covering of the sixth feast provides an answer not only for what we
do—we sin—but for what we *are*—"sin" (Rom. 6:6).

Sin is anything outside God's perfect will. God's perfect will for man,
from the beginning, has always been that man should be a sinless being
who reveals the beauty of Christ's likeness. Since we *are* rebellious and
sinful, we *are* outside God's perfect will and we *are*, therefore, sin. We commit **sins** because we are **sin**. In Christ's redemption God has provided an

answer for both our problems! At the beginning of our walk God gives us the covering of Christ's blood, which forgives our **sins**; at the end of our walk He gives us the covering of His blood or very life in a far deeper way. His blood deals with our **sin** and changes the way we live and walk.

In the Holy of Holies there was a wooden box called "an ark." The wood of that box was **covered** within and without with gold (Ex. 25:10-11). In order to dwell in the manifest glory of God that resides in the Holy of Holies, we must be conformed to the pattern that is revealed in that place. Like the ark, most of the furnishings of God's dwelling were made of wood that had been covered with gold, silver, or bronze. What does wood symbolize in the spiritual realm? We have seen that throughout the Bible trees are a symbol of men (e.g. Is. 61:3). Therefore, the wood from which His furniture is made is symbolic of men who have been cut down by His Word and by the work of the cross in their lives. However, neither God nor the world is interested in seeing "wood"—man's life that has been dealt with by the cross. They do not want to see the "wood" of humanity, even though it may have been crucified or cut down. Instead of seeing "wood," they want to see the beauty of "gold." Gold covered most of the furnishings in the Tabernacle; it is a symbol of the Lord Himself. "Yes, the Almighty will be your gold..." (Job 22:25 NKJV). We must "put on Christ" (Rom. 13:14) and cover what we are with the beauty of what He is.

Throughout the six steps in the Tabernacle we find wood furnishings that have been covered with gold on the **outside**. Not until we have completed the sixth step and have entered the Holy of Holies do we find a box of **wood that has been covered with gold on the outside and the inside!** *This* is the "covering" the Day of Atonement provides for us. It not only covers what we are outwardly—our **sins**—but it also covers what we are inwardly—our **sin**. *This* is what Jacob, the sixth man of faith, actually experienced. He experienced a spiritual change whereby the very life and nature of Christ not only covered what he was outwardly—his sinful **actions—but also what he was inwardly—his sinful nature**. God fully plans "to cover" us with gold on the sixth feast, as the word "atone" means. This is precisely the hope the Lord sets before us on Day Six of Creation. On that Day, a man in God's own image is placed *within* our earth! We should rejoice in God's plan for us and in His willingness and ability to finish this work in us.

Seeing the tragic condition of His Church, Jesus counsels us to **buy** from Him "**gold** tried in the **fire**" (Rev. 3:18; see also verses 14-17). Nothing could be more graphic. We must replace what we are—dross— with what He is—gold. When He says that we must *"buy"* gold, He shows us that it will cost us something. This gold must be tried in **fire**. Peter informs us that this "fire" that tries our gold symbolizes the times of tremendous affliction and suffering we share with Christ (1 Pet. 1:7; 4:12-14). Those who understand this and long to be eternally rich are able to accept the daily work of the cross with joy and thankfulness, instead of with complaining and resistance.

The spiritual "needlework" of this sixth feast, the Day of Atonement, continues. Another part of the yearly celebration confirms that this sixth feast deals with what we *are* (sin), not only with what we *do* (sins). The high priest would lay his hands on the head of a goat and confess over him all the sins of the nation, thus "putting them [their sins] on the head of the goat" (Lev. 16:21 NKJV). That goat was then led out into the wilderness and left there, symbolically carrying with him all the sins of God's people (Lev. 16:21-22). This act is absolutely filled with significance.

First, a goat is a symbol of rebellion, or the sinful human nature. After the priests had laid hands on the goat, it carried all the sins of God's people (Lev. 16:22). Paul says that our "old man," or sinful human nature, is the very "body of sin" (Rom 6:6). Like the rebellious goat, it is laden with sin.

Each year on the day all Israel was afflicting their souls with fasting, they would release the goat into the wilderness and leave him there. All this was to symbolize the fact that their rebellious old man had died and was left behind in the wilderness as they suffered afflictions of the journey from Egypt to Canaan. The old generation literally died there, and a new generation, symbolic of the new man (Christ in us), finished the journey and entered the rest of God that Canaan represents. Consequently, we again find the truth within this sixth feast that God must afflict our flesh and crucify us together with Christ in order to free us from sin and welcome us into the rest of the seventh Day. One day each year, Israel recalled this message as they left the goat in the wilderness; only on that day could the high priest enter the Holy of Holies to represent the entire nation of Israel before God.

It is extremely important to understand that the Day of Atonement has nothing whatsoever to do with the forgiveness of sin. It is the first feast, the Passover, that grants us forgiveness through the shed blood of the Passover Lamb. The purpose of this sixth feast is to show us how sin is actually *removed* from our lives; how we actually get the victory over sin so that we are no longer the slaves of sin. Jesus said that we are slaves of sin if we commit sin; a slave cannot dwell in the Lord's house or dwelling place—the Holy of Holies (Jn. 8:34-35). Therefore, for us to **dwell continually** in the **fullness** of the Lord's presence, our sin must be dealt with—it must be *removed* from us and not only forgiven.

One of the glorious promises that John the Baptist spoke concerning Jesus, the Lamb of God, was that He would "take away" the sin of the world (Jn. 1:29). This is much more glorious than simply forgiving our sins. The angel Gabriel said that Jesus would save us *"from"* our sins. This is far more glorious than saving us *in* our sins! The sixth feast, as well as the sixth step in the other groups of seven, reveals how sin is **taken away**. We *must* accept the sufferings and death of the cross in order to conquer it. The crucifixion of our old man is finally and fully accomplished as we come to the end of our wilderness journey. By then, what *we* are has decreased to zero and what Christ is has increased within us, filling every part of our temple with His glory. Few Christians are really willing to lay down their lives; but oh, what glory awaits us when we do! Paul leaves little doubt about this process and the resulting victory when he says, "Knowing this, that our old man is crucified with him, that the body of sin might be destroyed, that henceforth we *should not serve sin. For he that is dead is freed from sin.* Now if we be dead with Christ, we believe that we shall also live with him [in the Holy of Holies]...Likewise reckon ye also yourselves to be dead indeed unto sin, but alive unto God through Jesus Christ our Lord" (Rom. 6:6-8,11).

Let's consider one final thread of truth in God's needlework. The sixth man of faith, Jacob, is intimately linked with this sixth feast. He reveals the sixth step because he was a man who received the divine "covering" of gold. His life was truly covered within and without by the very life of Israel—Christ Himself. Being covered "without" is not enough, nor is it God's ultimate goal for us. God is not seeking people who attempt to manifest the nature of Christ on the outside, in the eyes of men, while being filled on the inside with hatred, envy, strife, and lust. This characterized the lives of the Pharisees (Mt. 23:27-28). This cannot please the Lord because His place of abode is the inner chambers of our being. Like the ark, we must be covered with gold inside and out so that His glory may be seen by Him in ways and places that others may never see. He wants us not only to *act* humbly, but to *think* humbly (Rom 12:3).

By the end of his life, Jacob was this kind of saint. He knew the "affliction" (or "humility") of the Day of Atonement. He not only had been afflicted over and over by his Uncle Laban, but he also had experienced the humiliation and death of the cross in another way—the weakening of his thigh. Surely the Bible mentions this natural detail because it reveals truth about Jacob's spiritual life. He no longer walked in pride, trusting in his own abilities and strength. This was the sixth man of faith, a man in whose heart God's redemptive work had been completed—a man who could enter rest.

The Lamb That Was Slain

Now let us ask: How does the creation of Adam on the sixth Day of Genesis 1 reveal the suffering and death of Christ? How does it reveal affliction and humiliation? These things are definitely found on the sixth Day, but they are present in the most unexpected place and in the most amazing way. At the moment the Lord created Adam on the sixth Day, someone was already paying a price in suffering, humiliation, and death that cannot be measured by human standards. To understand who it was, we must understand something about time and eternity. The Bible reveals that God lives at all times in the past, the present, and the future. This is why the writer of Hebrews, speaking of entering God's rest, declares, "...the works were finished from the foundation of the world" (Heb. 4:3). At the very moment the Lord created the world and the life of man, He *finished all the works* (past tense) that are necessary (present tense) for us to enter the rest of His seventh Day. This includes His greatest work of all, the cross. Therefore, Christ is called "the Lamb that *was* slain [past tense] from the creation of the world" (Rev. 13:8 NIV).

At the moment the Lord created man, He not only knew that man would sin, but He was actually witnessing that sin, since He was living in the future. Not only was the Lord witnessing the condition of man; He was also *finishing* the work that would provide the only way possible to bring man back into the rest man would lose through sin. Christ was already offering Himself as the slain Lamb. The Lord's plan for His people *cannot* fail because every detail was planned, executed, and finished before the Creation. God does not expect us to understand this. He only asks us to believe it and to be assured that every necessary work for our complete redemption and our entrance into His rest was finished since the beginning. What joy this should give us!

Can we fathom the love that He revealed at Creation? Some have asked, "Since God knows the future and He knew that man would fall into sin, why did He continue with His plan to make man?" This is simply the wrong question to ask. The correct question is, Since God knows the future and He knew that man would fall into sin, and that the only answer for that sin would be for Him to personally carry man's sin and experience the suffering and death of Calvary, how could He have possibly continued with His plan knowing the price He would have to pay? There is only one answer to this question: The Lord made us regardless of the cost to Himself because He was motivated by a love that is beyond human comprehension—a love that does not take self into consideration or allow its personal well-being to influence its decisions. Love for His Bride moved the Lord to pay the price for her from the beginning. This divine love will continue to embrace us until it has brought us back into His glorious rest!

Only God can accomplish the work of the sixth Day in our lives. Yet, we can cooperate with Him as His Spirit moves upon us to fulfill this sixth step. Like Jacob, we should expect and accept the spiritual travail associated with suffering, as well as the spiritual travail associated with intercession. When the Spirit moves upon our hearts to intercede, we must not refuse to yield our time and strength to this spiritual travail. Offering Him our time and strength for this purpose is a precious way of offering our lives as an acceptable sacrifice to Him. Besides the travail of intercession, the Spirit will bring spiritual travail in the form of suffering. May we understand that this travail will also bring us new life and the rest of Day Seven. Those who accept both these aspects of travail, as Jacob did, will receive the blessing Jacob received—the light of the Sun shining upon us!

Jacob's Cattle and the Sixth Day

It is interesting that the Lord created cattle on the sixth Day, along with man. In the Bible, cattle represent at least two things: sacrifices and men. First, cattle were chosen by God to become **sacrifices** of the highest order upon His altar. Second, **men** are likened to the Lord's cattle (Lk. 13:15-16; Ezek. 34:31). Both of these thoughts will have significance for our spiritual lives when the last Adam takes up residence within our earth on the sixth Day.

First, the highest and costliest sacrifices God has ordained will ascend from our earth as we build Him altars. Spiritual travail is one of the costliest of all sacrifices. Nevertheless, our God is a good God. Not only will God provide us with opportunities to offer these acceptable sacrifices to Him, but He will also provide the grace we need to offer them; on the sixth Day, He will even provide the cattle we need for the offering as well!

Second, in terms of the souls of men (His cattle), this sixth Day will begin a time of unprecedented fruitfulness in our lives. This fruitfulness will be intimately related to the spiritual sacrifices that will be ascending from our lives (Phil. 2:17; Eph. 3:1; 2 Cor. 4:8-12). These sacrifices of suffering will cause many cattle to be brought forth through our earth. We will be more fruitful than ever before, yet we will also experience the divine rest of Day Seven. Is it any wonder then, that Jacob, the sixth man of faith and the man of travail, experienced the supernatural multiplication of cattle in his life during a time of great suffering? (See Genesis 31:7-13.) Do we still long to be fruitful even if bringing forth spiritual children involves travail, an inescapable process that nature itself reveals?

Babies, Fathers, and Travail

Let us now move on to Day Seven to discover the spiritual blessings that flow through the mature saint. Before we do, let's consider a few of the major differences between a babe in Christ and a spiritual father. The Scriptures speak in a number of places about babies and fathers (1 Cor. 3:1; 4:15; Heb. 5:13; 1 Jn. 2:13).

Obviously, there are tremendous differences between a baby and a father in their understanding and physical strength, but also in their physical, emotional, and spiritual maturity, in their abilities to reason and communicate, and in their capabilities to contribute to society. Another outstanding difference is far more fundamental. A baby *receives* life whereas a father *gives* life. By definition, a father is someone who has become a source of life for another. A father is not only the **initial** source of life for the child, but also the **continuing** source of life until the child reaches maturity. The father gives his love, his time, his strength, and his finances, receiving very little in return. If we accept the biblical concept that a man and wife are one flesh and one body, then together, as a unit, they "father" a child. To do so they first give themselves to an intimate love relationship where there is an actual impartation of life. Later, they travail to bring forth a new life. The father, too, is involved in the travail to bring forth life.

If we apply these concepts to our spiritual lives, it should be clear that a person can be a spiritual father only if *the* source of life, the Lord Himself, has been formed within him. The Lord is the *only* source of life in the universe. We cannot birth new life without Him. The life of Jacob and other intercessors reveal that our travail for the sake of others provides the opportunity for the Lord's life to actually come forth through us and be imparted to those around us. When the life of Christ, the last Adam, fills us and shines forth through us, we will know the blessing of His rest and all that the seventh Day promises. It's just ahead!

Chapter 17

Day Seven—His Rest

Unlike the blessings of the first six Days, the divine blessings associated with the rest of Day Seven are so extensive that an entire chapter of Genesis is devoted to describing them. These are the blessings that come to us when the last Adam is within us, living in the garden prepared for Him by the Spirit of God. We do well to remember that, according to Hebrews 4:1, we are called to enter **His rest**, not our rest. Hebrews goes on to reveal that the garden within us is also **His garden** (Heb. 6:7). When He comes to dwell within us, all the benefits of **His** rest are shared with us. We become partakers of the life of the One who walks in continual spiritual rest.

Genesis 2 *begins* with a revelation of God's rest—He rested from His works (Gen. 2:1-3). It also *ends* with a revelation of rest, symbolized by the marriage of Adam and Eve (Gen 2:21-25).[1] Many other details found in Genesis 2 are sandwiched between these two revelations of rest. Through a closer look at those details, we can discover that they are all directly related to the great blessings that come to us when we enter the Lord's rest.

Just like the seed we discussed in Chapter 3, every revelation of rest in Genesis 2 contains so much truth that a separate chapter could be written on each. Scriptures from all over the Bible have sprung from these wonderful seeds of truth. This Chapter is intended to present but an overview of the glorious hope the Lord sets before us. Therefore, we will limit ourselves to a brief look at the principal revelations of His rest—the rest He longs to share with us, His creation.

---

1. We need to recall here that marriage is referred to as rest in Ruth 1:9 and that marriage, rest, and Canaan all refer to the same thing—our inheritance, or the goal of our journey as discussed in Chapter 4.

The Nature of God's Rest

1. God Rests From All His Work

"Thus the heavens and the earth, and all the host of them, were finished. And on the seventh day God ended His work which He had done, and He rested on the seventh day from all His work which He had done" (Gen. 2:1-2 NKJV). One of the great theological debates that has raged for centuries is whether or not the Believer can conquer sin during his earthly life, before he goes to Heaven. There are those who declare that, because of what *we* are, we must sin every day in word, thought, and deed until we get to Heaven. Likewise, there are those who assure us that there is a place in God where we can have victory over sin in this present life. The answer to this debate is as unbelievable as a classic "Believe-It-Or-Not." The answer is that both sides are completely right! To reconcile both sides, we need to understand what the Bible has to say about "Heaven," and what it means to go there.

The Bible makes it very clear that there is a literal place called "Heaven." [2] Someday the Church will physically go there to live. The Bible also confirms the truth found in the old saying, "Heaven is where Jesus is." This saying is actually quite profound. Jesus doesn't need to go to Heaven to be in Heaven; no, Heaven always dwells where Jesus dwells. If He is here, Heaven is here with Him. If He is a million light years away, that is where Heaven is. Of course, the Lord is omnipresent, existing everywhere at once. Why then are we not experiencing Heaven right here, right now? Because our *sins* have separated us from Him (Is. 59:2). Sin will always bring separation, even between God and His own people. Sin *must* be dealt with—not only the forgiveness of sin found in the Passover, the first feast, but also the removal of sin that we saw in the Day of Atonement, the sixth feast.

The Lord Jesus told Nicodemus, "No one has ascended to heaven but He who came down from heaven, that is, the Son of Man *who is in heaven*" (Jn. 3:13 NKJV). This is an amazing statement for a human being. Jesus became a man in every sense of the word and was like us in every way (Heb. 2:17; Phil. 2:7-8). Yet, near the beginning of His earthly ministry as He talked face to face with Nicodemus, Jesus said that He was already in Heaven. He did not say that He *had been* in Heaven or that He *would* be there. He told Nicodemus that at that very moment He was in Heaven.

---

2. Ps. 14:2; Mt. 18:10; Acts 1:11; 3:21; 7:55-56; Heb. 9:24; Rev. 4:1; 5:3; 11:12; 15:5.

Could Jesus have been referring to a very real experience, or was He speaking symbolically? Could He have been referring to what had happened to Him in the Jordan River? "At that moment *heaven was opened, and he saw* the Spirit of God descending like a dove and lighting on him. And a voice from heaven said, 'This is my Son, whom I love; with him I am well pleased' " (Mt. 3:16b-17 NIV). In the Jordan, Jesus both saw into Heaven and heard the Father's audible voice. Many of us have assumed that the heavens closed again once the Spirit had descended, but that is not the case. That day Jesus entered a spiritual realm and remained there until the end of His earthly life. We know this because the Lord affirmed that He did and said only the things He saw the Father doing and heard the Father saying (Jn. 5:19; 8:28).

When Joshua and Israel passed through that same Jordan many years before, the commander of the armies of Israel visibly appeared to Joshua and took command. (It is noteworthy that "Joshua" and "Jesus" are the same names in Hebrew.) This was immediately after Israel had been circumcised, a symbol of the work of the cross to destroy their flesh (Josh. 5:2-3;13-15; Col. 2:11-12). Baptism is also a symbol of the work of the cross to destroy our flesh (Rom. 6:3-6). Immediately after Jesus was baptized, He too met with His Commander—the Father. From that day forward, Jesus simply followed instructions and saw the glorious results that changed the course of the world. He experienced what Paul would experience many years later when he was caught up to the third heaven (2 Cor. 12:1-5). Paul's experience of entering the heavenly realm was so real that he was unable to tell if he was in his body or out of his body. After this experience, Paul, too, was used to change the world.

Are not the Lord Jesus and Paul both examples for us? Should we not experience the same thing they experienced?[3] Obviously, we should—but

---

3. I realize that some sectors of the Body of Christ teach that the supernatural experiences of Paul and the early Church were only for that time, to establish the Church. This doctrine has many serious flaws. First, Paul tells us that he is an example for future Believers (1 Tim. 1:16). If we are not supposed to live like Paul lived, then he is not an example in at least some areas of his life. Who has the authority to tell us which areas those are? Second, if the foundation of the early Church was with the power and signs of the Holy Spirit, are we saying that the foundation of the churches that are founded today should be different? Paul declares that the foundation of the Church is apostles and prophets (Eph. 2:20). One of the root problems with the false doctrine that rejects the supernatural manifestations of the Spirit today is that it does not recognize the apostolic and prophetic ministries as valid ministries today. However, in the same Book of Ephesians, Paul goes on to say that these ministries will continue **until** we have **all** come into maturity and perfection—not only until the early Church was established! (Eph. 4:11-14)

when will this happen? It happens in the seventh step in the Tabernacle of Moses as we pass through the veil that separates us from God's manifest glory and presence that reside in the Holy of Holies. At that moment, we stand before Him with nothing separating Him from us. This can only happen if the veil, which is a symbol of the rending or death of man's flesh, is rent (Heb. 10:20).[4] Only circumcision, or the cutting away of our flesh, can bring us into the literal presence of our commander. Those who enter the Holy of Holies are, in reality, entering the heavenly realm in such a real way that, like Paul, they are unable to discern whether they are there in body or in spirit. At that time, it will be evident that the Lord's life and character are dwelling within them. Once we take that seventh step, Jesus will be in control to command us as He commanded Joshua. As happened with Paul, even the physical world around us will feel the effects of His Shekinah glory—the glory found in the Holy of Holies. That glory will turn the world upside down. Yes, Heaven is where Jesus is, and He is everywhere. Our problem is that a veil separates us from that glory. That veil is our flesh and its works, and those works are sin (Heb. 10:20; Rom 6:6). That veil must be rent!

Elijah also knew the glory of the Holy of Holies. He announced to Ahab that he was standing before the God of Israel (1 Kings 17:1). No wonder he had the authority to shut up Heaven for three and a half years (Lk. 4:25). At the burning bush, Moses also experienced what happens when we are brought into the glory of the heavenly realm. There, he found himself standing on holy ground, the same spiritual place Joshua found (Josh. 5:15). At that point, Moses' life was filled with the power and authority of Heaven; after that the world was never again the same. God changed it through Moses. This experience came to Moses only after many years of preparation, after he had finished his own 40-year wilderness journey, where his flesh and its ways were crucified. Before Israel ever faced the dealings of the wilderness, Moses had to leave behind his own old man in the wilderness so he would no longer lean on his own strength and wisdom, but the Lord's. Only then He could deliver Israel by the arm of God, not by his own arm which he used to kill an Egyptian 40 years earlier.

---

4.   Hebrews 10:20 tells us that the rent veil was symbolic of the rent flesh of Christ, but it also tells us that we are to enter the Holy of Holies by "the way" that He has opened for us. We can only enter if we follow in His footsteps, taking up our cross and allowing our own flesh to be rent or crucified as His was. This is the message of First Peter 2:21.

Just as happened in Moses' day and in Paul's day, the world order is soon to be changed again. We are definitely coming into a "new world order," but it will not be patterned after the schemes and ideas of today's politicians. We are on the threshold of the greatest outpouring of God's glory on mankind that the world has ever witnessed! The Lord's visitation and direct intervention in the affairs of this world will soon usher in His eternal Kingdom and the physical return of the Lord Jesus Christ. The Lord Himself will preside over the "new world order!" Will we have a part? Much depends on whether or not we believe that the fullness of His life can actually be formed within us. Do we believe that the creative power of the Spirit during the "redemptive week" can prepare our earth to be a dwelling place for Christ, the last Adam?

I repeat an important warning: We *must not* base our doctrine on tradition, personal experience, or the experience of those around us. The measure of God's glory that will soon be seen resting upon the Church has never been granted before. A new day is about to dawn, a day that has never been experienced. This was also Joshua's experience. As he was preparing to cross the Jordan into Canaan, the Lord spoke to him, "...you have not passed this way before" (Josh. 3:4 NKJV). As God's people, we need to heed this message today as never before. The Body of Christ will soon cross a spiritual Jordan and enter the rest and inheritance of a spiritual Canaan. We have not passed this way before! Only those who have the faith to believe for greater things than what past generations knew will be used to lead others when the new day dawns. Hebrews sets before us the hope of receiving something that the fathers of our faith never received. The great men of faith "obtained a good report through faith"; but, they did not receive the promise: "God having provided some better thing for us, that they without us should not be made perfect" (Heb. 11:40). Your hope and mine should be nothing less than "Christ in us" (Col. 1:27).

As I said, both sides of the great theological debate over whether or not we can conquer sin in this present life are correct. Yes, we will definitely sin every day in word, thought, and deed until we enter Heaven; and yes, there is a place in God where we can have victory over sin in this present life. That place is the heavenly realm Jesus, Paul, Moses, Elijah, and many others experienced while still on earth. That place is the Holy of Holies, the seventh step in the Tabernacle. That place is the rest of God, Day Seven, where we no longer labor under the burden of our own sinful works, where we are no longer slaves to sin. That place was found by Joseph, the seventh man of faith. He not only came to the kingdom and ruled over men, but he ruled over his own sin.[5] He ruled over his passion, pride, and self as is seen by his dealings with Potiphar's wife, his brothers, and even Pharaoh himself, whom he loyally served even when he had opportunities to do otherwise. Yes, if we enter the Lord's rest, we will have rest from our sin and our sinful nature. The cessation of our own works as God ceased from His is one of the first blessings we find in Genesis 2 as we come into His rest. (Compare Hebrews 4:10.)

Imagine how sad the eternal testimony of some will be when they physically go to Heaven and have finally been perfected, as every saint will be sooner or later. The essence of their testimony will be, "By the grace of God I am now perfect. While I lived on earth, I did not believe that God's grace was sufficient to conquer the sin in my life. I unknowingly glorified Satan and sin by believing that Satan's influence over me, and the power of my own flesh, were too great for the power of His grace." God, in His kindness, promises to wipe away all tears; surely this testimony would cause some tears. Oh, may we be convinced that the cross of Christ can destroy what we are and conquer Satan's power over our lives today, just as He did for the whole world 2,000 years ago! If we do not believe this, we may go to Heaven someday, but we will not enter Heaven in this life. Our unbelief will allow the veil of flesh and its sin to keep us from the Holy of Holies. Let's pray, "Lord, help our unbelief!" (Mk. 9:24)

2. The Man From Dust

"And the Lord God *formed man of the dust* of the ground, and breathed into his nostrils the breath of life; and man became a living soul" (Gen. 2:7). God will form within us the life of the last Adam, the Lord Jesus Christ, from the very same material He used to form the first Adam—the ashes or dust of our earth. In Numbers 19:17, the burnt offering is reduced to "ashes." This is the same Hebrew word that is translated as "dust" in Genesis 2:7.[6] If we long for the Lord to form the life of Christ within our earth, we must provide Him with some ashes. They come from experiences of the cross, from ourselves as living sacrifices as we allow His altar to reduce what we are to ashes (Rom 12:1). If we understand this, we will

---

5. Please note that I am not promoting the doctrine of "Kingdom Theology," which teaches that godly men will ultimately take over the world whether the Lord comes physically or not. Although we are already in His Kingdom today in a spiritual sense, a day is coming soon when that Kingdom will be manifested on this earth in a physical, literal way. That will only occur when the Lord Jesus physically comes again, just as has been promised. See Acts 1:11 and Revelation 19:11–20:6.

6. In fact, in Numbers 19:9,17, the most common Hebrew word used to refer to the ashes of the altar is used interchangeably with the Hebrew word translated as "dust" in Genesis 2:7.

consider the suffering and death of the cross in our lives to be a tremendous blessing. Our sufferings become an opportunity to give the Lord some ashes, the raw material from which His very life is formed in us. Only as we decrease can He increase in us.

Sadly, the ashes used to form His life in us are very rare material in the lives of God's people today. Choosing the afflictions of Christ, as Moses did, is never an appealing message; neither is it popular (Heb. 11:25). Throughout history, very few of God's people have chosen that way. Choosing affliction may be less popular today than at any other time in man's history. Many Believers have bought into the message that assures them they need not suffer anything for Christ, yet our God is still the One who gives "beauty for ashes" (Is. 61:3). But do we have any ashes to exchange for His beauty? Are you allowing the Holy Spirit to reduce what you are to ashes? This is a painful process, but those who have caught a glimpse of His beauty know that it is well worth it. We must not wait until Day Seven to permit the work of the cross to begin in us. In fact, we will see in Chapter 20 that the cross operates in each one of the seven steps. Without the cross, not one single Day can be completed. No wonder Paul advised the Philippians, "For to you it has been *granted* on behalf of Christ, not only to believe in Him, but also to suffer for His sake" (Phil. 1:29 NKJV). We have been *"granted"* this blessing! Let's get back to the cross.

A fear of death was Israel's problem in the wilderness (Ex. 20:19). It is still our problem today. Hebrews 2:15 explains why most of us spend our entire lifetime in bondage to sin and Satan: We are afraid to die. We can only know true liberty from sin and the flesh when what we are has been reduced to ashes. Isn't it tragic that we are so afraid of the cross—the death the Lord has chosen for us—that we often spend our entire lives under the bondage of Satan? We accept Satan's rulership because we are afraid of what will happen if Christ rules over us unconditionally! Only a deep love for Him and a complete trust in His heart of love for us can cast out that fear because "perfect love casts out fear..." (1 Jn. 4:18 NKJV). Since we are afraid to experience His *death*, we do not come to experience the fullness of His *life* or His rest.

Christ, our example, revealed the process of receiving beauty for ashes in His daily walk. He invited His disciples to **follow** Him and **die daily** on the cross (Lk. 9:23-24). He must have been dying daily Himself, as did Paul many years later (1 Cor. 15:31). If we are interested in this way of life, Isaiah tells us how this works, practically speaking, in our everyday life. He gives us insight to Christ's daily walk:

The Lord God hath given me the tongue of the learned, that I should know how to speak a word in season to him that is weary: he wakeneth morning by morning, he wakeneth mine ear to hear as the learned. The Lord God hath opened mine ear, and I was not rebellious, neither turned away back. I gave my back to the smiters, and my cheeks to them that plucked off the hair: I hid not my face from shame and spitting (Isaiah 50:4-6).

How many of us would like to hear the Father's voice the first thing every morning? Wouldn't that be wonderful? Israel didn't think so. They were afraid they would die if they heard His voice again (Ex. 20:19). Imagine this. Most of us plead with God to allow us to hear His voice because we think His voice will bring us life; here we find Israel saying that His voice would bring them death! Either Israel missed the point or we are missing it today. Unlike most of us, the Israelites had heard God's audible voice. Could it be that they heard something in God's voice that we have not yet heard, much less understood?

Can we begin to imagine what Jesus must have heard each morning? Maybe we have assumed that the Father's daily wake-up call was a message of the day's coming victories—how many lepers Jesus would cleanse that day, how many dead would be raised, or how the multitudes would gather to hear His words. But Isaiah doesn't make any sense if that was so. In the next verse He declares, "The Lord God hath opened mine ear, *and I was not rebellious*, neither turned away back" (Is. 50:5). Who would ever consider rebelling against the Father's voice if His message concerned the glorious victories just ahead?

The next verse in Isaiah explains the Father's daily early-morning message for His Son. It was along this line: "Son, today there will be many in the multitude who will reject what You are teaching them. Some will spit in Your face. Others will mock You. Some will even smite You with sticks and throw stones at You. You will bear much reproach and rejection today for My name's sake. You have the power to vindicate Yourself, but instead, I am asking You to show them how much I love them. Are You willing to do that, Son, to please Me?" Day after day, Jesus accepted the word that brought death to His own human desires; and day after day, without effort or work, resurrection life and power from above flowed to the needy. In fact, lepers *were* cleansed, the blind *did* receive their sight, the deaf *did* hear, and the dead *were* raised. The ashes of His sacrifice were exchanged for the beauty of Heaven's life.

The Lord's glorious life always flows from our death. There is simply no other way. The degree to which I die to my way, my rights, and my will *today* will be the degree to which His life flows through me *today* to those around me. He offers us the life of the last Adam and shows us the way to enter that life. Is it any wonder that Israel never wanted to hear His voice again? For those who love this world, death to the flesh is too high a price to pay for something they are really not interested in—the Lord's life. Is it any wonder that Paul said he gloried in the cross? (See Galatians 6:14.) Everything he longed for was granted to him through that cross.

First, the Creator forms the last Adam in us out of the nothingness of ashes; then He breathes into that New Man the breath of **life**—His life! It was God's "breath" that caused even the dry bones to live when Ezekiel prophesied to them (Ezek. 37:5,9). The Hebrew word "breath" in Ezekiel 37 is most often translated as "Spirit" or "spirit." When the Lord forms the ashes of our living sacrifice into the beauty of Christ's life within us, His breath causes us to become a Spirit-breathed and Spirit-controlled people. As the divine breath becomes our breath, great things are accomplished. *This* is rest.

3. The Tree of Life

"And out of the ground the Lord God made every tree grow that is pleasant to the sight and good for food. The *tree of life* was also in the midst of the garden, and the tree of the knowledge of good and evil" (Gen. 2:9 NKJV). The tree of life is one of the great mysteries of God's Word. It is also one of the most awesome and glorious of His truths. The tree of life was, and continues to be, the source of life for man (Gen. 3:22; Rev. 2:7). When man lost access to the tree of life through sin, the Lord, in His kindness, immediately showed fallen man the way back to that tree. The last verse of Genesis 3, immediately after man's fall, is a revelation of that way: "So He drove out the man [from Eden]; and He placed cherubim at the east of the garden of Eden, and a flaming sword which turned every way, to guard *the way to the tree of life*" (Gen. 3:24 NKJV).

Cherubim were not placed there to hide or destroy the way to life, but rather to preserve and protect that way. The sword, which is a symbol of God's word or truth, also protected the way. When the Lord Jesus came, He said that He is the way, the truth, and the life. We find this three-fold revelation as early as the first chapters of Genesis: He is the **way** back to the tree of life; He is the **truth**, or sword, that puts an end to our life and ways so that His life and ways can fill us; and He is the tree or source of **life** itself.

Immediately after the fall, Abel found his way back to the tree of life through worship. It is extremely significant that the first lesson God gave humanity after their separation from the tree of life concerned offering worship to Him (Gen. 4:1-5). A Hebrew reader of the Scriptures finds it easy to make the connection between giving the Lord an offering and finding the way back into His presence. One of the principal Hebrew words for "offering" comes from the Hebrew verb meaning "to draw near," or "to approach." [7] Therefore, from the Hebrew language, we understand that giving an offering is the God-given "way of approach" to a holy God. Unfortunately, many in the Church today have not yet learned the lesson that Cain teaches us. Cain's offering was not accepted by the Lord. This shows us that offering something to the Lord is not enough. Our offering must be acceptable to God. He does *not* say that, as God's priests, we are called simply to offer spiritual sacrifices to God. Peter affirms this truth when he says that we are called to offer spiritual sacrifices that are *acceptable* to God (1 Pet. 2:5). As Cain discovered, offering sacrifices and offering *acceptable* sacrifices are two very different things. There is a prevalent attitude today that God accepts any offering, given in any way, as long as we are sincere. The Cain and Abel story gives us a different message.

Two different forms of worship were also the crux of the problem among God's people in Elijah's day. As you may remember, Elijah offered worship that called down fire from Heaven, unlike the worship of the rest of God's people. Therein Elijah rescued God's people from false worship and restored them to their God. Jesus promised that Elijah would come again and restore all things before the Lord's own coming (Mt. 17:10-11). If the Lord must send Elijah again to restore His people, God's people must have again forsaken true worship. Elijah will reveal the God-ordained way to draw near to the tree of life and experience the fire of God afresh.

Jesus Himself warned all humanity about the seriousness of worship. He told the Samaritan woman that she and her people definitely worshiped, but they did not know what they were worshiping (Jn. 4:22). Old Testament Israel is both a negative and a positive example for Christians (1 Cor. 10:1-11). Throughout Israel's history, people of God have often worshiped demons, thinking they were worshiping God (Lev. 17:5-7; Deut. 32:15-17; 1 Cor. 10:7). Could this possibly happen to God's people in the New Testament?

The heavenly battle for true worship can also be seen in the Lord's temptation in the wilderness. Satan offered Him all the kingdoms of the world for one act of worship! (See Matthew 4:8-9.) Why would Satan do this? He certainly considers worship to be far more important than most of us do today! By His response to Satan's temptation, the Lord revealed

---

7. See Leviticus 1:2. The principal Hebrew word used for the offerings of Leviticus comes from the verb "qarab," which means "to draw near" or "to approach." See *Strong's Hebrew Dictionary*, #7133 and #7126.

God's attitude toward worship. Jesus treated worship as a decisive issue in life. Why else would the issue of Cain and Abel's worship be the first thing recorded in the Scriptures after the fall of man? Why, also, would the issue of Christ's worship be part of the first scriptural record of Christ's life after His baptism? Do we really understand the importance the Lord places on this matter? David, the man after God's own heart, understood. He avowed, "His praise shall continually be in my mouth (Ps. 34:1b).

When we enter the Lord's rest on Day Seven, the tree of life will be found in the garden within our earth. This tree of life within us becomes a source of food for the last Adam, who has been formed in our earth and placed in our garden to tend and keep it (Gen. 2:15 NKJV). He eats the fruit of this tree. Proverbs declares, "The fruit of the righteous is a tree of life" (Prov. 11:30a). Is it possible that the Lord could actually seek and find fruit from *us*? Almost 2,000 years ago, He came and sought fruit from the fig tree and the vineyard, both symbols of Israel. When He found no figs on the fig tree, He cursed it; when He received nothing from the vineyard, the keepers were removed (Mt. 21:19,33-44). Will the Lord find the fruit He seeks from our lives? We understand from Hebrews 6:7-10 that our earth must also produce fruit for the One who cultivates it.

Maybe we thought that the tree of life was primarily for *us* to eat from. We, with others, will definitely eat from it on Day Seven, but let us remember that this is *His* rest and *His* garden. The tree of life is in our garden primarily for the benefit of the last Adam, who dwells there. We simply enter the joy of *His* rest and participate in its blessings and life. The Lord declares that His lover *is* the garden (Song 4:12). Later, when other daughters of Jerusalem (Believers) have no idea where to find His presence, she knows where He is. She tells them her secret: "My beloved is gone down into his garden, to the beds of spices, to feed in the gardens…" (Song 6:2). Oh, that we would become a garden where His presence continually dwells!

The Lord also speaks to His lover, "I am come into **my garden**, my sister, my spouse: I have gathered my myrrh with my spice; I have *eaten my honeycomb with my honey*; I have drunk *my wine* with *my milk*" (Song 5:1a). This is the Lord's garden and the Lord's food; and He is the One who is eating. Where does He find these wonderful fruits He seeks? "*Thy lips*, O my spouse, drop as the **honeycomb: honey** and **milk** *are under thy tongue*" (Song 4:11a). This is obviously spiritual food—which in the spiritual realm is the Word of God. Jeremiah testifies, "Thy words were found, and I did eat them" (Jer. 15:16a).

Have you ever feasted on the word of God that has come from the lips of one of God's servants? Just as we eat the words that come from the

Lord, whether directly from *His* mouth or indirectly through one of His servants, the Lord eats the **words** of life that come from *our* mouths as we worship in Spirit and in truth. In fact, the "honeycomb" He finds in His lover's lips is explained for us in Proverbs by Solomon, the one who best understands the symbolism he used in the Song of Solomon. He explains, "Pleasant words are as an honeycomb" (Prov. 16:24a). Solomon also explains that, for the Lord, "a wholesome **tongue** is a **tree of life**" (Prov. 15:4a).

There it is! Our **tongue** actually becomes the **tree of life**, and the tongue is the source of the fruit the Lord seeks from our garden! Later, in Solomon's Song, the Lord likens His lover to a tree from which He receives fruit (Song 7:8). So, too, the righteous person in Psalm 1 is *"like a tree* planted by the *rivers* of water, *that bringeth forth his fruit* in his season; his *leaf* also shall not wither..." (Ps. 1:3). In the end of God's dealings with man, the four thoughts that are emphasized in this verse are again joined in one verse. We are shown a **tree** that is planted by a **river**. It brings forth **fruit** in its season, faithfully yielding its fruit every month. We are even given a revelation of its **leaves**: They are given for the healing of the nations (Rev. 22:2). Will we be a tree of life planted by the river of life that gives the Lord fruit when He seeks it?

In Song of Solomon 7:13, we find that the lover actually prepares her fruits and has them laid up at her gates, ready to give them to her Beloved when He comes: "...at our *gates* are all manner of pleasant fruits, new and old, which I have laid up for thee, O my beloved." Spiritually speaking, our gates are the gates of praise (Is. 60:18), showing us that praise is our means of entrance back into the Lord's presence. No wonder it was so important for Abel!

Is praise important to you also? The Lord satisfies His spiritual hunger and thirst as He partakes of the fruit of our lips prepared for Him at the gates of praise. He revealed this wonderful truth when He was with the woman of Samaria at Jacob's well (Jn. 4). After a long journey, Jesus and His disciples were **thirsty** and **hungry**. While the disciples were buying **food**, Jesus asked the Samaritan woman for a **drink**. He then explained to her what the real hunger and thirst of the Creator are. He tells her, "...the true worshippers shall worship the Father in spirit and in truth: for the Father seeketh such to worship Him" (Jn. 4:23). The Lord also reveals in other Scriptures the spiritual food for which He hungers. For example, the Lord assures the psalmist that He is not interested in a calf ("bullock") and its blood for food and drink. If He were hungry (as we understand hunger) He would not tell the psalmist; but, He tells him to offer a sacrifice of thanksgiving and to **pay his vows** to the Most High (Ps. 50:9-14). (A study of the ten times that the word "vow" appears in the Psalms reveals that it is speaking about offering praise to the Lord. For example, in Psalm 61:8, the psalmist explains, "So **I will sing praise** to Your name forever, that I may daily **perform my vows**" [NKJV].) The woman at the well did not understand that praise is the spiritual food and drink the Father seeks from us. *This* is what satisfies the Lord's hunger and thirst.

The prophet Hosea beautifully brings together in one short verse all the concepts we have been considering. There he exhorts us to "*take with you words*, and turn to the Lord: say unto him, Take away all iniquity, and receive us graciously: *so will we render the calves of our lips*" (Hos. 14:2).[8] How do we offer the Lord a calf? By taking words and using our lips to speak to Him. Hebrews 13:15 also brings these thoughts together: "By him therefore let us offer *the sacrifice of praise* to God continually, that is, the *fruit of our lips* giving thanks to his name." Yes, the husbandman who tends the garden in our earth definitely seeks fruit from the tree of life found in our garden. He seeks the fruit of our lips; He seeks His living word in our mouths, words spoken by the Spirit. This is the blessing David experienced. He said, "The Spirit of the Lord spake by me, and *his word* was in my *tongue*" (2 Sam. 23:2). No wonder David became one of the greatest worshipers in Spirit and in truth of all ages. He knew how to satisfy the hunger of the Almighty. Surely, if we learn to satisfy Him, He will satisfy us, as He did the woman at the well!

A tree of life is found in our garden on Day Seven. Will the last Adam find fruit on it when He comes to our garden seeking it? Will He find on our lips the living word offered in spiritual worship? This word is not only the *written* Word—quoting Scriptures is not enough. This does not satisfy others, nor does it satisfy Him. Rather, we must become oracles or mouthpieces for the living, spoken word (1 Pet. 4:11). This is the word that *proceeds out of His mouth*, and that He places within our own mouths also. This is the word Jesus referred to when He said, "The words that I *speak* unto you, they are spirit, and they are life" (Jn. 6:63b). This is the word Peter referred to when he said, "Lord, to whom shall we go? thou hast the words of eternal life" (Jn. 6:68b). This is the bread of life that descends from Heaven (Jn. 6:48-50).

---

8.   The KJV is one of the few translations that properly translates the Hebrew word for "calves" or "bullocks" here. This is the same word used in Psalm 50:9, translated as "bullock." It appears 133 times in the Old Testament and always refers to the animal. It is consistently translated as "calf" or "bullock" by all versions, except in this verse in Hosea 14:2.

One of God's main goals throughout our wilderness journey is to teach us to live by this word that *proceeds from His mouth* (Deut. 8:2-3; Mt. 4:1-4). Of course, on Day Seven, God will continue to speak to us through the written Word; but in the glory of the Holy of Holies, the seventh step in the Tabernacle, we will hear His audible voice—as did Jesus, Moses, Samuel, Paul, and many others.

The question is, Will we render to the Lord the fruits He seeks from the tree of life He plants within us? What if the woman at the well had not been willing to give the Lord a drink? What if she had been too busy? If so, she never would have drunk from the well of living water. What if the poor widow had not prepared a cake for Elijah? (See First Kings 17.) She and her son were dying of hunger. How could she afford to feed the prophet from the little she had? Yet if she had not made that great sacrifice, she would have died of hunger in the famine. However, because she sacrificed, she never lacked bread and oil for her household or for any other hungry person who came under her roof. What if Abraham had not invited the Lord to come in and dine at his table? (See Genesis 18.) He may never have heard the living word that brought forth Isaac, the son of promise. What if the two on the way to Emmaus had been too tired after a long journey to welcome a stranger into their abode to eat with them? (See Luke 24:13-32.) Their eyes would never have been opened to see the glory of the resurrected Lord.

Are you too busy to offer daily words of thanksgiving and praise to a thirsty Jew? Are you too famished in your own spiritual life to minister to the Prophet of Israel with worship in Spirit (oil) and truth (flour)? Is it always too late, or too early, or are you always too tired to invite the Stranger whose words have burned in your heart to come into your house and spend time with you? That's all right. He understands. There's always another house just down the road that has supper already prepared for Him, and another garden not far away. The owner is just hoping that the *Well from which Jacob drank* will pass by there today to meet him as He met the Samaritan woman. Don't worry. He won't go hungry...but *you* will! Then you will miss the glory of His presence. You see, when we give the Lord fruit from the tree of life that grows in our garden, He gives *us* fruit from that tree in return. In fact, when we open our door to His knock, He comes in and sups with us and we with Him (Rev. 3:20). When we take time to speak words of love and praise to Him, He takes time to speak living words to us. He is always willing to speak to those who are willing to take time to speak to Him.

His cry to us is, "Won't you make Me a cake first?" (1 Kings 17:13) He also cries to every true lover, "let me see thy countenance, *let me hear thy voice*; for sweet is thy voice, and thy countenance is comely" (Song 2:14b). Most of us feel spiritually weak because we lack the bread of Heaven, the living word. How can we have the privilege of hearing His voice if we do not respond to His longing to hear our voice? I have a suspicion, based on experience, that the more He hears my voice, the more I will hear His voice. The more He eats from the tree in my garden, the more I will eat from that tree also. We know how wonderful it is for us when He speaks a word of love to our hearts. Indeed, it is a word of life from the tree of life. Might we then expect that he, too, finds joy in hearing our words of love for Him? This is the bread He also seeks because He is like we are. He is hungry for our love.

Something else happens as we give the Lord an offering of love as Abel did. For those who long to develop the habit of speaking to the Lord in love and praise, He promises, "Open your mouth wide, and I will fill it" (Ps. 81:10b NKJV). This promise is made in the context of praise. The Lord is telling Israel that He has ordained worship to be a statute, a law, and a testimony in them (Ps. 81:1-5 NKJV). In this context, He promises to fill our mouths—but with what? With natural food? Obviously not. Nor is He speaking about filling the mouth of a preacher who didn't prepare a message before speaking. If we open wide our mouths in His presence, He will fill them with the praise and worship that will satisfy His hunger and thirst.

We are incapable of worshiping "in spirit and in truth" because in ourselves, we possess neither the spirit nor the truth with which to worship Him. If we will just open our mouths, however, and "take words," as Hosea 14:2 admonishes us to do, then He will give us both the truth and the anointing oil of the Spirit to satisfy His heart with heavenly worship. He asks us to take the tiny bit of flour (truth) and oil (Spirit) that remains in our house and make Him a cake first, not only once, but every day. Then, everything we give the Prophet of Israel will be multiplied and returned to us. We must start by opening our mouth through an act of our own will. Many times this involves a sacrifice. We must begin by using our mouths to give Him some little expression of truth about who He is, what He does, or what He has said. We might also begin our praise by singing a song to Him. As we continue, suddenly He will come and fill our mouths with an inspired and anointed expression of praise. Thus, He makes something out of nothing in this area of our walk also! David proclaimed that the Lord "satisfies your mouth with good things, so that your youth is renewed like the eagle's" (Ps. 103:5 NKJV). This is the path to spiritual renewal. We will also be able to say with David, "The Spirit of the Lord spake by me, and *his word* was in my *tongue*" (2 Sam. 23:2).

God's response to our true worship will revolutionize our lives. As the fire falls upon our altar of worship and the Lord fills our mouths with the living word, we find Christ Himself, the living Word. Have you sought the Lord, at times, without finding Him? Have you longed to meet with Him, but you just have not known the secret? The Apostle Paul tells us where the seeking soul can find the Lord: "Say not in thine heart, Who shall ascend into heaven? (that is, to bring Christ down from above:) Or, Who shall descend into the deep? (that is, to bring up Christ again from the dead.) But what saith it? The *word is nigh thee, even in thy mouth*, and in thy heart" (Rom. 10:6b-8a). All born-again Believers declare that Christ is in their hearts. But how many times have you heard it said that Christ, the Word, can be found in our *mouths*? That is what Paul tells us here! As we use our mouths to offer the Lord a sacrifice of worship, He visits us, meets with us, and feeds us with fresh truth as the Spirit of revelation comes upon us. This was always the experience of any true priest in the Old Testament. He ate and was satisfied from the very same lamb he offered on the Lord's altar (1 Cor. 10:18; Heb. 13:10).

If there is a lack of spiritual food in our churches or our lives, maybe we have taken the importance of offering sacrifices of worship far too lightly. In some places, worship is treated as an add-on that isn't very important in the life of the local church or in the private lives of its members. One evidence of this is that in many churches the youth of the congregation are in charge of the music and worship. Apparently, the "mature" saints do not consider worship to be something they need to be overly concerned about or directly involved in.

David, a man after God's own heart, saw it differently. He, with the prophets of Israel, chose the songs that were to be sung by God's people, played the instruments, and led the worship services.[9] Under David, the most mature leaders were in charge of this vital area, *not* the youth! Too often in the Church today the attitude is that God is happy to accept anything that is offered to Him in any way we choose, as long as it comes from a sincere heart. The story of Cain should have been sufficient to correct that grievous error from the beginning, but Jude 11 warns that many in the Church still go in "the way of Cain." How tragic!

It is *His* word in our tongue that becomes a tree of life for the Lord Himself, that causes our sacrifice of praise to become a joy to His heart. He alone is the source of any and all sacrifices that are **acceptable**. The great worshiper, David, understood this and confessed, "But who am I, and

---

9.   David, Asaph, and men like them wrote Israel's hymnbook, the Psalms. See First Chronicles 15:16-17 and 25:1.

who are my people, that we should be able to offer so willingly as this? For *all things come from You, and of Your own we have given You"* (1 Chron. 29:14 NKJV). The mystery of the tree of life is very similar to the mystery the Lord Jesus posed to the Pharisees about the Son of David. He assured them that Christ is David's son, or in other words, a fruit of David's own life. He adds that David called his own son, "Lord," then He asks them, "Therefore David calls Him 'Lord'; how is He then his Son?" (Lk. 20:44 NKJV) One of the great mysteries of God's ways is that a fruit of our lives can actually be the Lord Himself. This is the fruit He seeks from the tree in our garden. Only that which is divine can satisfy the Divine One.

The Lord says to His lover, "Thy lips, O my spouse, **drop** as the honeycomb: honey and milk are under thy tongue" (Song 4:11a). This word "drop" actually means "to speak by inspiration," or "to prophesy."[10] This is the only way the fruit of our mouths will be a delight to His heart as they are in the Song of Solomon. They must be offered under the inspiration of the Spirit. The Lord promises that this will happen if we open wide our mouths. Little by little we will learn to speak to Him by inspiration. Soon this will affect the way we speak to others, individually or in a group. People will take note that we have been with Jesus because there will be spiritual food in our house for all the hungry. Unfortunately, people will also take note if we have given our mouths to words of condemnation, criticism, unthankfulness, and murmuring. When we do, our tongue becomes a source of death instead of a tree of life. Both "death and life are in the power of the tongue" (Prov. 18:21a).

As we learn to yield our tongue to His worship, the anointing of the Spirit will flow, and we, too, will be able to say, "Eat, O friends; drink, yea, drink abundantly, O beloved" (Song 5:1c). Not only will the Lord's hunger be satisfied by the words of our mouths but also the hunger of many others—His friends. When we have reached Day Seven, any hungry heart will be able to eat from the tree of life, the living Word, that has been placed within us. As we offer unto the Lord sacrifices of praise, the fruit of our lips, **He** eats, **we** eat, and **others** eat. As we become a tree of life for Him, He becomes a tree of life for us, as well as for others through us. *This is rest.*

4. Rivers Flow From Our Innermost Being

"Now a river went out of Eden to water the garden, and from there it parted and became four riverheads" (Gen. 2:10 NKJV). In 1978 my wife and I, along with our four children, moved to Guatemala, Central America, to begin a new chapter in our lives. Shortly after arriving there, I was

---

10. Micah 2:6; *Strong's Hebrew Dictionary*, #5197.

driving along a main thoroughfare in Guatemala City and approaching the busiest intersection in the city of almost 2 million people. I noticed that up ahead of me a small airplane was descending. I was not familiar enough with the city to know that this airplane had begun to descend immediately after takeoff—with no place to land safely! As the airplane crash-landed in the street, the biggest ball of fire I had ever witnessed exploded a short distance in front of my vehicle. In that instant, I had a strong impression that I "just happened" to be at the scene of this accident by divine appointment. I was one of the first to approach the burning wreckage.

The four occupants, North American missionaries, had died almost instantly. Someone had been with the pilot's wife at the airport just before they took off and the pilot's wife had expressed the deep longing of her heart to be with the Lord. Her longing was granted within 15 minutes of that conversation!

There were several personal things the Lord spoke to me as I stood there and observed the tragedy. In addition, the Lord gave me a vision of a jet crashing. As I received the vision, I understood that He was forewarning me about a future tragedy that would come to Guatemala. I also understood that by "divine appointment" He would use that future crash to speak to me again. A Guatemalan jet did, in fact, crash a few years after that vision, killing all 100 people on board. It was a terrible tragedy for many families and a great sorrow for the entire nation. It was a very difficult time for me personally because I knew all three members of the flight crew. I had received many hours of flight instruction from the captain who died in the crash, and had also flown on one occasion with the first officer.

Possibly the most awesome message the Spirit of God gave me at the scene of that small airplane crash came as I turned around to return to my vehicle. For ten minutes my attention had been glued to the crash and to what the Lord was speaking to me. But, as I turned around, I was absolutely awestruck by what I saw. At least 20,000 people had gathered at the scene of that accident in a matter of minutes! This was possible because of the high volume of traffic that flowed through that intersection and because the surrounding buildings were mostly commercial, including a large shopping center. People were pressed together everywhere—on the highway, on the sidewalks, on the overhead pedestrian crosswalk, on the grassy areas, and on the roofs of the surrounding buildings. I was not only awestruck by the number of people who gathered but also by the rapidity with which they seemed to materialize out of thin air! In that instant, the Lord said to me, "They gather here today because they have been brought face to face with the reality of death; but the day will soon come when even greater multitudes will gather in this way because I will bring them face to face with the reality of My resurrection life. When people die tragically, multitudes gather; but when people are raised from the dead by the power and glory of My Spirit, even greater multitudes will gather, and they will want to hear the message My people will have to share with them about life. My rivers of life will soon be flowing throughout the land!"

Oh, how the Church and the world need the mighty rivers of life that will flow through those who finish their journey and come into the glory and rest of Eden! According to Ezekiel, those rivers will bring life wherever they go. He writes, "And it shall be that every living thing that moves, wherever the rivers go, will live. There will be a very great multitude of fish, because these waters go there; for they will be healed, and everything will live wherever the river goes" (Ezek. 47:9 NKJV).

Two thousand years ago, on the great day of the Feast of Tabernacles, the **seventh** feast, Jesus cried out in the Temple, "If any man thirst, let him come unto me, and drink. He that believeth on me, as the scripture hath said, out of his belly shall flow rivers of living water" (Jn. 7:37b-38). According to Genesis 2, rivers flow from the garden within us on **Day Seven**. And Jesus links the flowing of rivers from within us to the seventh feast, the Feast of Tabernacles. Jesus said that rivers will flow in the lives of those who believe on Him in accordance with the Scripture.[11] The first Scripture that reveals the way we must believe on Him is the Creation account. If we believe in that revelation enough to allow the Creator to accomplish His will in us, then our life in God will one day experience the flow of His mighty rivers.

There is nothing I could say about the rivers of God that could compare with what many different Scriptures tell us about them. If we will only believe and obey, here is what God promises us:

"And the Lord shall guide thee continually, and satisfy thy soul in drought, and make fat thy bones: and **thou shalt be like a watered garden,** *and like a spring of water, whose waters fail not* (Isaiah 58:11).

"When the poor and needy seek water, and there is none, and their tongue faileth for thirst, I the Lord will hear them, I the God of Israel will not forsake them. I will open rivers in high places, and fountains in the midst of

---

11. Note that Jesus is not quoting a specific Scripture here. There is no Old Testament Scripture that specifically says rivers will flow from us. Rather, Jesus is saying that if we believe on Him in accordance to what the Scriptures reveal, then the rivers will flow.

the valleys: I will make the wilderness a pool of water, and the dry land springs of water" (Isaiah 41:17-18).

"And he shewed me a pure river of water of life, clear as crystal, proceeding out of the throne of God and of the Lamb. In the midst of the street of it, and on either side of the river, was there the tree of life" (Revelation 22:1-2a).

5. Not My Will But Thine

"And the Lord God commanded the man, saying, Of every tree of the garden thou mayest freely eat: but of the tree of the knowledge of good and evil, thou shalt not eat of it: for in the day that thou eatest thereof thou shalt surely die" (Gen. 2:16-17). Although the first Adam failed to obey the will of his Father as it was expressed in this command, the last Adam (the Lord Jesus Christ) never fails. He lives to do the will of the Father. He said, "For I came down from heaven, not to do mine own will, but the will of him that sent me" (Jn. 6:38). Wherever He goes, it is always to do the will of the Father. When He comes to take up residence in the garden of our hearts, it is always to do the will of the Father. Much of the reason we lack rest in our spirits and "labor and are heavy laden" (Mt. 11:28) is that we have a will of our own that has not yet died; therefore, we struggle feverishly to reach the long and short-range goals of our own will.

At this very moment, is there a storm of doubt, worry, fear, or uncertainty about something in your heart? Do you lack His deep peace and rest within? If you take a moment to analyze the root of your concern, you will almost certainly discover that your own will and desires are involved. If your conflict is spiritual, it could be that the root of your unrest is personal ambition—seeking to reach your own spiritual goals instead of seeking God's perfect will for your life. Is your conflict financial? Then the root problem could be that you do not want to lose something you already have. Those who understand the Lord's heart know that He *never* takes anything away from us unless it is to make room for something better. On the other hand, maybe you are struggling to find the money to buy something you do not yet have. If the Lord wants you to have that thing, no one on earth can keep it from you. However, if He does not want you to have it, then you do not really need it. It won't do you any good because you will be out of His will if you have it. It will almost certainly lead you into greater problems than you already have.

Some might say, "But you don't understand. My need is for food—I have to eat!" This is an oft-heard declaration that is totally false. We do *not* have to eat! If He chooses to withhold His provision in this area, then we have an option that the strong will of some has not allowed them to even consider—fasting until we die of starvation. Eating is not essential; doing the Lord's will is. Fear not! The psalmist had never heard of anyone who had died of starvation while doing the Lord's perfect will (Ps. 37:25). I have not either. Have you? The question is, Are we willing to submit to His will for our lives today or do we insist on doing things our way?

My wife and I have been in situations where we had no money and literally no food for weeks on end. No one ever knew it. We did not survive those times by turning into spiritual beggars, telling people how bad off we were or that we were "living by faith." Declaring this to others in our time of need is usually just a subtle way of asking them for an offering. It is also generally proof that we are not living by *our* faith, but rather, we are living by the faith of others as we seek their financial help. We did not survive our times of financial need by going into debt either. We did not borrow one penny. I do not share this to honor ourselves, but rather, to honor the only One worthy of honor. We are still alive because the One who is the source of provision still rules in the affairs of men! *He* decides what happens to us. Neither circumstances nor men decide. He still has his "ravens" that can bring us bread each day without even knowing what they are doing. Again, the issue is, Are we willing to do His will or are we demanding our own way and will?

You might say, "Brother, you make it sound like doing the Lord's will sometimes requires being radical or even fanatical!" The night Jesus was betrayed, His sweat was as great drops of blood as He agonized over how radical the will of the Father was at that moment. He was facing the agony of the worst experience of suffering and death that man has ever known. He was also facing the prospect of being separated from His loving Father as He took upon Himself the sins of the whole world from all ages. In Gethsemane, when He prayed to the Father, "Not my will, but thine, be done" (Lk. 22:42), the Father's will required something more radical than you or I will ever face! Yes, there are times in our lives when doing the Father's will is a costly proposition, but do we want to spend the rest of our lives struggling hopelessly to accomplish our own will in our own way? Or do we long for the rest that comes as Jesus takes control and chooses every detail for us? Allowing Him to take control brings rest to our hearts.

About 30 years ago, my spiritual understanding was partially opened to the depths of truth that are found in the Lord's prayer. (See Matthew 6:9-13.) I realized that His prayer is really a pattern prayer, each part of which is filled with the essential ingredients of effectual prayer. Several years ago, after I had shared on this theme for several Sunday mornings,

Pastor Rene Bertholin, one of my associate pastors, experienced a heart-rending tragedy. With his wife and their three boys in the car, he was driving on a rainy night in Mexico. As they were rounding a curve, a bus coming downhill at high speed on their side of the road hit their car. Rene's entire family perished in the crash, and he was hospitalized in critical condition. In spite of the medical risks involved, it was decided to fly him to a hospital in Guatemala, along with the bodies of his four loved ones. The funeral was to be held during the upcoming Sunday morning service at our church.

None of us could begin to share the agony my friend, brother, and co-worker was experiencing. In the midst of death and sorrow, I longed to share a message of life and encouragement with the church and the family members. I just naturally assumed that the series of teachings on the Lord's prayer would be interrupted, until I realized that the next part was, "Thy will be done in earth as it is in heaven." What a prayer for a situation like Rene's! Most of us are very willing to pray, "Thy will be done in [our] earth," as long as His will for us involves blessing, joy, and prosperity, but do we have enough trust in His loving heart to accept sorrow, trials, and even death, knowing that He is incapable of choosing anything but the very best for us?

The Lord's presence came to comfort us that Sunday morning. The gloom turned to glory—not because of my message, but because of the testimony I shared about Rene himself. I had been traveling at the time of the accident and was unable to go to the place in Mexico where Rene was initially hospitalized. Therefore, I requested that several other leaders of the congregation go to be with him. When they arrived, the doctor in charge cautioned them not to tell Rene that his entire family had passed away. His condition was so critical he might not survive the shock and sorrow. They agreed not to tell him. When they entered the room, Rene was conscious. To their chagrin, one of the first things Rene wanted to know was about his family. Rene's friends felt that, as Christians, the only thing worse than telling Rene the truth would have been telling him a lie. The leader who had been closest to Rene for many years reluctantly shared the news about his family.

Physically, Rene was suffering excruciating pain from multiple injuries and several broken bones. However, upon hearing that he had lost his entire family, he was overcome by inexpressible grief. In spite of all this, Rene's first reaction was to pray. His prayer was very short but obviously from the depths of his spirit. He said, "Father, many times I have committed them into Your hands. I give You thanks now for having taken them to be with You." Rene's next reaction was to begin to sing a song of worship to the Lord. The glory of God filled the room and touched each of their hearts in an awesome way. They all joined in the chorus Rene was singing and ended by worshiping the One who is unchanging love, regardless of what our hearts might tell us in the midst of our raging storms and our darkest nights. Rene's reaction was not that of a man who flippantly prays, "Lord, Thy will be done." This was the reaction of a man who had learned that God's will for His children is *always* best, and our own will is *never* best.

In the depths of a trial like Rene's, not everyone would react the same way. You might say, "I am afraid I would not be able to accept the Lord's will for my life in a situation like that." You may be right if you judge by your present level of spiritual maturity, but God wants to take you on to spiritual maturity and the rest found on Day Seven so that neither loss nor gain can change your love for Him. This is His desire for all His children. Those who come to that place in God do not merely accept, or endure, the Lord's will. They do not simply grit their teeth and wait for something better. In that seventh Day they have come into the rest of the One who could say, "I *delight* to do thy will, O my God: yea, thy law is within my heart" (Ps. 40:8). They know that His will for their lives is always *best*, not just good or acceptable. There can be no lasting rest in our spirits until this knowledge is planted deeply in our hearts. This is true because life is in a constant state of change. From our earthly point of view, change is sometimes for the better and other times for the worse. If we belong to God, *every* change is for our good! A deep assurance of this fact brings rest to our spirits even as the storms of life rage about us. Along life's journey, we all too often struggle for *our* way; but those who have entered the rest of the last Adam always pray with Him, "Father, Thy will be done." *This* is rest.

6. Adam Names the Animals

"And out of the ground the Lord God formed every beast of the field, and every fowl of the air; and brought them unto Adam to see what he would call them: and whatsoever Adam called every living creature, that was the name thereof. And Adam gave names to all cattle, and to the fowl of the air, and to every beast of the field" (Gen. 2:19-20a). Can we begin to imagine the tremendous divine wisdom that Adam manifested as he named the animals? We have no way of knowing how many he named. In fact, to this day no one is even sure how many different species of animals are on the earth. Estimates vary wildly between 3 million and 100 million.[12] One thing is certain—when God brought the animals to Adam,

---

12. Randy Fitzgerald, "When a Law Goes Haywire," *Reader's Digest*, September 1, 1993, p. 52.

their names must have been on the tip of his tongue. If he would have had to deliberate about each one for very long, he would still be naming them today! Have you ever noticed that he made all these decisions before God gave him Eve as a helper? What a project this would have been if there had been two opinions for every animal!

In the life of the last Adam, Christ, we see that when His Father brought people before Him, He supernaturally knew them immediately and frequently gave them a name that reflected His knowledge of their character. He said to Simon, "Thou art Simon the son of Jona: thou shalt be called Cephas, which is by interpretation, A stone" (Jn. 1:42b). Not only did Jesus supernaturally know Simon's name but He also knew the name of His father Jona. Even more glorious—Jesus knew who Peter was spiritually from their first meeting. Shortly afterwards, Jesus also knew who Nathanael was, saying to him, "Behold an Israelite indeed, in whom is no guile!" (Jn. 1:47b) It is not clear exactly what happened in Jesus' first encounter with Nathanael, but it was such a revelation of supernatural knowledge that it caused skeptical Nathanael to respond, "Rabbi, You are the Son of God! You are the King of Israel!" (Jn. 1:49 NKJV) Jesus supernaturally knew the character and lives of each of His disciples, and He gave them different names based on His divine knowledge. He even knew that Judas was a devil (Jn. 6:70).

As we come into the rest found on Day Seven, we will discover that the last Adam will give us supernatural wisdom to know people and see situations as God knows and sees them. How could it be otherwise once the heavens are opened to us and we see the spiritual realms as God sees them? Just imagine how many church splits, conflicts of character, conflicts of interests, and other problems could have been avoided if only we had been able to see people as the Lord sees them! This is granted to those who enter His rest; this will also *bring* great rest to us and to those around us.

7. Married to the Last Adam

"And Adam said, This is now bone of my bones, and flesh of my flesh: she shall be called Woman, because she was taken out of Man. Therefore shall a man leave his father and his mother, and shall cleave unto his wife: and they shall be one flesh" (Gen. 2:23-24). Did you know that God's purpose for your life is that you become one with Christ, the last Adam, to such a degree that He calls you bone of His bone and flesh of His flesh? The Lord pleads with His people, "Turn, O backsliding children, saith the Lord; for I am married unto you" (Jer. 3:14a). The Apostle Paul also tells us that we are married to the Lord. He writes, "For no man ever yet hated his own flesh; but nourisheth and cherisheth it, even as the Lord the church:

For *we are members of his body, of his flesh, and of his bones.* For this cause shall a man leave his father and mother, and shall be joined unto his wife, and they two shall be one flesh. *This is a great mystery: but I speak concerning Christ and the church"* (Eph. 5:29-31).

Paul did not try to explain the glory of this relationship or rationalize its beauty. He simply accepted the reality of this call and said that it is a "great mystery" (Eph. 5:32). Ruth 1:9 refers to marriage as rest. A successful marriage certainly does bring rest to our lives. It brings love, unity, fellowship, provision, protection, strength, fruitfulness, purpose, and many other blessings that bring rest and peace to our spirits. No wonder the Lord ordained natural marriage to be a revelation of our heavenly marriage with Him. He could not have used a more graphic way to reveal the blessings of being joined to the Lord Himself! Of course, all the blessings of marriage are infinitely multiplied when we become one flesh with an infinite God. Even if the Lord has not chosen a natural marriage relationship for you, what you have lost is nothing compared to what is available in Him. Paul, the bachelor, surely believed this! (See First Corinthians 7:1,7,32-34.)

Marriage also provides us a wonderful opportunity to learn to live for the sake of someone else, instead of living only for ourselves. Living for self is a way of life that always destroys rest in our spirits because we live in a continual battle to get what we think will be best for us. Daily we have the opportunity to give ourselves for our spouse and children, in unfeigned love, as we lay down our rights, desires, plans, and purposes. Learning to do this faithfully usually requires many years of practice, and unfortunately, it is sometimes never learned. The Lord laid down His life for His wife (us), and He calls us to do the same for others. This is especially true for any earthly husband who longs to be like Christ. Paul exhorts, "Husbands, love your wives, even as Christ also loved the church, and gave himself for it" (Eph. 5:25). From this verse, Paul goes on to apply this self-giving, selfless love to the relationship between Christ and the Church (Eph. 5:28-32). He explains that we are all members of Christ's flesh, and no one has ever hated his own flesh. The implication here is clear: As Christ gave Himself for us, we should give ourselves for Him and for others. We should love and care for the other members of His "flesh and bones"—the Body to which we belong. When we come to Day Seven, the way we care for and love the Body of Christ will be automatic because Christ will be dwelling within the garden of our hearts. In a real sense, we could say that on Day Seven it will be "second nature" for us to give ourselves for others. This is the way the Lord has always been; it is also the way He will always be when He lives in and through us. This will bring rest to us and to others.

8. Naked and Not Ashamed

"And they were both naked, the man and his wife, and were not ashamed" (Gen. 2:25).

They were not ashamed because there was nothing to be ashamed of in their lives. As long as they had nothing to cover or hide, the desire to cover what they were was simply never felt. In fact, the very concept of being naked was foreign to them. They had never seen anyone wearing clothes before. They did not even know what nakedness was! It had never been defined or experienced by anyone.

Would it be possible for someone who had never heard of the game of baseball to comprehend that "the runner was out at third base"? The concept simply would not register in their minds. To have told Adam and Eve that they were naked would have caused the same perplexity. Nakedness was so foreign to them that after they had sinned, God asked Adam, "Who told thee that thou wast naked?" (Gen. 3:11a)

The moment Adam wanted to hide something from God and others, he felt a need to cover and hide himself. This is the sensation we call "nakedness." We know that fig leaves did not do the job because even after he used the leaves to cover himself, Adam said that he was naked when God entered the garden (Gen. 3:7,10). Fig leaves could not cover the guilt and sin that only the Lamb can cover. Standing in His light, our spiritual nakedness is never covered by our own efforts. Only He can clothe us, and an animal, representing the eternal Lamb of God, had to die to do so (Gen. 3:21).

What a glorious way to end the divine revelation of His rest in Genesis 2: "They were naked and not ashamed!" Oh, the rest He has prepared for those who follow on to know the Lord. It is real rest when we can walk before the Lord and others in such a way that we never have to cover or hide anything! Paul experienced this walk. He testifies, "And herein do I exercise myself, to have always a conscience void of offence toward God, and toward men" (Acts 24:16).

The spiritual place where we never feel a need to hide anything can *only* be found in Christ. God didn't take away Adam and Eve's fig leaves without giving them an answer for their nakedness. The Lord clothed Adam and Eve with skins obtained through the death of another. If we love righteousness, there are so many areas of our sinful lives that we would like to keep out of sight. When we begin our Christian walk in Christ, these sins are all forgiven and covered by the blood—the Lord does this daily if necessary. Later, our iniquities are removed from us when the work of the crucifixion of the old man is finally complete on Day

Six. On that Day, the very life and nature of the last Adam fills our earth, covering us within and without with the gold of His nature. Only *then* can we enter rest without feeling a need to cover what we are. When the Lord's life covers us, we have no need to be ashamed of what He does or says in and through us. There is nothing to hide. *This* is rest.

You Can Enter Rest Today

Are you waiting with great expectancy to experience an instantaneous change sometime in the future that will bring you into the rest found on Day Seven? Wait no longer. Although we will only experience the **fullness** of His rest when the **fullness** of Christ is formed in us, we can **begin** to enter a measure of His rest today. This is true regardless of which of the seven Days we are presently experiencing. Please do not misunderstand. This is not a contradiction of what I said in the beginning. God must complete the work of each Day to His satisfaction before we can move on to the next Day. Of course, besides experiencing God's rest, the greatest glory that is associated with Day Seven is that the Lord Himself fills our earth with "all the fullness of God." Before we reach Day Seven, we will not yet be channels through which the **fullness** of Christ is revealed; nevertheless, each new Day will bring us into a new and deeper rest. Although we long for the day when His glory covers all the earth, the prospect of experiencing a continually deeper measure of rest should greatly encourage the pure heart that longs to rest from its own works and ways. How do we enter an ever deeper rest in our spiritual lives?

The characteristics of the Lord's rest that are revealed on Day Seven are basically virtues that have become part of our spiritual lives on previous Days. In fact, God does **no work** whatsoever in our earth on Day Seven. Rather, the rest of Day Seven is simply the fruit of His work in our lives on the other six Days. When the last Adam finds a resting place and comes to dwell in our garden, it will be a garden that has already been prepared by the six previous Days of God's creative work.

For example, how can we know the rest that comes with obedience to the Father's will on Day Seven if we do not learn obedience to Him as He makes a separation between the works of darkness and the works of light in our lives on Day One? The foundation for this aspect of rest is laid in our lives on Day One. On that Day, as we allow Him to deal with us according to *His* list of priorities, we enter a **measure** of rest. As we receive grace to be changed, we cease from our own works in at least some areas. Each time we do, we experience greater rest in our spirits.

We also experience a new measure of rest on Day Two as the Lord leads us into doctrinal purity and truth. Our spirits will be brought into greater rest as we are set free from the bondage of doctrinal error on Day

Two. The spirit of error brings doubts and uncertainty to us, for which truth is the only answer.

God's work in us on Day Three is also part of the foundation of rest. On Day Seven, we will be able to satisfy the hunger of the last Adam only if God has planted the fruit trees in our earth on Day Three, along with the tree of life. This third Day also offers us greater depths of spiritual rest as the fruits of the Spirit replace the pride, jealousy, hatred, and strife of our own hearts.

On Day Four we receive a revelation of the glory of the Lord; we also see Him in His Body. This brings us into a depth of communion with Him and others that we have never before known. That intimate communion with Christ and His Body prepares us for the marriage of Day Seven. Oh, what rest becomes ours on Day Four when we begin to treat others differently because we know that Christ is living in His Body!

On Day Five the waters bring forth an abundance of life. This prepares us to experience the rivers of water that will flow from our innermost being on Day Seven. Those rivers will bring life wherever they flow as we open our mouths and speak forth a mighty Word of life as a trumpet of God. On Day Five, we begin to expend less effort and enter greater rest as we learn to minister from the flow of the water of life!

On Day Six we experience the covering of gold or the covering of the divine nature and life as the last Adam is formed in our earth. That reality will prepare us to experience the blessing of being naked without being ashamed. In other words, at that time we will have nothing to hide from God or man. This is a wonderful and new measure of rest that comes to us on Day Six.

If we allow the Lord to bring us into the ever-increasing spiritual maturity that is revealed through these six Days, the time will come when the Spirit will lead us to our personal Jordan River experience. At that moment, the anointing from Heaven will descend and abide with us just like the Lord Jesus received the Father's anointing when He was baptized in the Jordan. Then the Anointed One will take up His abode in us, but He will not dwell in a house that is filled with turmoil. He seeks a house that is filled with His peace and rest. David cried to Him, "Arise, O Lord, into thy **rest**" (Ps. 132:8a).

The Lord found a resting place in David. He seeks one in us also. The Spirit lovingly prepares that place throughout the six Days of the "redemptive week." Regardless of what Day you are presently experiencing, **now** is the time to allow Him to bring you into a deeper measure of spiritual rest. You need not wait; you *must* not wait!

Chapter 18

A Treasure in Vessels of Clay

"I didn't come to this Bible school to work in a vegetable garden. I am called to preach, not to cultivate vegetables," declared one of the Bible school students in the Philippines. During his two years of study, this student made it clear that he was not willing to work. I didn't have much hope for his future. I had never seen God really bless a lazy person in the ministry. The Lord always seems to choose hard-working people like Ruth, Elisha, Peter, and Paul. I was very surprised, therefore, when this young man was chosen to pastor a large church. Shortly afterwards, the news came that he had been arrested and was locked up in a national prison. His desire for an easy life, obtained in an easy way, led him to commit criminal offenses.

Long before this young man actually began to pastor the church, it was rumored that the church property was the site of an ancient Chinese burial ground. Authentic Chinese artifacts from the Ming Dynasty (14th century) were bringing a very good price in the Philippines. The only real problem was that like most nations of the world, the Philippines considered ancient artifacts to be part of their national heritage, and therefore government property. Those who were caught buying or selling them on the black market were not very popular with the archaeologists from the national museum. Selling artifacts was precisely the crime that brought a long vacation in prison for this young "pastor" who didn't like to plant vegetables or do anything else that involved hard work. The more he heard the rumor about the church property being a burial ground, the more his interest grew in Chinese artifacts. Therefore, one night under the cover of darkness he decided that digging in the soil wasn't such bad work after all. In fact, he enjoyed it so much that from the first night on, he worked quite hard digging just about every night. The rumor proved true, and this young man found himself in the middle of a very lucrative business.

One of the last artifacts he dug up was just a common, unpainted clay pot. It was worth thousands on the black market, and he already had a buyer for it when the police came to take him to jail. Imagine that—just a common old clay pot that was no different from the pots sold almost anywhere in the Philippines. Those pots sold for a few pesos, but this pot was worth thousands! Why? Simply because there were people on earth who were willing to pay such an exorbitant price for it. The value of a thing is determined by what people are willing to pay for it, not by the value of the materials used to make it. This pot came from the very same soil that many other clay pots came from. They had been formed and baked in much the same way and were all used for the same purposes. Nevertheless, people were gladly willing to pay an unbelievable price because they saw value in it that was far beyond what the human eye could see or appreciate. Those who buy such things sometimes do so because of who owned them in the past—either famous, infamous, or ancient people. The location from which something is rescued or dug is another reason for paying a ridiculously high price for an otherwise common object. For example, things that are rescued from the Titanic are considered priceless. Therefore, exorbitant prices can sometimes be demanded and collected for very simple things. These things often become status symbols or trophies of one's financial resources. They definitely make a statement. They carry with them a message from their past, as well as a message about their new owner.

Did you know that God looks upon us as clay pots? The New Testament calls us "jars of clay" (2 Cor. 4:7 NIV). The only thing that makes us valuable in this world is God's willingness to pay an incredible price for us. The price He paid was infinite—the life of His own dear Son! The enormous price He paid was given not because Satan once owned us (though he *is* infamous), but because of the depths of sin from which we were rescued, depths that no one else could have reached! Our redeemed lives definitely make a statement and carry a message. We are trophies of God's grace. We also reveal His infinite resources of love, mercy, and forgiveness. We are indisputable proof of what the Lord is really like.

To each of His purchased vessels the Lord assigns a sublime purpose. We were not purchased only to be conversation pieces for the heavenly hosts. Instead, He puts us to good use in His Kingdom. Intrinsically, a clay pot is of little value, but the treasure God has placed within the clay pot is most precious, indeed. Paul declares that we have a *"treasure* in jars of clay" (2 Cor. 4:7 NIV). This treasure from Heaven is the Lord Himself. The Creator has decided that we will become His dwelling place, or His eternal habitation.

Can we fathom the depths of meaning in this divine decision? The Almighty God of Heaven and earth decided to dwell forever in lowly men—clay pots. This definitely makes a statement about God's nature. What humility! What condescension! What love! Even the universe is too small to serve as His house (1 Kings 8:27). Couldn't He have chosen something better for His eternal dwelling? Something more glorious? Something more precious? Yes, He could have chosen something better and far more glorious. In fact, being God, He could have chosen something entirely different. Still, He could *not* have chosen something more precious because He has made us infinitely precious in His sight by paying an infinite price for us. Like one who buys ancient artifacts, He sees a value in us that goes far beyond what the human eye can see or appreciate. When we are yet lumps of clay He sees the finished product of His creative work. He envisions His own glory and life formed within us.

The Glory Within the Clay Pots Is Christ

As the Apostle Paul explains, the glory God could see in us is Christ's own life. Paul prays that we will **know** what the hope of our calling is, which is "Christ in you, the hope of **glory**" (Col. 1:27; see also Eph. 1:16-18). Paul also wants us to know *"the riches of the glory of his inheritance in the saints"* (Eph. 1:18b). Remember, the inheritance is two-way: God inherits us and we inherit God. Only Christ within us can make us to be a worthy inheritance for our God. Later, in Ephesians 3:3-6, Paul goes on to speak of a wonderful divine **"mystery,"** which is that the **inheritance** will be received by Gentiles and Jews alike. Just as Colossians 1:27 explains that "Christ in us" is our hope of glory, so, too, it explains that "Christ in us" is the "riches of the glory" of God's inheritance among the Gentiles and Jews (in other words, the "mystery"). Paul writes, "To whom God would make known what is the *riches of the glory* of this **mystery** among the Gentiles; which is Christ in you…" (Col 1:27). The Lord is not seeking an inheritance that consists merely of clay pots—us—but also of the treasure that fills those pots—Christ's life formed within our earth.

Clay Pots Become His Resting Place

What do clay pots that become His dwelling place have to do with the rest found on Day Seven? Jesus said, "Foxes have holes and birds of the air have nests, but the Son of Man has nowhere to lay His head"

(Mt. 8:20 NKJV). The Son of Man seeks a place where He can rest. He seeks a dwelling place. For Him, as well as for human beings, a dwelling place serves as a resting place. The psalmist proclaims, "For the Lord has chosen Zion; He has desired it for His *dwelling place*: 'This is My *resting place* forever; Here I will *dwell*, for I have desired it' " (Ps. 132:13-14 NKJV). Will we be that place? Will the last Adam find a garden in our earth in which He can dwell and enjoy rest?

From the beginning, the Lord has sought rest. In Genesis 2:2, we find that God entered rest before anyone else. In Hebrews 3–4, rest is likened to the goal of our spiritual journey. Over and over it is referred to as *"His* rest." For example, we are promised the gift of "entering into *His* rest" (Heb. 4:1). We must understand that it is *His* rest we enter and not our own. The Almighty will finally find a place to rest when He has finished His creative work in each of us individually, as well as in His Church corporately. This dwelling place is revealed at the end of the Book of Revelation: "And I heard a loud voice from heaven saying, 'Behold, the tabernacle of God is with men, and *He will dwell with them*, and they shall be His people. God Himself will be with them and be their God. And God will wipe away every tear from their eyes; there shall be no more death, nor sorrow, nor crying. There shall be no more pain, for the former things have passed away' " (Rev. 21:3-4 NKJV). *This* is real rest. This is a place of no pain or sorrow (no travail) and no death; therefore, there can be no sin because sin always brings death. In this passage, **this rest** is directly associated with the fact that we have become the Lord's dwelling or *His* place of rest. Therefore, **this rest** will only come to each of us as we personally become a tabernacle of God—His eternal dwelling. The fullness of His rest cannot be entered or experienced without the fullness of Christ dwelling in us. Christ must be fully formed within our earth on Day Six so that He can occupy His dwelling place in the garden of our hearts on Day Seven and share His rest with us. Otherwise, there will be no rest for Him *or* for us. There will be no Day Seven. The rest of God is primarily for *His* benefit, not for ours. Of course, the benefit for us is incalculable when He finds a resting place in us. Could there be a greater joy than to become a place for the Son of man to lay His head?

Are you seeking a place of rest, as Christ does? Since the fall of Adam in the garden, mankind has a deep inner longing to find again a place of rest for his spirit. Man will never find it until, and unless, the Lord first finds a place of rest within him. David understood this when he gave the Lord an invitation to enter His place of rest: "Arise, O Lord, to Your resting place, You and the ark of Your strength" (Ps. 132:8 NKJV). David was more concerned about the Lord finding rest than he was about finding rest for himself. His goal was unselfish. In the same psalm, he vowed, "Surely I will not go into the chamber of my house, or go up to the comfort of my bed; I will not give sleep to my eyes or slumber to my eyelids, until I find a place for the Lord, a dwelling place for the Mighty One of Jacob" (Ps. 132:3-5 NKJV).

The Lord found in David a place to rest, but this did not happen by chance. David became the Lord's dwelling place because one of David's primary goals in life was to prepare the Lord a place within his heart. He could, therefore, invite the Lord to find rest within him. The Lord's dwelling place is prepared in us as we submit to the work of the spirit during each successive Day in the "redemptive week." May we, like David, submit to the Spirit's work. **May our primary goal in seeking rest be an unselfish one, that is to provide a place of rest for God, not only ourselves.** God can place within our hearts this unselfish longing to satisfy the heart of the Son of Man by providing a place of rest for Him.

Providing rest for another was the desire of the Shunammite woman. Due to her unselfish concern for Elisha, she said to her husband, "Please, let us make a small upper room on the wall; and let us put a bed for him there, and a table and a chair and a lampstand; so it will be, whenever he comes to us, he can turn in there" (2 Kings 4:10 NKJV). She was a barren woman, but as she provided a place of rest for the Lord's servant, new life and joy came to her home. Soon she was no longer barren, and she gave birth to a son (2 Kings 4:12-17). This same life and joy is available to the spiritually barren who provide a place of rest for God within their hearts.

In this manner one of God's wonderful goals for man in His Kingdom is fulfilled: Man's spiritual house becomes a place of spiritual rest for the Lord **and for others in His Body.** This is what the Shunammite's house became for Elisha in the natural. Isaiah prophesies, "See, a king will reign in righteousness and rulers will rule with justice. *Each man* will be like *a shelter from the wind and a refuge from the storm,* like streams of water in the desert and *the shadow of a great rock in a thirsty land*" (Is. 32:1-2 NIV).

Is our only goal in entering rest to find for ourselves His peace, safety, shelter, and calm in the midst of the storm? God wants our self-centered goals to die and be replaced with God-centered goals. These goals must also include the Lord's Body, His people. Selfishness cannot cohabit with rest because selfishness is never satisfied or content. It must die! How wonderful it would be to become a person like those mentioned by Isaiah—a shelter and refuge for others in their storm, and the shadow of a **great rock** for people who are hurting! This can only happen if *the* Rock, the Lord Jesus Christ, dwells within us. He is the only one who can bring peace and rest to others in their storms. In this day of unparalleled spiritual and natural turmoil, He desires to do that for others through us. Once our earth is "filled with all the fullness of God" (Eph. 3:19 NKJV), He will accomplish that goal.

Selfish goals are never reached on the heavenly path to glory. This is true even if they may be "spiritual" goals. On the other hand, grace will always be granted to those whose motive is to be a blessing to the Lord and to His Body. We were created for His benefit, not our own. Paul declares that "all things were created by him, and *for* him" (Col. 1:16b). Is God being selfish then, by centering everything in Himself? No. Quite the opposite. The fact is, unless everything is centered in Him, there can be no rest because He alone is totally unselfish. When Christ was on earth, He spent 33 years denying Himself and taking up His cross daily, as He lived to serve God and others. He never lived to serve Himself (Rom. 15:3). The only reward He received for serving others, and for being the poured-out One, was to be crucified by those He came to serve. Afterwards, He ascended to His throne to reign forever. Enduring 33 years of continual, selfless giving may seem like a relatively small price to pay for the joy of reigning eternally. As Believers, we, too, should expect to experience the death to self that the Lord's own people will inflict on us from time to time. When others treat us unfairly, do we comfort ourselves with the thought that a short lifetime spent serving others is a small price to pay for the joy of reigning with Christ and being served forever? If so, we have missed the message of the cross that Christ continually lived and preached.

As Christ came to the end of a life that had been lived for others, He declared, "He that hath seen me hath seen the Father" (Jn. 14:9b). What did Jesus' disciples see in His life? What do we see in His life? His 33 years of self-denial were not the price He had to pay to reign; nor were they spent simply to give us a demonstration of how to live a spiritual life. No, Jesus spent those years showing us what the Father is really like. If His disciples saw the selfless, self-giving Christ, then they had seen the Father Himself because He is a Father who continually gives Himself for others. Like every man who becomes a real "Dad" on this earth, the Lord lives for His children, not for Himself. During His short life on earth, Christ was revealing the way the "Lamb slain from the foundation of the world" (Rev. 13:8) lives His life *continually*, and not only for His 33 years on this earth. He was revealing what He was, and is, and always shall be throughout eternity. He is infinitely unselfish, and therefore, His life alone can bring real rest to man's selfish heart. Aren't you thankful that everything is centered in Him?

Many years ago, the Lord invited His disciples to be like Him—to be people who live only for others and never for self, neither in this life nor the life to come. Today, He still invites willing hearts to embrace the same walk of love. Is that kind of life appealing to you? Some have their sights set on "being the boss" instead of being a servant; or, at least, on finally being served rather than serving. A selfless life is never appealing to our flesh, our earthly man. Ever since Eve, "the mother of all living" (Gen. 3:20), allowed ambition to enter her heart, human nature has continually sought to be "number one." Maybe our deceitful hearts have been willing to endure the unpleasantness of being on the bottom of the pile today because we harbor the hope of being on the top tomorrow. Can you imagine what Heaven would be like if the goal of all was to be on top and to be served? We should rejoice that those in Heaven have all been conformed to Christ's likeness and example. Like Him, they have become servants who delight in serving others.

The suffering and death of the cross in this life is not a test to see if we have what it takes to reign. It is not a time to "grin and bear it" with the hope of a better day. No, the cross of Christ is a God-given way to kill the flesh with all its ambition and self-love so that we may learn to give ourselves for others, both in this life and the life without end. Is this unappealing to you? Compare, for a moment, the earthly, carnal, selfish life with the heavenly, Christ-like, selfless life. In this natural life there is only one person on earth who is constantly looking out for what is best for me. That person is me. Our way of life in this world is "every man for himself." How ugly! Do our spirits long for rest from that selfishness, or would we prefer to live that way forever in Heaven? Thankfully, Heaven will be quite different because God's ways are far above our ways. In all Heaven there will be only one person who will *not* be looking out for what is best for me. That person will be me. Everyone else in Heaven will be concerned about what is best for me, and I will be concerned about what is best for every one of them. One of the wonderful realities of God's ways is that what is best for others *always* turns out to be what is best for me also! Therefore, if we learn to seek what is best for those around us, we will also end up getting what is best for ourselves.

Which do you prefer: to be cared for by just one self-centered, egotistical person, or to be cared for by all the selfless hosts of Heaven? Are you willing to pay the price to live in that glorious realm? That price is to learn to live for others and not for yourself in this present life. Are you willing to apply this to your life in a practical way today by beginning to live for others—for your family, friends, coworkers, and casual acquaintances? Only as you learn this lesson will you know the real rest of Day Seven. If you never learn this lesson, you will not be ready to reign with Christ, the Servant of servants.

Could that be why Paul says, "If we suffer, we shall also reign with him"? (2 Tim. 2:12a) Are we willing to suffer the injustices and reproaches of others and still keep on loving them as the Lord did for us? Each time we do, a little more of what we are dies, and a little more of the selfless One is formed in us. If we are willing to suffer the death to self that Christ's cross offers us, we will live and reign with Christ forever. If we learn to become servants, we will be ready to reign in Heaven. In Heaven, those who become kings and priests will be continually concerned about what they can do for others, instead of being concerned about what others can do for them.

This was the experience and attitude of Joseph, the seventh man of faith in Genesis. He definitely knew what it was to suffer at the hands of his brothers. Sold for a slave, he suffered one injustice after another. After years of God's dealings in his life, he was ready to reign. Only then did He ascend to a place of rulership in Egypt. Years later, when his brothers bowed before him and sought his help, he was willing to serve them and care for them for the rest of his life. He did not seek vengeance for the injustices they had committed against him. He didn't even force them to be his servants, though he could have. Instead, he cared for them, and all Egypt, from his position of glory and authority.

At the end of our journey toward spiritual maturity, the hallmark of our lives will not be the power and authority to do miracles and cast out demons, nor will it be our ability to preach mightily anointed messages that cause multitudes to gather. Although these things will definitely be manifested in our lives, as they were in the life of Christ, our example, they will not be our crowning glory. Power is not what draws us to the Savior. We are drawn by His demonstration of love for us in that He died on Calvary's tree to redeem us. When we reach maturity, others will be drawn to the Savior through us for the same reason—a demonstration of love (Jn. 13:35). The hallmark of our lives will not be the glory of the Lord's power revealed in us, but the glory of His unfeigned love for the brethren that flows through us. We will never be called to rule over others, until we first love them and give our lives for their welfare and blessing. This was Joseph's experience. That is what any normal father does for his children. Even more will this be true in the life of a mature saint—a *spiritual* father!

While it is true that we should never bring people under condemnation as Sister Most Holy did to John, we will find as we mature in the Lord, that the Lord will use us from time to time to correct and counsel others to keep them from making disastrous mistakes. This is one of the many responsibilities of a natural or spiritual father toward his children. Rarely, however, will we be commissioned to disciple another in this way unless we have first shed tears of intercession for them before the Lord, in the secret place.

"Unfeigned" love for others is something that we reveal in the secret place when we think no one is watching. It cannot be measured by how we act toward people in public. It is *genuine* love, not a front or pretense. The same is true for our love for the Lord. It cannot be measured by how we are in public, how we preach, pray, or praise when others are present. It is revealed only by how much we seek Him and love Him in private.

Judah manifested unfeigned love when he and his ten brothers stood before Joseph, the ruler of Egypt. Judah still did not know that this very powerful ruler was actually their "missing" brother for whom their father had mourned for years. He didn't know that they were standing before the very man they had sold into slavery 22 years before—at Judah's suggestion! But Joseph knew.

Joseph also knew that all the brothers had agreed with Judah's suggestion because Joseph was Rachel's son. Rachel was the only wife Jacob, their father, really recognized and accepted as his true wife. It seemed that Jacob considered the mothers of the other brothers to be mere concubines. The brothers were sure that as long as Joseph, the favorite son, was alive, they would not get their fair share of the family inheritance. They solved their problem by getting rid of Joseph. Then the brothers realized that they had another problem—Benjamin, the only other son of Jacob's beloved Rachel. It seemed obvious that Jacob, their father, would choose him to take Joseph's place as the family heir. Then came the severe famine that forced the brothers to go down into Egypt to buy food. There they found themselves standing before Joseph, the brother they had sold. God had exalted him in spite of what his brothers had done to him. (Man *never* decides our position in life; God does.)

Then, because something very strange had just happened, it appeared that young Benjamin would have to remain behind in Egypt as a slave. Joseph's own cup had been found in Benjamin's sack. It appeared that Benjamin was a thief. In fact, this was the work of Joseph, who was only seeking to prove his brother's hearts. He had ordered his steward to secretly place his cup in Benjamin's sack. By now Benjamin had become the only obstacle keeping the half-brothers from getting what they considered to be their rightful share of the inheritance. Their feelings about the inheritance were, and still are, common to humanity. Family inheritances almost always cause strife. Surely the brethren would consider Benjamin's fall into slavery to be a confirmation of what they had always felt. They were sure that Benjamin *was* a thief. After all, he was going to take more than his fair share of their father's estate!

Judah and the others had no way of knowing that the very brother they had betrayed was listening and weighing every word and action. Joseph had heard, first hand, what was in their hearts those many years ago when they had sold him. Now he waited to see if Benjamin would have to drink the same cup of suffering he, Joseph, had drunk at their hands. This is why the cup had been placed in Benjamin's sack. Joseph wanted to know if his own cup of suffering also belonged to Benjamin. He wanted to know if the brethren themselves would choose to make it Benjamin's cup also!

The question was, Did the brothers still harbor their same old envy, bitterness, and hatred? If they did, they now had the perfect opportunity to rid themselves of the only brother who was still a threat to their selfish goals. How easy it would have been for them to abandon Benjamin in Egypt. They could have said, "Yes, we sinned by selling Joseph into Egypt, but it was God who dealt with Benjamin. God has surely looked upon our situation and judged justly. He knows that our father has shown partiality to those two boys. Now they both have gotten what they deserved. They have both become slaves in Egypt!" (When false motives are in our hearts, how easy it is for us to fail a test. Under those circumstances, we tend to see things from our own perspective instead of God's!)

As Joseph waited for their decision, Judah came near to him and began to speak. Joseph could hear much more in Judah's words than anyone else in the room. This is what Joseph heard: "My lord, please allow me to speak to you from what is in my heart. My father had only two sons from the only woman he accepted as his wife. He loved those boys with all his heart. Many years ago one of them was taken from him, and ever since, we have witnessed just how much he really loved him. He mourns for him to this day. You, my lord, told us that we could not see your face again unless our youngest brother, Benjamin, was with us. At first, our father was unwilling to send him but because of the severity of the famine, he finally had no choice. If you send us back without Benjamin, our father will go down to the grave with sorrow. His very life is bound up in this boy. All the rest of us together don't mean as much to him as this beloved son. We could never comfort him, and I could never endure seeing his great sorrow. I would sorrow with him. You see, many years ago we were men who were very jealous of our two brothers, and we deeply resented our father's partiality. We thought that he was being unfair to us. All that has changed now. We recognize that we are not worthy to be called his sons. We know that it is a privilege to belong to this family. We have all sinned grievously against our father, but we love him now, and therefore we love what he loves. If he loves Benjamin and prefers him above the rest of us, then so do we. In fact, I love Benjamin and my father so much that I plead with you, my lord, that you would permit me to take the place of my brother in his slavery. Please allow me to be a slave in Egypt so that my brother can be with his father."[1]

Do we understand why Joseph wept upon hearing Judah's heart? To witness the grace of God that can change a hate-filled, murderous heart into a selfless, loving heart would cause any tenderhearted person to weep for joy. How could Joseph do otherwise when he saw the depths of the unfeigned love of the brethren that Judah had? Judah was offering his own life that another might live! Joseph wept to see how all the selfish struggles and ambitious strivings to get ahead of others had ceased in Judah's heart. What rest!

We can be sure that this was not the first time Joseph wept over his brothers. If Joseph had not travailed in intercession for them, if he had not prayed and wept for those who had despitefully used him, his heart would have become like their hearts once had been—filled with hatred and bitterness. As Joseph wept and prayed for them year after year, his heart was changed, as were theirs. This is why Jesus admonishes us to pray for those who despitefully use us (Mt. 5:44). In so doing, we will become children of our Father in Heaven. If we do not follow this counsel, we will very likely become children of the devil, like the people Jesus spoke to in John 8:44.

In other words, whether or not we travail and weep over those who have mistreated us will decide how we end up treating them and others. We will end up being either children of God filled with the nature of Christ, or children of the devil filled with the nature of Satan, who was a murderer from the beginning (Jn. 8:44). It is our choice. If we travail for others, we will become vessels of clay filled with Heaven's treasure. If we become embittered against those who have mistreated us, we will become vessels of clay filled with the evils of hell. If Joseph had not wept in travail

---

1.   The basis of this narrative is found in Genesis 44:18-34. However, some of the details of what was really being said, or at least, what Joseph was hearing, and what was in the heart of Judah, are found in Genesis 37–43; Luke 15:11-19; and First John 3:1,16; 4:9,20-21.

for his brethren, he would never have wept with joy upon seeing their transformation. Yes, God could still have changed Joseph's brothers, but Joseph would have remained unchanged. Bitterness would have caused him to kill them all at his first opportunity, and Joseph would have been the only brother who would have gone to hell! Instead, they were *all* changed, and Joseph was willing to feed and care for them instead of judging them.

Joseph is a wonderful revelation of the last step in the "redemptive week." His journey to becoming the king's emissary and his principal authority in the kingdom is what spiritual maturity is all about. Joseph ruled over all Egypt, but everything he did was directed toward the blessing and salvation of others. His great authority was used to bless others; all his greatness was directed toward providing bread for the hungry. When we compare Joseph's rulership and his goals in life with King Saul's rulership and aspirations, we see why the seventh man of faith in Genesis is a wonderful revelation of true rest.

Saul struggled to receive honor. He lived with a continual fear of losing his kingdom (1 Sam. 18:6-9). He would do anything to hold onto his kingdom, including murdering God's priests (1 Sam. 22:17-18) and consulting a witch (1 Sam. 28:7-25). The things he gave others were given with false motives—to buy their loyalty (1 Sam. 22:7-8). He sought for the sympathy of those around him (1 Sam. 22:8). His kingdom and his own vessel of clay were both filled with turmoil.

Joseph was just the opposite. He was not afraid of losing his kingdom because God had given it to him. He no longer sought the loyalty or help of man because he had learned from the butler that the arm of flesh will fail us, and the help of man is vain. (He had ministered to the butler hoping to gain his friendship and loyalty. The butler rewarded him by forgetting him [Gen. 40].) Neither did Joseph run after the honor of man. He had sought and found Potiphar's honor, only to discover that man's instability may turn today's honor into tomorrow's disdain on the strength of just one false accusation (Gen. 39). Instead of seeking the sympathy of his brothers, Joseph told them that God had sent him to Egypt, not them (Gen. 45:4-5). With his heart filled with love, he freely helped everyone around him, knowing that God had called him to do so (Gen. 45:5-8).

Saul knew only continual torment, fear, jealousy, and strife. Joseph knew the divine rest of a heart that had died to self and was alive to God and others. Unfeigned love for God and others is the fulfillment of all the righteousness of God's law (Gal. 5:14). *This* is real rest, and it comes only when the treasure of Heaven finds a resting place in our clay pots, filling them with His life and His selfless nature.

Chapter 19

Unfulfilled Promises?

Have you ever had difficulty reconciling some of the promises found in the Bible with your own personal experience? Maybe you have even been afraid to admit that some of the promises you are holding on to do not seem to be working in your situation. Are you afraid to confess it openly and accept the reality of your situation? Do you fear that someone might label your acceptance of reality as a "negative confession," or worse yet, "unbelief"? I have known numerous Believers who have desperately hung on to Scriptures concerning healing for someone. They simply refused to accept reality until after their loved one had died. In some cases, the results have been disastrous as they struggled with condemnation for their own lack of faith. Others have actually become spiritual shipwrecks by totally rejecting faith in Jesus Christ. Either way, they blame someone for their failure—ususally themselves, but all too often, God Himself.

Let's place the blame for our frequent spiritual devastation where the Lord places it. Through the prophet Hosea, He tells us that a lack of knowledge brings destruction to God's people (Hos. 4:6). Knowledge of truth, or God's law, is part of what Hosea is speaking about in this context (Hos. 4:1,6), but Hosea is far more concerned about our lack of the "knowledge of God" Himself (Hos. 4:1). In the final judgment, God will speak to *many* who have accomplished *many* wonderful works in His name—even supernatural works—telling them that He never *knew* them (Mt. 7:21-23). Their problem will not be that they failed to hold on to a promise of God with unwavering faith until they received the answer, but that they lacked a personal relationship with the Lord. They never got to know the Lord!

If obtaining the fulfillment of a promise of God by faith is what pleases the Lord, the greatest men of faith listed in His Word all failed to please Him. We find a list of those great men of faith in Hebrews 11. We are given this summary of their lives: "And these all, having obtained a good report through faith, **received not the promise**" (Heb. 11:39). The balance that this Scripture brings to the oft-preached extreme message of faith is urgently needed in the Church today. Not one of these saints of faith received the promise he was believing for! His faith, however, *did* accomplish the most important thing in life—it pleased the Lord. The Lord tells us through this Scripture that each of these saints "obtained a good report." As in Abraham's life, the result of their faith was an intimate relationship with God. Their faith didn't always cause them to *receive*, but it did cause them to *know—to know the Lord and to know how to please Him in this life.*

Does it not matter, then, whether or not we ever receive the fulfillment of the Lord's promises? Of course, it matters greatly, partly because God's name and reputation are at stake. He is a covenant-keeping God, and He wants the whole world to know that. Therefore, although Abraham did not possess even one city in Canaan during his lifetime, he and his descendants will soon inherit it all, along with all the earth (Rom. 4:13). It is important, then, that we stop pretending we are receiving the fulfillment of certain promises when, in fact, we are not. This does not glorify our covenant-keeping God in the eyes of the world. Who are we kidding with our "positive confession"? Does anyone believe us any more than they believe little six-year-old Billy when he insists that his father allows him to take the car out into the city on drives by himself? Why do we find it impossible to believe Billy? Because we know that his feet don't even reach the car's pedals. Even if they did reach, he can't see over the dash to steer the car. Just as we receive promises from our heavenly Father, Billy receives promises from his earthly father. Maybe his father has promised him that one day he will be permitted to drive the car. For that promise to be fulfilled, all Billy needs is more maturity. The only thing that hinders us from receiving the fulfillment of God's many promises is the maturity that comes with time and training.

We can and must continue to believe God's Word. We can be sure that He will fulfill every jot and tittle, but not necessarily today, and maybe not even during our lifetime. To pretend that we are already receiving the fulfillment makes us seem just as ludicrous to the more mature folk as Billy seems to them. Not only that, but far from revealing our great spiritual maturity, such claims only reveal how immature we still are. They do not glorify the Lord; rather, they often cause the world to conclude that God's way is foolish, and only the foolish and gullible believe in His way. Wouldn't it be wiser and more humble to say, "I have not yet seen God fulfill this promise, but I know that He *can,* and I know that He *will* in His time and way"?

Let's consider just a couple promises that the Lord has made and ask ourselves if we are personally experiencing their fulfillment today on a regular basis. He promised, "Verily, verily, I say unto you, **Whatsoever** ye shall ask the Father in my name, he will give it you" (Jn. 16:23b). Do we always receive everything we ask the Father to give us? Another promise Jesus gave is that those who "believe" on Him "shall lay hands on the sick, and they shall recover" (Mk. 16:17-18). If the sick are not healed when you lay hands on them, is this proof that you do not really believe Him? Believing is the basic requirement to be born again (Jn. 1:12-13; Acts 16:31). Multitudes of people who believe, and therefore are truly born again, have not yet seen the sick healed when they lay hands on them. Why is this?

Understanding that some promises have simply not yet been fulfilled in our lives brings peace. There is no need to justify ourselves or God by trying to explain why promises like these, and others, are not yet working for us.[1] It is amazing to hear the many excuses that are used "to get off the hook" when the laying on of hands for healing does not produce results. Many solve their dilemma by saying that the sick person was not healed because he or she simply did not have enough faith. Imagine how the sick person feels after hearing that! Now he not only has one problem but two: Not only is he sick, but he also feels that he is displeasing the Lord because of his lack of faith (Heb. 11:6). We have not brought blessing to him if we leave him under that condemnation! If our desire is to give the impression that we are spiritually mature, or if we actually believe that we are mature, then we will likely find a reason for the seeming failure that does not incriminate ourselves. In some cases, no one is to blame. Usually it would be kinder and humbler to simply admit that we still need more of the Lord in our own lives.

Although there were times when the Lord Jesus did not heal certain sick people, we never find Him saying, "Their problem is that they don't have enough faith to be healed." He did not place people under that condemnation. If our example had done so, then maybe we would be justified

---

1. It is true that God can sovereignly choose to use even a new-born Christian to bring healing through the laying on of hands. This experience does not prove that a person is mature. On the other hand, a mature person can fully expect that healing through the laying on of his hands will be part of his normal Christian experience even if he has not been used in that way in the past.

in doing so also. In fact, even when there was so much unbelief in Nazareth that He marveled at it and was unable to do any mighty works there, He still laid hands on the sick and they were healed! (Mk. 6:1-6) Jesus didn't say that if the *people* we pray for believe, *then* we can lay hands on them and heal them. He said we can do that if *we* believe. Even the great unbelief of the people of Nazareth did not stop the flow of healing—because Jesus believed when He laid hands on the sick! Nevertheless, we can expect that there will be times when, just like the great men of faith, we have faith, yet still do not receive.

The Lord sovereignly decides when and how He will fulfill His promises in our lives, just as much as He decides when and how the promise of the Second Coming will be fulfilled. Furthermore, very often a humble recognition that many of God's promises require more maturity than we currently have is even more pleasing to the Lord than if we have the faith to receive the answer! This attitude may actually demonstrate more genuine faith than our receiving the fulfillment of a promise would demonstrate. This attitude proves that we believe God will continue His great work in our lives and He will bring us into a far more glorious walk with Him than we are experiencing presently. An added blessing we receive by humbling ourselves in this way is that God gives grace to the humble (Jas. 4:6). The more we humbly admit our need before God and man, the quicker our need will be met. Humility moves God to give us new grace to advance on to the next Day of His creative work in our lives.

There is an extremely important fact in the life of Christ, our example, that is sometimes overlooked. Although the Lord Jesus was the only begotten of the Father, He never did one single miracle during the first 30 years of His life, and He never saw even one sick person healed. How do we know that? First, because we are told that His first miracle was to turn water into wine at the beginning of His ministry (Jn. 2:11); and second, if He had previously manifested His glory in Nazareth, the people there would not have been surprised at His ability to speak gracious words when He returned to them after His first year of ministry (Lk. 4:16-30). If they had already seen His ability to heal the sick, how could they have been surprised at His ability to speak? This brings us to a question. How could He have seen so many needy people around Him without doing anything to help them?

The Lord could not manifest the glory of the Anointed One until He had received the anointing of the Father in the Jordan River. We have already considered this pivotal moment in Jesus' life, but we now need to understand how it applies to our lives and the rest we enter on Day Seven. While it is true that we can experience many miraculous works of the

Holy Spirit in and through our lives as the Spirit prepares our dwelling for the last Adam during each of the Days of Creation, it is equally true that there are many glorious promises and mighty works that the Lord will **not** do in and through our lives until after Christ, the Anointed One, has been formed in our earth on Day Six. If the Anointed One is not present to do these things in and through us, they will not be done.

Have we hoped to be able to do the works of the Anointed One ourselves someday, without Him? Unfortunately, many of us in the beginning of our walk would do just this if we could. The immature soul is often led more by human compassion than by the will of God. If we had sufficient power without sufficient maturity and wisdom, human compassion could easily move us to meet every need around us, whether it was God's will to do so or not. This world desperately needs to see the power of God in operation, but it needs to see the beauty of the Lord's character even more. Fortunately, because of His loving heart, the Lord only entrusts to us an amount of power that will not harm us or others. If we had any more, we would most likely wreak havoc on His Kingdom and upset His purposes.

For example, with sufficient power, we probably would have healed Lazarus if we had been there when he was dying. He was a good man whom the Lord loved greatly. So why let him die? Unlike what we would do, Jesus only healed when He was told to do so by His Father. Besides endangering God's purposes, possessing power without sufficient character and maturity almost always brings pride and spiritual ruin to those who have it. The Lord Himself manifested no power until the anointing from Heaven came upon Him at the Jordan. Of even more importance is the fact that even He could not go to the Jordan until the Spirit of God had finished preparing Him and He had come into maturity.

Is it possible that we have assumed there is some sort of shortcut for us—a shortcut that wasn't available to the Lord? Have we believed that we can arrive at the goal by some way other than *the* Way, without following the example He has given us? We must enter His rest, Day Seven, in the same way He entered it. Rest requires a maturity that comes with time; it also requires a total dependence on the Father. In order to partake of the rest of Day Seven, we must finish our journey and learn to *lean* on Him, as Jacob learned. We must learn to be *led* by Him, instead of *working* for Him in our own way and our own strength.

The high calling of God is not that we be equipped to work for Him, but that we permit Him to work through us. We have been called to **enter His rest** (Heb. 4:1 NKJV). Entering His rest means for us exactly what it meant for the Lord. On Day Seven, God "ceased from **His own works**," as

Hebrews 4:10 explains. This verse goes on to explain that if we have entered His rest, we have done the same. We have ceased from *our* works.

What are our works? Paul defines them as the works of the flesh (Gal. 5:19). They are the works we are capable of doing ourselves. Since our old man is the very body of sin (Rom 6:6), sin is the only work we are capable of doing in ourselves. Sin is anything outside God's **perfect will**. For this reason, Paul defines sin as anything that is short of God's glory in our lives, or anything that is unlike Him (Rom 3:23). What we are as fallen man is actually outside the Lord's **perfect will** because His will for man is that we be like Him, filled with His glory. No wonder Paul also declares, "For I know that in me (that is, in my flesh,) dwelleth no good thing" (Rom 7:18a). Regardless of how wonderful my work may appear in man's eyes or in my own eyes, it will always fall "short of God's glory" and is, therefore, defined by Paul as "sin" (Rom. 3:23).

The *root* of my tree—that is, the *source* of my life is my problem. The tree and its root always determine the fruit (Mt. 3:10; 7:16-20). Every work of man, regardless of how wonderful it appears to be, is always contaminated by one or more of Adam's characteristics (the things found in our root) which are pride, ambition, self-centeredness, false motives, love of praise, concern for our own well-being, desire to be someone, desire to be accepted, desire to be loved and appreciated, etc. This nature is the spiritual cyanide that poisons every piece of fruit we can possibly produce in ourselves. It doesn't take much of this cyanide in the food we serve others to kill them if they eat it! Does something in our hearts long for rest from the works of our flesh that are poisoned by the evil root of fallen man?

The only answer for our condition is this: What we are must decrease so that what He is might increase in us. The Creator cannot make something out of nothing in our lives if we are still something. He can only make something out of nothing if we are reduced to nothing! As we have seen, God's work is completed in us on Day Six. The "Jacob" in us dies, and "Israel" takes up His residence. The crucifixion of the old man is finished, and the resurrection life of Christ dwells within us. Only then can we enter His rest on Day Seven. In a beautiful and humble way the Lord Jesus exposes the secret to His strength, as Samson once did. It wasn't found in His hair, but rather in His heart. It was a direct result of His attitude of heart—resting and trusting in His Father. He declares, "Most assuredly, I say to you, *the Son can do nothing of Himself*, but what He sees the Father do; for whatever He does, the Son also does in like manner" (Jn. 5:19 NKJV). He also said, "The words that I speak unto you I speak not of myself: but *the Father that dwelleth in me, he doeth the works*" (Jn. 14:10b). These are definitely some of the most humbling revelations in the entire Bible.

The Lord Jesus Christ said that *He could do nothing,* yet we so often think that we are capable of working for the Lord and accomplishing something for Him. Jesus had to come to the place of total and absolute dependence on His Father. Thus, He came out of His wilderness experience "leaning upon His Beloved" (Song 8:5). It was the Father who did all the works through Him. He did nothing. *This* is rest—*His* rest. We enter and partake of this rest only as Christ is formed in us and placed in our garden. When He comes to dwell in us, we no longer work. He reveals *His* nature in us, allowing the Father to do everything in and through us. The Father alone works. This is the rest and life that Jesus revealed—the rest and life He offers us. This rest is also the source of His strength within us: "In returning and *rest* shall ye be saved; in quietness and in confidence shall be your *strength*" (Is. 30:15b). As we rest in Him, placing our confidence in Him rather than leaning on our own abilities, we will know a strength that is far greater than Samson's. David cried, "Arise, O Lord, into thy *rest*; thou, and the ark of thy *strength*" (Ps. 132:8). When He comes to dwell in the place of rest we have prepared for Him, His strength comes with Him. David prepared a literal tent or dwelling place for the ark of God at his home in the city of Jerusalem (1 Chron. 15:1,12). Far more important, David himself became a **spiritual** tent, or dwelling place, for God's presence and life. It is no wonder David became one of the mightiest men in history. He was a resting place for the Lord and for His strength. David learned to place his confidence in the Lord, not himself. This is reflected in the way he always sought counsel from God before entering battle. Have you lost a few spiritual battles lately? If so, you need to learn to lean on the Strength of Israel in a greater way. He has never lost a battle yet, and He never will!

The Apostle Paul refers to this same attitude of trusting the Lord's strength in Second Corinthians 12:9-10: "And he [the Lord] said unto me, My grace is sufficient for thee: for *my strength is made perfect in weakness.* Most gladly therefore will I rather glory in my infirmities, *that the power of Christ may rest upon me.* Therefore I take pleasure in infirmities, in reproaches, in necessities, in persecutions, in distresses for Christ's sake: for *when I am weak, then am I strong.*" Only when we become weak in our own estimation and cease to have confidence in what we can do are we really strong. Only then will the power of Christ "rest" upon us. The Greek word Paul chose to use here for "rest" could very well be a reference to what King David experienced. It actually means that Paul became a "tent or habitation" for the power of Christ (*Strong's Greek Dictionary*, #1981). The Lord found a dwelling place in him. When Christ is in us and we are in Him, all God's promises are fulfilled. Paul declares, "For all the promises of God **in Him** are Yes, and **in Him** Amen, to the glory of God **through us"** (2 Cor. 1:20 NKJV). As long as we still live part of our lives in the flesh and part in the Spirit, not all the promises are "amen" in our lives, only part of them are. When we live in *Him* alone, and He lives in us, then *all* the promises are fulfilled. *This* is rest.

Chapter 20

For Those Who Glory in the Cross

The Lord began His work on Day One in darkness (Gen. 1:2). If He is going to work with us, He has no other choice because as fallen human beings, we are darkness (Eph. 5:8). From Day One onward, we discover that the "evening" or darkness is mentioned first, and a new morning comes afterwards. In other words, not only does Day One begin with a time of darkness but also every other Day begins that way. This is made evident by the phrase, "the evening and the morning were the first day...the second day," and so on (Gen. 1:5,8,13,19,23,31).

From Genesis 1 and other Scriptures, we understand that the Lord works in the spiritual darkness of our lives to bring us into the light of a new Day. Time after time, the Spirit of God draws near to us to accomplish a deeper aspect of God's creative work within us. Each time, He brings light to another area of darkness. Until He lightens our darkness, we continue to experience spiritual darkness in that area. In fact, every untouched area of our lives is in such darkness that we are not even aware of our need for His light there. Most of us have met other Christians whom we consider to be lacking in certain areas. Far from seeing their need, they most often are offended if we even suggest that they might lack in their spiritual lives. This is one of several reasons why the Lord rarely calls us to address the weaknesses of others. That is the work of the Holy Spirit, not ours. Others are no different than we are. We are all incapable of seeing our need without the help of the Holy Spirit.

If we trust the Lord, He will bring us and others out of darkness and into light, as Isaiah promises, "Who is among you that feareth the Lord, that obeyeth the voice of his servant, that walketh in darkness, and hath no light? Let him trust in the name of the Lord, and stay upon his God" (Is. 50:10). He will be faithful to move upon our earth to bring forth in us a greater revelation of the "light of life" (Jn. 8:12). He visits our earth Day after Day precisely to bring us that light of life, as Second Samuel 22:29b declares, "the Lord will lighten my darkness." Let's yield to His gracious work in our hearts, whatever the cost, so that we will continually know deeper realms of joy in His presence.

Darkness or nighttime experiences speak of times of trial or difficulties. Concerning our spiritual nights, the psalmist assures us, "Weeping may endure for a night, but joy cometh in the morning" (Ps. 30:5b). Why does Genesis 1 reveal that God's order for each Day in our lives is first darkness, then the light of a new morning? Is the Lord giving us a message that the work of each redemptive Day begins with the valley of the shadow of death—a death to self? Let's consider for a moment the seven steps as they are revealed in the Tabernacle of Moses. There we find that the death of the cross must indeed be our experience as we begin each of the seven steps. Life out of death is one of the most important themes in the Word of God. We can only know the power of His resurrection life if we have first been conformed to His death (Phil. 3:10-11). We will never come into the light of life in a given area of our lives unless we have first experienced the darkness and suffering of the cross of Christ in that area. Before He can fill us with what He is, He must empty our vessels of what we are—reducing us to nothing. The message of the cross is so important that the only thing Paul shared with the Corinthian church (and presumably all the other churches as well) was "Jesus Christ and Him crucified" (1 Cor. 2:2 NKJV). In this chapter, we will discover that the message of the cross is an important part of every one of the seven steps of the Tabernacle of Moses.

Accepting by faith the redemptive work Christ accomplished for us at Calvary is **essential** and also **sufficient** for our eternal salvation. With this faith in our hearts, we have access into Heaven even if we were to die while still being spiritual babes. Nevertheless, if we want to reach maturity, we must do more than merely *accept* the work of redemption He accomplished for us on the cross. We must also be willing to become *identified* with that cross and be *conformed* to the death of His cross if we are to know the power of His resurrection life. Paul's longing was, "That I may know him, and the power of his resurrection, and the fellowship of his sufferings, **being made conformable unto his death**; if by any means I might attain unto the resurrection of the dead" (Phil. 3:10-11). Paul also declares, "For we who are alive are always being given over to death for

Jesus' sake, so that his life may be revealed in our mortal body" (2 Cor. 4:11 NIV). We can experience the fullness of His resurrection life only after we have first experienced the sufferings and death of the cross.

Portions of God's Word like these and many others sometimes illicit the question, "How could the Word of God, which was ordained to bring us life, end up bringing us death?" This is precisely the dilemma Paul deals with in Romans 7:10: "And the commandment, which was ordained to life, I found to be unto death." This dilemma is also one of the principal reasons Israel rejected their Messiah 2,000 years ago. They were looking for the Kingdom of God in the form of victory over Rome and all that Rome represented. They passionately hated the Roman soldiers who desecrated their holy land. Day after day, they suffered the cruel occupation of God's land by these uncircumcised Gentiles. Frequently they saw their countrymen being executed Roman style—hung on a cross and left to die. The cross can be likened to the electric chair in our day, although the cross was much crueler. It came to be a symbol of Rome and its ways. It was deeply despised by all who considered themselves to be part of God's family.

Then along came a poor carpenter from Nazareth who preached a powerful message to Israel with mighty signs to confirm His teachings. Multitudes began to gather around Him, and many chose to be His permanent followers. His disciples longed to follow the Lamb wherever He went; they desired to be just like Him. How wonderful it was to hear the voice of God in Israel again, to hear the word of life resounding in the countryside and in the synagogues! It was wonderful, that is, until the day the living Word announced to them that if they wanted to be His followers, they would have to take up a cross and die with Him.

Not even Peter could accept this message! This was the most absurd thing anyone had ever heard! Peter and the others did not yet understand that from the very beginning of time the Living Word has always spoken a message of death to the flesh. The enigma is that the Word of life brings death to the flesh. This is part of the price of being near Him, of being like Him. How can we be like Him unless we die so that He can live within us? The Lord revealed this truth to man from the very beginning when He placed cherubim with flaming swords to guard the way to the tree of life. Those who want to eat from the tree of life and live with God forever must choose to walk the way that leads back to that tree of life. They must be willing to face the terrible work of that flaming sword, which destroys every trace of the fleshly life. Our fleshly life and the

Lord's life can never live together in peace within us. *Our* tree *must* be cut down by that flaming sword!

As we progress through the seven steps of the Tabernacle, we will discover a fresh revelation of the cross in each of the different parts. Then we will understand two truths. First, each part gives us a revelation of the beauty of the crucified Savior, reminding us that **He gave His all to gain us**. Second, it extends an invitation to us to become identified personally with that particular step in the Tabernacle. As we advance from one place in the Tabernacle to the next, our high priest reveals to us how He has ministered in each place and what He has accomplished there. He invites us to become faithful priests in His house by following His example, and by ministering according to the pattern He has revealed through His own priesthood in the Tabernacle (Heb. 9). He invites us to deny ourselves, take up our cross, and follow in His steps—**an invitation to give our all to gain Him**. Imagine that! The Almighty gave the infinite riches of the Prince of Glory to gain a worthless beggar like me, and the only thing He asks in return is that I unreservedly give the life of this beggar to gain the Prince of Glory. What an exchange! What a plan! What a redemption! What a God! As the well-known hymn proclaims, "Love so amazing, so divine, demands my life, my soul, my all."[1]

The Cross in the Door

The door to the outer court was made of fine linen woven with blue, purple, and scarlet (Ex. 26:36). Throughout the Bible, scarlet is a symbol of the shed blood of Christ. It is related to man's cleansing from sin, which only the shed blood can accomplish (Lev. 14:4; Heb. 9:22). It is also related to the salvation of Rahab and her house (Josh. 2:18). So, in our very first step—the door of the Tabernacle—we see the death of the cross.

The cross is indirectly seen in the purple that is also part of the door. It is the color of royalty. The Romans dressed Jesus in purple and placed a crown of thorns on His head to proclaim Him, in a mocking way, the King of the Jews (Mk. 15:17-18). Today He is the King, and He wears the crown and the purple of Heaven's royal One! According to Hebrews, Jesus was crowned King by the Father because He suffered the death of the cross. "But we see Jesus...now crowned with glory and honor *because he suffered death...*" (Heb. 2:9 NIV). The Apostle Paul assures us that we will also partake of the authority and kingship of purple, but only if we are first willing to partake of His cross. "If we suffer, we shall also reign with him" (2 Tim. 2:12a).

---

1.   Isaac Watts, "When I Survey the Wondrous Cross."

Do we want to be saved from hell by taking the first step in our spiritual walk with Christ? Even this beginning step requires the self-denial and death to self that the cross brings. A modern "gospel" that is sometimes preached today tells the sinner that he can go to Heaven if he just believes in Christ, even though he continues to follow in his own sinful way. This is not the gospel of the Bible. The first step or first Day requires that we accept both Jesus' work of redemption and also Lordship over our lives. It has been well said, "If He is not Lord of all, then He is not Lord at all."

The first part of this false "gospel" is true: If we simply believe on the Lord Jesus Christ, we will be saved (Acts 16:31). The problem arises with our definition of "believing." Suppose I am very ill and I visit a doctor who tells me that unless I take a certain medicine I will be dead by tomorrow. What would I do? Some might answer, "Well, of course, you would take the medicine!" This is certainly true *if* I really believe what the doctor has told me. If however, I have no confidence whatsoever in the doctor's diagnosis, and I decide that the doctor is a quack, it is very likely that I would not take the medicine. I would probably seek a second opinion. It is all a matter of whether or not I really have faith in the doctor.

The same thing applies to "believing" on the Lord Jesus Christ. If I really believe His Word, I will follow His instructions! By not submitting my life to Christ's Lordship and guidance, I am proving that I do not have real, genuine, saving faith. James 2:14-26 declares that faith without works is dead. James concludes, "Ye see then how that by works a man is justified, and not by faith only" (Jas. 2:24). This part of the New Testament is sometimes ignored. James is not telling us that we are saved by works. No, he is saying that we are saved only by true faith, but that the presence of true faith in our lives is proven by our works of obedience. When Abraham offered Isaac on the altar, he gave us a beautiful example of how true faith inspires obedience.

The door of salvation demands a death to my way as I begin to obey the great Physician's instructions, often against my own plans and wishes. Salvation is *not* as easy as many Christians seek to convince their prospective converts. There is a great price to pay! It is true that salvation is totally free; it is equally true that it will cost us everything! We thus can well understand why Jesus would say, "Because narrow is the gate and difficult is the way which leads to life, and there are few who find it" (Mt. 7:14 NKJV).

The Cross in the Laver

The laver was filled with water. Israel understood that the source of water in the wilderness was the smitten rock, a symbol of the crucified

Savior (Ex. 17:6; 1 Cor. 10:4). In fact, they very likely filled the laver with water from that smitten rock. As far as we know, it was the only source of water they had when the Tabernacle was erected—although it is true that, just before Israel drank from the smitten rock, they drank for a short time from the bitter waters of Marah. Those waters had been made sweet when Moses cast a tree into them (Ex. 15:23-25). The tree is another biblical symbol of the cross (Gal. 3:13). This, too, shows that without the cross, the water of His Word is not granted to His people. As we have discussed, we only receive truth when we obey, and obedience usually requires death to *our* way.

Do you desire to be cleansed daily by the "washing of water by the word"? (Eph. 5:26) Each day the laver acted as a mirror, revealing any blemishes that the priests had. It also provided the water that could deal with those spots and cleanse the priests. Jude 23 speaks about our garments being "spotted by the **flesh**" (our own sinful works). As priests, we should not attempt to approach the Lord until we have spent time washing at the laver so that the spots caused by the works of the flesh can be dealt with.

In addition to comparing God's Word to water, the Bible also compares it to a sword (Heb. 4:12). In our spiritual lives, the work of His water and the work of His sword are very much the same. They both deal with the flesh. Through washing, His water frees us from the defilement caused by our flesh, and through spiritual circumcision His sword frees us from the flesh also.

Israel learned in the wilderness the same lesson that Christ's disciples learned—that God's Word brings death to the flesh. For this reason they pleaded with Moses, "Speak thou with us, and we will hear: but let not God speak with us, lest we die" (Ex. 20:19). Israel never understood the blessing of willingly submitting to the spiritual death of the sword of God's Word. Like many Christians today, Israel thought that the sword was to be used primarily to destroy the enemy or to convince others that they were God's people and were, therefore, right. Unfortunately, very few understood that the sword was given by God to destroy their own fleshly ways. From the beginning, God has used a flaming sword so that the way to the tree of life would be protected from defilement and so that no unclean thing would be able to walk that way (Gen. 3:24; Is. 35:8). Very few in Israel were permitted to enter God's rest or Canaan because very few were willing to submit their worst enemy—their own flesh—to the Spirit's sword. Of course, as Jesus said, those who lose their life end up saving it (Lk. 9:24b). Israel learned this truth because those who submitted to the work of God's sword finally did enter His rest—Joshua, Caleb, and the new generation. Jeremiah tells us, "The people that were left of the sword found favor in the wilderness; even Israel, when I went to cause him to rest" (Jer. 31:2b ASV).

In the laver, the water is not the only symbol that speaks of God's dealings with the flesh through the cross. The cross is also revealed through brass (or "bronze" in some versions of the Bible), the material the laver was made from. Brass is associated with the judgment of God—more specifically, God's judgment against sin—a judgment that was revealed at the cross of Christ. This is evident from the brass serpent that was placed on a brass pole during Israel's wilderness journey (Num. 21:9). Israel was saved from death by snake bites if they just looked to the brass serpent on the brass pole. Jesus said that this was a symbol of His death on the cross (Jn. 3:14). He was made sin for us (2 Cor. 5:21) and died under God's judgment against sin (Is. 53:4-5).

Another biblical example where brass is associated with judgment is found in the story of the rebellion of the 250 Israelites under Korah, Dathan, and Abiram (Num. 16:1-2). After the fire of God's judgment had consumed them, their brass censers were beaten into plates and placed in the Tabernacle as a memorial of God's judgment (Num. 16:35-40). When God judged Goliath through the boy David, Goliath was covered with brass. The Scripture mentions this four times (1 Sam. 17:4-6).

The laver is a wonderful place if we are longing for more of the Lord, but our flesh will certainly die there. Our fleshly ways will be revealed by the Word, judged by the Word, and cut away and washed away by the Word. Upon hearing this, if we are hungry for God, our spirits cry, "Amen, Lord! Let it be so. Let the laver do its work!"

The Cross in the Brazen Altar

Do we long for Him to give us beauty for ashes? (Is. 61:3) To make something beautiful out of nothing in our lives? The altar is the place where we are reduced to ashes. There is scarcely a detail about the altar that does not, in one way or the other, symbolize the cross of Christ. Hebrews 13:10-13 directly links the suffering and death of Christ on the cross with the death of the sacrificial animals on the altar. Of course, the altar is the place where the blood of the sacrifice is poured out. Consider also that the altar was made of wood. Wood comes from trees, and trees speak of humanity (Is. 61:3; Song 2:3). As we have previously observed, wood is the product of a tree that has been cut down or has died.

The wood of the altar is then covered with brass. This speaks of humanity under the judgment of God. The cross was a revelation of God's judgment on humanity (Is. 53:4-5). What mercy Christ has provided by facing that judgment in our place to save us from hell! The fire on the altar speaks of the Holy Spirit, through whom Christ offered Himself on the cross (Heb. 9:14). Likewise, it is the Holy Spirit at work in us who brings us to the crucifixion of our flesh (Rom. 8:13) because no one can choose this path without supernatural enabling. Will we accept His help if He offers it to us? In our estimation, is the beauty of Christ's likeness worth the suffering of the altar that reduces us to ashes?

The Cross in the Candlestick

Like Moses, many of us long to see the glory of the Lord (Ex. 33:18). Is the privilege of entering the light and glory of the Holy Place worth the price that must be paid? As he entered the Holy Place, an observant soul might have noticed that the pieces of furniture found there were arranged in the shape of a cross. Are we willing to become personally identified with the first piece of that furniture, the candlestick? The candlestick was made of "beaten gold" (Ex. 25:31). Gold speaks of the life and nature of God: "The Almighty will be your gold" (Job 22:25a NIV). This gold has been under the hammer of God, which is symbolic of Christ—the divine one—who on the cross suffered the blows of God's hammer of judgment against sin. The oil for the candlestick was the product of beaten or pressed olives (Ex. 27:20). The Bible compares olives to God's people (Is. 17:4-6). The anointing oil is extremely precious to the Lord because it comes from lives that have been pressed and beaten by His dealings—the dealings of the cross of Christ. Without beating there can be no oil in the Lord's temple, nor can there be a candlestick that gives light!

The Cross in the Table of Showbread

A true Believer not only hungers for the Bread of the Lord's presence but also desires to become a channel for that living Bread. The Lord wants to make us bread for the nations (1 Cor. 10:16-17; Ps. 14:4). The bread on the table of showbread is an unbelievably graphic revelation of the sufferings and death of the cross. Of course, Christ is the bread of life that is represented by the bread. At this table, He invites us to submit to the process that He experienced to become bread for others. Do you desire to be granted the privilege of feeding the hungry hearts around you? The process is awesome. First, after the wheat is grown, it must be cut down. Next it is threshed and it is ground into fine flour. After that, it is mixed with water and other ingredients and is kneaded. Then it is placed in the fire. Finally, it is broken or cut into pieces, chewed, and swallowed. This is the cross! This will make us into bread for others. The table that holds the showbread also reveals the cross since like the altar, it is made of wood. Unlike the brass-covered wood of the altar, however, this wood is covered with gold, a symbol of the divine nature. The "wood" of the altar is under the influence of God's judgment—brass; but the "wood" of the table is under the influence of God's nature—gold. One aspect of His nature is to provide bread for others through the daily death of self (Jn. 6:51; 2 Cor. 4:12). We will be used to do the same if our own nature or "tree" dies and is covered by the gold of Christ's nature.

The Cross in the Altar of Incense

One of the longings of my heart for over 30 years has been that the Lord would grant me the grace to dedicate myself to one of His favorite ministries—intercession. The Book of Hebrews refers to this, assuring us, "Therefore He is also able to save to the uttermost those who come to God through Him, since He always lives to make intercession for them" (Heb. 7:25 NKJV). He is able to draw us into the secret place of the Most High and permit us to become identified with the altar of incense. There, the Lord will pour through us divine intercession for our families, the Church, and the world as we learn to intercede as He intercedes (Rom. 8:26-27). If the God of the universe has chosen to dedicate Himself to this ministry, then there must be a joy and delight in it that we know nothing about. After all, He does have a choice with what He does with His life! The altar of incense gives us an idea of the cost involved in true intercession.

An altar carries with it the connotation of sacrifice; of course, the fire found on the altar of incense strengthens that concept. This altar, like the brazen altar and the table of showbread, was made of wood—symbolic of humanity that has been cut down by the cross. The incense that was offered there represents prayer (Ps. 141:2; Rev. 8:3-4). The incense was made of ingredients that are symbolic of the suffering and death of Christ on the cross (Ex. 30:34). Stacte is drops of myrrh. The Scriptures link myrrh with Jesus' death by telling us that He was buried with myrrh (Jn. 19:39-40). Onycha comes from the muscle of a shellfish; when the shellfish loses that muscle, it has lost its very life. Galbanum has a pungent odor that causes tears, and frankincense is associated with the **brazen** altar and the sufferings of Christ because it was placed on the fire of the brazen altar along with every meal offering (Lev. 2:1).

These spices not only reveal the life of one who has become a living sacrifice to God (Rom. 12:1), but they also reveal the cost of true intercession. Real prayer and intercession involve laying down our lives for others. The time and physical effort that are spent in prayer are an acceptable sacrifice and a sweet savor that rises before the Lord. Besides this sacrifice, intercession can literally involve the risking, or even the giving, of our own lives for others. Jesus reveals this as He interceded for humanity in the garden of Gethsemane. As He poured out His soul before the Father, His sweat was as great drops of blood (Lk. 22:44). The life is in the blood (Gen. 9:4). Spiritually speaking, He was pouring out His life through intercession.

Abraham actually risked his life as he interceded for his nephew Lot, "bargaining" with God to spare Sodom from destruction (Gen. 18:25-32). Abraham was definitely sailing in uncharted spiritual waters at that moment. Had anyone else ever stood before the Almighty in His moment of wrath, trying to reason with Him? Abraham knew that God was burning with anger toward Sodom and Gomorrah, and he probably thought it was not a good time to approach Him, but to have waited would have meant death for Lot. How could Abraham be sure that God's anger would not fall on him if he stood in the way of God's judgment?

Moses also risked his life for the children of Israel as he interceded for them on Mount Sinai. God told him to stop hindering His wrath, and to allow Him to destroy all Israel. Instead, Moses stood between God and Israel and interceded for God's people, pleading that God would not destroy them (Ex. 32:10-14). Therefore, the altar of incense is both a beautiful and an awesome revelation of the giving of one's life for others. That, too, is the cross of Christ.

The Cross in the Ark of the Covenant

Once a true lover of the Lamb has experienced the manifest presence of the Lord, he can no longer find real satisfaction in anything less or anything else in this world. As we have mentioned, the only way into the Holy of Holies, where that manifest presence continually dwells, is through the rending of the veil of flesh (Heb. 10:19-20). In the Holy of Holies we find the ark of the covenant, the last and most glorious revelation of the cross.

The ark was a wooden box, covered with gold both inside and outside. Again, being wooden, the ark symbolizes humanity cut down and covered with the gold of the divine nature. The literal presence of God dwelled upon the ark (Ps. 99:1). When we consider what was inside the ark, we discover that it symbolizes the human heart. According to Hebrews 9:4, there were three things inside the box: 1) the tables of the Law that the Lord had give to Moses on Mount Sinai, 2) a pot of manna, and 3) Aaron's rod that supernaturally budded after being dead. By explaining the significance of these three things, the Bible gives us a clear under-standing of what the ark represents. The tables of stone on which the Law was written are symbols of the tables of flesh found within the human heart (2 Cor. 3:3; Heb. 8:10). The manna (Israel's bread) is a symbol of the Word of God (Deut. 8:3), and the pot of manna inside the ark is a symbol of the Word we should hide in our hearts (Deut. 30:14; Ps. 119:11). The rod of Aaron that came to life and produced fruit after being dead is a symbol of Christ's resurrection life. We were once dead in trespasses and sins, but the resurrection life of Christ has raised us up together with Him, giving us a new life with new fruit (Eph. 2:1-6). Therefore, the ark is a graphic revelation of the human heart that has been prepared to be a resting place for the Lord.

Possibly the most beautiful revelation of the cross that is found in the Holy of Holies is the mercy seat. The mercy seat was a solid plate of gold that covered the ark like a lid (Ex. 25:17-22). Much more than just covering the ark, the mercy seat actually made a separation between the presence and glory of God that rested continually upon the ark, and the ark itself that was under the mercy seat. In our spiritual life, the mercy seat is the only thing that comes between a holy God, who is a consuming fire, and our human heart, with all its weaknesses (Lam. 3:22). The mercy seat was made of pure gold, telling us that only divine mercy can cover and protect Adam's race. His mercy not only covers us but it also decides who will ac-tually dwell with that consuming fire (Ps. 65:4). When the mercy of God has been placed upon our lives as the mercy seat was placed on the ark, we will be permitted to dwell where He dwells and rest where He rests—in the Holy of Holies! (See Psalm 23:6 and Romans 9:15-16.)

The Source of God's mercy is the cross. There has never been a greater revelation of mercy than Calvary. When Christ suffered the consequences and condemnation of the righteous law of God against sinners, taking our guilt and punishment upon Himself, He paid the price for our "atone-ment" or "covering." God's law demands the death of every sinner (Ezek. 18:4). The sentence of the law is the same for all mankind. The divine mercy provided on Calvary's tree can now cover us, or atone for us, so we do not have to face the mortal sentence of the law as we stand before the righteous Judge.

As we see the cross in the Holy of Holies, surely we are thankful that He was willing to suffer and pay the price for our salvation. Each of us should ask ourselves, "Am I willing to be identified with the cross that is revealed in the mercy seat? Does a longing for the glory of the Lord so fill me that I am willing to carry the cross for His sake as He did for me?" He carried the cross to win us, and He now asks us to carry it to "win" Him (Phil. 3:8c-10).

Not only are we called to carry the cross to win Him, but also to win others. Since His nature is to carry the cross for others, that nature can be formed in us only as we do the same. Are we, like Christ, concerned enough for others to carry the cross for them, knowing that it will involve self-denial and personal suffering for us as it did for Christ? Are we willing to pray and fast so that others will be saved? Are we willing to go out of our way to help a needy soul find Christ?

When we become identified with the cross in the mercy seat, it sometimes involves something even costlier than self-denial. It sometimes involves covering the faults of others, instead of exposing them—often at a cost to ourselves. Doing so will sometimes make us look like the guilty ones, but we will never bear another's guilt to the extent that Christ did. He accepted the guilt of all our sins and died in our place!

A burden for others and a love for His likeness always go hand in hand. The world around us cries at your door and at mine, "Sir, we would see Jesus." Can we hear that cry? Will we follow in His footsteps as He lovingly leads us to Calvary's tree? If we do, the world will see Him again, through us, as He makes something out of nothing!

Chapter 21

The Feast of His Appearing

"Then the Jews sought him at the feast [of Tabernacles], and said, Where is he?...Now about the midst of the feast Jesus went up into the temple, and taught" (Jn. 7:11,14). Could this sudden appearance of the Lord in the Temple while His people were seeking Him have anything to do with what the prophet Malachi foresaw? He wrote, "And the Lord, *whom ye seek, shall suddenly come to his temple,* even the messenger of the covenant, whom ye delight in: behold, he shall come, saith the Lord of hosts" (Mal. 3:1b).

Is it possible that the Lord's sudden appearance in the Temple 2,000 years ago, during the very time of the **seventh feast,** was ordained to give us a message, and to link these two passages? Note that John 6 begins at the time of the first of the seven feasts—the Feast of Passover (Jn. 6:4). The Lord used that opportunity to reveal the spiritual significance of the Passover (Jn. 6:53): Christ is our Passover meal (1 Cor. 5:7). Then, John 7 begins at the time of the seventh feast—the Feast of Tabernacles (Jn. 7:2). It is apparent that the Lord chose to use the time of the Feast of Tabernacles to reveal the spiritual significance of that feast also. The most glorious aspect of the spiritual fulfillment of the Feast of Passover that Jesus revealed in John 6 was that **He** is the bread of life—broken bread that gives life to all who love Him. Surely the most glorious aspect of the fulfillment of the Feast of Tabernacles that He revealed in John 7 was His sudden appearance in the Temple to those who sought Him, and the glorious teaching that came forth from that appearance (Jn. 7:14,28,37-39). We could call the Passover, the "Feast of Broken Bread," and we could call Tabernacles, the "Feast of His Appearing."

When we have finally experienced the glory of the seventh feast, things will be different in our lives and in the world around us. At that time the Lord Jesus Christ will suddenly appear in His temple—in us! This glory awaits each of us, individually, if we allow the Lord to complete the work of the Six Days in *our* earth. Since each of us individually is a temple for the Lord (1 Cor. 6:19), there will be an individual fulfillment of Tabernacles in our lives. However, there is a glory that will come to the *entire* earth when the Lord finishes His Six-Day work of redemption in His Church, His corporate temple (Eph. 2:20-22). Very soon, in accordance with the divine timetable, there will be a corporate fulfillment of this seventh feast, the "Feast of His Appearing." What a glorious hope awaits the Church and this world when God's people finish the seven steps of their spiritual journey, when they experience the glory of God who dwells in His temple in the Holy of Holies. What a day it will be when "Christ in you, the hope of glory" is no longer simply a beautiful thought, but has become a glorious reality—when Christ has been formed in us to such a wonderful measure that we are filled with all the fullness of God!

To commemorate Israel's journey through the wilderness, the Lord gave a seventh feast, the Feast of Tabernacles (Lev. 23:34). This feast commemorated the fact that Israel dwelled in "booths" or "tabernacles" during their journey (Lev. 23:42-43). However, it commemorated something else. Celebrated yearly during the time of the **general harvest** (Lev. 23:39), the feast commemorated a mighty harvest, and therefore, the Lord called it the Feast of Ingathering (Ex. 23:16). He ordained it to be a yearly feast of great rejoicing as God's people enjoyed the new wine of the grape harvest and the oil of the olive harvest. Since it is clear that God was not offering Israel such a harvest during their wilderness journey, we understand that this feast was looking ahead to the harvest of Canaan that awaited them at the end of their journey, and that also awaits the Church at the end of its journey. Since the Apostle Paul assures us that Israel's journey to Canaan is an example for God's people in the last days (1 Cor. 10:11), we can be sure that God is promising us a mighty harvest also. We will enter Canaan, the fruitful land, and destroy the giants there who have continually sought to destroy God's plan for us.

As a mighty harvest is associated with the **seventh feast**, so a mighty harvest is one of the outstanding characteristics of Joseph the **seventh man** of faith. In Egypt, he gathered in such a mighty harvest that he was able to sustain and save the world during their time of great need. Maybe the Lord also wants to use you to bring His salvation to the world around you as you share with them the spiritual food you will receive through the mighty harvest of the seventh feast. When the Lord appears in His temple, there will be a mighty harvest of the "finest wheat" (Ps. 147:14)—the most precious teaching ever heard—and this will cause a mighty harvest of souls as multitudes flock to every spiritual storehouse that feeds the hungry.

Much has been written and spoken recently about plans to evangelize the entire earth before the year 2,000. That is good because missionary fervor and vision are essential if we are to have healthy churches. We must remember, however, that the mighty harvest of the **seventh feast** will be reaped only when the mighty Lord of the **seventh Day** is dwelling within us, His people. He alone can accomplish the work. Let's confess what Christ Himself confessed: "I can do nothing of myself!" (See John 5:19.) The last 2,000 years of Church history should teach us that we will never accomplish the goal of preaching the gospel of the Kingdom as a witness to all nations, unless the King is filling our lives (Mt. 24:14). How can we preach the gospel of Kingdom power, authority, and character if these things are not operating in our lives? If we are born again, we can preach the **gospel of salvation**, but we cannot preach and reveal the **gospel of the Kingdom** until we have reached the seventh Day and we have been filled with the Kingdom authority and character that Joseph, the seventh man of faith, experienced.

The Feast of Tabernacles serves as a continual reminder of the glorious hope that is set before us, and of the new day that is soon to dawn on the Church. This feast, which we are also calling the "Feast of His Appearing," is one of the three **principal** yearly feasts in which all the men of Israel had to **appear before the presence of the Lord** (Deut. 16:16).[1] It is extremely significant that they had to "appear before the presence of the Lord" during the feasts of **Passover, Pentecost,** and **Tabernacles.** The spiritual fulfillment of these feasts clearly requires that God's people be in His presence. A consideration of history and the Bible leaves little doubt what the Lord is saying to us. These three feasts revealed to God's people that there would be three times in their history when God would literally and visibly appear to them—times in which they would find themselves in His literal presence. The Feasts of Passover and Pentecost have already proved this to be true.

The events surrounding Israel's first Passover and their deliverance from Egypt were marked by the visible appearance of the Lord and His

---

1. Note that Scriptures sometimes call the first two feasts—Passover and Unleavened Bread—by the same name because they were observed one after the other during an eight-day period (Lk. 22:1; Mk. 14:1; Ezek. 45:21; 2 Chron. 35:17). The "Feast of Weeks" is the Old Testament name for Pentecost because it was celebrated after a period of seven weeks (Lev. 23:15-16).

direct intervention in the affairs of man to change the course of history. It all started with the Lord's visible appearance to Moses at the burning bush. Then, as God led Israel out of Egypt, He literally appeared to them in the cloud by day and the pillar of fire by night (Ex. 3:1-2; 13:21-22). If God had not literally appeared, there would have been no Passover; without a Passover, there would have been no deliverance from Egyptian slavery, and therefore, no Old Testament.

About 1,500 years after the first Passover, the Lord again intervened visibly in the affairs of man. Once again, His people were in His literal presence. This is the visible appearance of the Lord in the person of Jesus. As the Apostle John says, "And the Word became flesh and dwelt among us, and we beheld His glory" (Jn. 1:14a NKJV). Once again, all Israel was permitted to "appear before the presence of the Lord!" A principal fruit of that visitation was that God brought His people into the fulfillment of Pentecost in Acts 2. If God, in Christ, had not literally appeared, there would have been no Pentecost; without a Pentecost there would have been no New Testament.

During the "Feast of His Appearing," the Lord is going to intervene in the affairs of man once again by visibly appearing to His people. Just as in the other two feasts, He will **first** do so through prepared vessels as He manifests Himself in His temple, the Church. Once again, the glory God reveals in His people will bring about a change in the course of history. If the Lord does not appear again, there will be no fulfillment of the third great feast, the Feast of Tabernacles—the Feast of His Appearing—and there will be no millennial age where Christ reigns on the earth! We should all rejoice because the sovereign King of the universe has declared that there are **three** feasts in which His people will appear before Him, not just two! He will soon intervene to visit His people once more and to change the course of history!

The Feast of Tabernacles, also called the "Feast of Ingathering," was given by God as a yearly commemoration of the **end** of Israel's journey, when they entered the Promised Land. Of course, Israel did not finish their journey when they should have. Israel should have finished their journey and entered the blessings of Canaan at Kadesh Barnea. At that time Moses sent spies into Canaan to see the glory of Israel's inheritance. The spies came back with samples of the harvest of the land. They brought a cluster of grapes so large that it had to be carried by two men (Num. 13:23). It was the time of harvest, the time of the Feast of Tabernacles. Although Israel rebelled and did not enter Canaan at that time, from that day on they have celebrated the Feast of Tabernacles each year at the time of the general harvest, which includes grapes, pomegranates, figs, olives, and other fruits.

What does this unbelievably enormous cluster of grapes tell us about the land of Canaan or God's rest, and the harvest that awaits us at the end of our journey? The Lord compares men to grapes in several Scriptures. For example, He declares, "I found Israel like grapes in the wilderness" (Hos. 9:10a). What a graphic revelation the Lord gave us of the mighty harvest that will be found in the place of our spiritual inheritance. It took two men to carry the cluster of grapes! What a tremendous outpouring of glory is just ahead! The day will come when just *one* anointed call for sinners to repent will produce a cluster with so many "grapes" that the spiritual burden will require the ministry of two men!

The Lord gives us another way to visualize what is just ahead: In just one catch of fish, there were so many fish that two boats were filled to capacity and began to sink (Lk. 5:4-7). We are soon to enter a day of unprecedented fruitfulness. Like Jesus, we will seek to escape from the multitudes instead of seeking the multitudes, as so many do today. If you have to seek the multitudes, it clearly shows that you do not yet have what they long for. Before you can win the multitudes, you must first "win Christ!" (Phil. 3:9)

Pastors and leaders, there is absolutely no need for competition in God's Kingdom. In God's eyes there is only one real problem: "The harvest truly is plentiful, but the laborers are few" (Mt. 9:37b NKJV). In many places of the world, this does not *seem* to be the case. I know of some cities where there are neighborhoods with a church on literally every block. The problem is not a lack of competition to corral the few souls that have already accepted the gospel message. Obviously, there is plenty of that! The problem is that we cannot participate in the glorious harvest if we are not found in the *place* of the harvest. How can we experience the harvest of Canaan if we are still camped at Mount Sinai enjoying the fourth feast, the Feast of Pentecost? Or worse yet, how can we labor in the harvest of Canaan if we are still living in Egypt?

Some years ago, the Lord allowed my spiritual eyes to be opened to see the harvest as He saw it in a certain country of the world. As in many other places of the world, there were plenty of churches. Some of them were very large. There was also much competition between the different denominations and much jealousy between the pastors. As I saw God's harvest in that country, my heart almost broke because the harvest was literally untouched. In a spiritual sense, no one had yet reached the field where the harvest was waiting. The grain was mature and ripe—it was ready to fall to the ground—but the many ministers were still miles from the field, fighting over a few spiritual gleanings they were able to gather up from an almost burned-over field. Those ministers did not need to leave their physical location to reach that mighty harvest. They simply needed to leave their spiritual location. They needed to embrace the cross, deny their own selfish ambitions and goals, and continue their journey.

Can we feel the burden of the Lord's heart as He urges us, "Therefore pray the Lord of the harvest to send out laborers into His harvest"? (Mt. 9:38 NKJV) We must pray that laborers might be permitted to reach the place of the Lord's harvest. He will not ask spiritual babes to reap that harvest. How we need to see the Lord's harvest that is at the point of being lost for the lack of mature laborers who have entered the rest of Day Seven! If He opens our eyes to see it, we will pray, cry, and travail that the Lord would send laborers to the fields that He longs for His people to reap—laborers who have experienced the Feast of His Appearing.

Could there be anything more tragic than failing to reap the harvest that has been set before us? The failure to do so does not simply mean that many wonderful grains of wheat will fall to the ground and rot. The loss of this harvest involves eternal consequences far beyond our comprehension. It will mean that many souls of men will fall into the fires of hell, where they will be lost forever to suffer without God and without hope. Could this happen? Jeremiah must have seen it happening to a people somewhere when he recorded their cry: "The harvest is past, the summer is ended, and we are not saved" (Jer. 8:20). Lord, help us!

May the Lord give us the grace to lay aside our petty differences, our selfish goals, our strivings to build our own kingdom instead of His, so that we can hear the cry of God's heart for laborers to reap His harvest before it is lost. God's great harvest can only be *fully* reaped by those who have come into the seventh Day or the seventh feast—the Feast of His Appearing. In reality, He is the *only* One capable of reaping it, and He will do so when He appears in His temple.

Do you sometimes wonder where the Lord is? Does His presence seem to be missing from your life and from your church? Do you long to experience the glory of His presence? God's call to you is to continue patiently on your journey toward your inheritance—the Lord Himself. The Promised Land is just ahead! If you have not reached the **fourth Day**, the glory of His appearing awaits you there. An even greater glory awaits you when He appears on the **seventh Day**, because there is a vast difference between His appearance on the fourth Day and His appearance on the seventh Day. On Day Four He appears *to* us; on Day Seven He appears *in* us and *through* us. At that time, He will no longer be walking *with* us; He will be walking *in* us. He will be living in His temple.

Those mighty rivers that flow from Eden on Day Seven are not something the Lord offers only to the really important people on earth. During the great day of the Feast of Tabernacles, the Lord promised to give those rivers to *all* who are thirsty and believe on Him according to what the Scriptures reveal (Jn. 7:37-38). Do you believe that He can change your wilderness into a garden of Eden as He has promised to do? Isaiah prophesies, "For the Lord shall comfort Zion: he will comfort all her waste places; and he *will make her wilderness like Eden,* and her desert like the garden of the Lord" (Is. 51:3a). Do you believe that just as the Lord can give you beauty in place of ashes He can also give you Eden in place of a long wilderness journey? Do you believe that rivers will flow in your wilderness? (See Isaiah 43:19-20.)

If you feel less qualified today to be a channel for the mighty flow of His rivers than you felt at the beginning of your walk, you are actually closer to them than you've ever been. Rivers flow toward the low place, *not* toward the exalted places of our earth! By the time you finish your journey, you will feel even lower because you *will* be lower. You see, when Israel crossed over the Jordan into Canaan, they were literally at the lowest geographical place on the face of the earth. They were more than 1,300 feet *below* sea level! How else can anyone enter "Canaan," which actually means "the lowland" in Hebrew? (*Strong's Hebrew Dictionary,* #3667) "Canaan" comes from the word "humbled." The Lord has promised that in the great day of His appearing "the lofty looks of man shall be humbled, and the haughtiness of men shall be bowed down, and the Lord alone shall be exalted in that day" (Is. 2:11-19). The rivers will not flow from the mighty; they will flow from the lowly. There will no longer be great men leading God's people. Rather, a great God will be leading us from within the camp—from within the Temple! He will lead the hungry hearts through humble men—men who have found "the low place."

During the Feast of His Appearing in John 7, there were very few Jews in Israel who were not seeking Jesus. Some sought Him because they thought He was a good man; others sought Him to kill Him (Jn. 7:11-12,30-31,40-43). Everyone had heard of Him; He was the talk of the nation. Thus, for one motive or another, just about everyone wanted to see Him. At that moment, Jesus fulfilled, in measure, the prophetic word of Malachi who wrote, "And the Lord, whom you seek, shall suddenly come to His temple" (Mal.3:1b). Malachi did not say that they would all be seeking Him for the right motives. In fact, he goes on to ask, "But who can endure the day of His coming? And who can stand when He appears?" (Mal. 3:2a NKJV) As Malachi continues, he gives the idea that very few will survive the purging and purifying associated with the Lord's appearing (Mal. 3:2-3).

Few of God's people did actually survive the tremendous dealings of God in the First Coming. Does Malachi have a message for God's people today? The Scriptures show us that the glorious promises, as well as the awesome warnings, of Malachi's prophetic message will have an even greater fulfillment in the Second Coming than they did in the First. (Compare Malachi 4:5 and Matthew 17:10-13 for one example.)

Yes, the Jews were all seeking Him during the Feast of His Appearing, but seeking the Lord is not enough! Many of God's people are seeking Him today: some because of their pure love for Him, and others because of a love for self and this world. Some seek His blessing and power so they can reach the pinnacle of ministerial, spiritual, or financial success. Are you seeking Him for the right motive? If you seek Him in humility and lowliness, desiring that *His* name be exalted and not your own, and that *His* voice be heard and not yours, one day the irresistible rivers of His glory will begin to flow through you. If you seek Him because you want to sit at His feet and hear the words of life from the Master, He will suddenly appear in *your* temple and speak *to* you and *through* you words that will cause your heart and the hearts of others to burn with a deeper love for Him.

What must we do to reach the goal? No amount of effort on our part can bring us into the glory of His fullness in our lives. As Moses discovered, God alone decides who will receive His mercy to finish life's race with joy (Rom. 9:15). Paul concludes, "So then it is not of him who wills, nor of him who runs, but of God who shows mercy" (Rom. 9:16 NKJV). However, there is *one* thing that *we* can do. We can draw near to God in our hearts and ask Him for mercy. Mercy will cause us to react to our times of trial, affliction, and great need in the wilderness in a positive way that will please Him. As we have seen, many of God's people failed to finish their seven-step journey through the wilderness. They never entered God's rest, but we can learn from their mistakes in order to experience a better end than theirs. In the context of Israel's dismal failure in the wilderness and a warning to us to not repeat their mistakes, Hebrews 3–4 concludes this theme by giving us the answer to having a blessed end. We are exhorted, "Let us therefore come boldly unto the throne of grace, that we may obtain mercy, and find grace to help in time of need" (Heb. 4:16). Only mercy can enable us to react the right way when we are under the pressure of our "time of need." We are incapable of embracing the cross in ourselves, but His mercy can enable us to do so. For that reason, those who spend time drawing near to the Lord each day to receive the mercy and grace necessary to please Him will have a glorious end! Maybe you do not even have the grace needed to spend time with Him daily. Then start by asking Him for help even in this area. He is well able to draw you to Himself and *cause* you to run after Him (Song 1:4).

He has promised, "For the **earth** shall be **filled** with the knowledge of the **glory** of the Lord, as the waters cover the sea" (Hab. 2:14). Christ in you is the glory with which He promises to fill your earth. He promises that His people will be "filled with all the fullness of God" (Eph. 3:19 NKJV). The mighty Creator will appear in *your* temple and fill you with His glory if you allow Him to do whatever He has to do to make something out of nothing in *your* earth. In six Days, He will make you a new creation in Christ Jesus, and you will know the glory of His rest on Day Seven!

	7 DAYS OF CREATION	7 MEN OF FAITH	7 FEASTS OF THE LORD	7 STEPS IN THE TABERNACLE	7 STEPS TO MATURITY
1	Speaks light into darkness	Abel	Passover	Door	New Birth
2	Separates the waters from the waters	Enoch	Unleavened Bread	Laver	Purification of Doctrine
3	Waters recede and fruits appear	Noah	First Fruits	Brazen Altar	Fruits of The Spirit
4	Makes lights in the heavens	Abraham	Pentecost	Golden Candlestick	The Lord Appears
5	The waters bring forth abundantly	Isaac	Trumpets	Table of Showbread	His Word Fulfilled
6	Creates a man in His likeness	Jacob	Day of Atonement	Altar of Incense	Christ in Us
7	His Rest	Joseph	Tabernacles	Ark of The Covenant	The Rest of God

Bibliography

Baker, H.A., *Visions Beyond the Veil*, Springdale, Pennsylvania: Whitaker House, 1973.

Bennett, Ramon, *Saga*, Jerusalem, Israel: Arm of Salvation, 1993.

Bennett, Ramon, *When Day and Night Cease*, Jerusalem, Israel: Arm of Salvation, 1993.

Byers, Marvin, *The Final Victory: The Year 2000*, Shippensburg, Pennsylvania: Treasure House, 1994.

Collins, David R., *George Washinton Carver*, Milford, Michigan: Mott Media, 1981.

Davey, Cyril J., *The Story of Sadhu Sundar Singh*, Chicago, Illinois: Moody Press, 1963.

Fitzgerald, Randy, "When a Law Goes Haywire," *Reader's Digest*, September 1, 1993.

Lauersen, Niels, M.D., Ph.D., *It's Your Pregnancy*, New York: Simon and Schuster, 1987.

Logos Bible Study Software, Oak Harbor, Washington: Logos Research Systems, 1993.

Osbeck, Kenneth W., *101 Hymns Stories*, Grand Rapids, Michigan: Kregel Publications, 1990.

Richards, Lawrence O., *Expository Dictionary of Bible Words*, Regency Reference Library, Grand Rapids, Michigan: Zondervan Publishing House, 1985.

Strong, James, *Strong's Exhaustive Concordance*, Grand Rapids, Michigan: Baker Book House, 1977.

Vine, W.E., *An Expository Dictionary of New Testament Words*, Old Tappan, New Jersey: Fleming H. Revell Company, 1966.

THE FINAL VICTORY: THE YEAR 2000

by Marvin Byers.

Barnabas, Sir Isaac Newton, and many others predicted the same year for Christ's return! Did Barnabas, Paul's companion, and the early Church have an understanding of the times that we today do not have? Can God's timetable be understood? This book shares what these men declared and shows how the Scriptures and recent events in the Middle East confirm the accuracy of their understanding. Decide for yourself after you consider the facts!

TPB-336p.

ISBN 1-56043-824-X

(6" X 9") Retail $14.99

Hebron Ministerial Institute

Does your heart long to know the Lord in a deeper, more intimate way? The purpose, calling, and ministry of Hebron Ministerial Institute in the United States and Guatemala, Central America is to share vital keys from God's Word that will help hungry hearts experience the joy of His presence. Our vision is to share revelation on God's Word that ministers to the heart, not only impart academic information about His Word. The program consists of a complete two-year course. All the courses listed below are already available in Spanish by either video or audio cassette. Many of the courses are also being made available in English on both video and audio cassette. For those who are able to dedicate two full years to the study of God's Word, Hebron offers a complete bi-lingual Ministerial Institute in Guatemala, Central America. The modern facilities include housing for both single and married students.

The curriculum includes a complete study of the books of the Bible, along with many other related subjects needed for effectual and victorious Christian living. Some of those related subjects covered in the two year course are listed below:

- The Tabernacle of Moses
- The Journey of Israel
- The Priesthood
- The Offerings
- The Feasts
- Foundational Doctrines
- The Tabernacle of David and Praise
- Women of the Bible
- The Holy Spirit and His Gifts
- Doctrine of God
- Doctrine of Man, Sin, and Salvation
- The Names of God

- The Fruit of the Spirit
- Life of the Pastor and Practical Ministry
- The Principles of the Kingdom
- The Cross
- Marriage and the Family
- Bible Geography
- Customs of Bible Times
- The Hope of the Christian
- Christian Ethics
- Prayer
- Homiletics
- Hermeneutics
- Church Government

- The Local Church
- Divine Guidance
- Apostolic Principles for a Ministry
- Numerology
- Typology
- The Relation Between the Beginning and Ending
- Evangelism
- The Fear of God

For more information write to either of the following addresses:

Hebron Ministries
Section 0374 P.O. Box 02-5289
Miami, FL 33102-5289

Hebron Ministries
P.O. Box 765
Mount Clemens, MI 48046-0765

Hebron Ministries
2203 E. 11 Mile Rd.
Royal Oak, MI 48067

Or call:
1-800-LAST-DAY (1-800-527-8329) in the U.S.
or
33-26-15 in Guatemala City, Central America